DUCK AND COVER

DUCK AND COVER

Civil Defense Images in
Film and Television from
the Cold War to 9/11

Melvin E. Matthews, Jr.

McFarland & Company, Inc., Publishers
Jefferson, North Carolina, and London

LIBRARY OF CONGRESS ONLINE CATALOG DATA

Matthews, Melvin E.
Duck and cover : civil defense images in film and television
from the Cold War to 9/11 / Melvin E. Matthews, Jr.
p.   cm.
Includes bibliographical references and index.

ISBN 978-0-7864-6587-3
softcover : 50# alkaline paper ∞

1. Civil defense in motion pictures. 2. Motion pictures —
United States — History — 20th century. 3. Civil defense on
television. 4. Television programs — United States — History —
20th century. I. Title.
PN1995.9.C514 M38 2012   2011039759

BRITISH LIBRARY CATALOGUING DATA ARE AVAILABLE

On the cover: Bert the Turtle from the 1951 U.S. civil defense film
Duck and Cover

Manufactured in the United States of America

McFarland & Company, Inc., Publishers
Box 611, Jefferson, North Carolina 28640
www.mcfarlandpub.com

Table of Contents

Preface

Growing up in Rockville Centre, Long Island, after World War II, future presidential historian Doris Kearns Goodwin experienced firsthand the impact the Cold War had on her and her friends. For them, the Cold War wasn't a vague notion. Given the realities of the age — school air-raid drills, the advocacy of bomb shelters, and the viewing of the unnerving civil defense films in school — how could it have been otherwise! Goodwin's generation was the first to face the undeniable fact that everyone and everything that made up their entire world could be instantaneously destroyed.

In school, Goodwin and her fellow classmates practiced two kinds of drills. In the first, predicated on the assumption that the bomb was nearby, everyone fell to the floor, face down under their desks, elbows covering their heads and their eyes closed. Should there be sufficient time for everyone to take cover from an attack, the second drill called for the teachers to guide the students into the school corridor and down into the basement, where the students were then instructed to lean against the wall and fold their arms over their heads. "We were told to practice the first drill ... at our homes at night, so we would be prepared to fall out of bed and onto the floor with maximum speed," Goodwill recalled. "Between the practice 'atomic fallings,' and the hundreds of prayers I said each night for my own account, for the poor souls in purgatory, and for my family and the Dodgers, it is a wonder that I ever got to sleep."[1]

Despite the fact that there would be no survivors in the event of a direct hit on Goodwin's hometown, civil-defense authorities confidently assured everyone that, with 12 minutes' notice and with well-organized civil-defense mechanisms established, casualties in her community could be diminished by 50 percent. A film Goodwin saw in school described a self-contained underground shelter that could be built in one's backyard at a cost of less than $2,000. For those who couldn't afford such protection, the same film recommended a more feasible alternative: transforming an existing basement into a shelter, equipping it with supplies and a first-aid kit. Civil-defense volunteers would play significant roles in an emergency, as air-raid wardens and auxiliary policemen, and directing people to emergency shelters.

On those occasions when the entire community took part in "Atom Attack Tests,"

> All pedestrian and vehicular traffic was brought to a halt when the siren rang. Thousands of volunteers were mobilized, including Boy Scouts and high-school seniors, to act the role of casualties and evacuees. Victims were carried to emergency hospitals; makeshift shelters were supplied with cots and blankets. In one location, volunteer firemen fought to subdue a blazing pit of oil, nearly blinded by thick "smoke" provided by a fog machine that belonged to the Public Works Mosquito Division. Others fought a simulated apartment-fire without the aid of water, on the assumption that an atomic blast would put the water mains out of service. The films and demonstrations were not meant to frighten us, we were told, but to prepare us. No amount of preparation, however, could hide the gruesome fact that an atomic bomb would kill tens of thousands of people, and, as the leader of the Soviet Union, Nikita Khrushchev, would later express it: "The living would envy the dead."[2]

Rather than focus her attention on "such Macabre thoughts," Goodwin instead sought to find a shelter suitable for her family and friends that could be reached within 12 minutes. She found just the right hideaway one day when she was shopping for her mother in a delicatessen. On this occasion she went to the basement to find a cardboard box her mother required for storage purposes. Upon seeing a metal door at the far end of the basement and asking what it was for, Goodwin learned that beyond the door was the basement of the soda shop, and that all the stores were joined together; she immediately had an idea: all the doors could be opened, creating a single block-long rectangular space that could furnish both entry to the stores and supplies above, and underground housing for an entire neighborhood. Not wasting any time, Goodwin visited every store in the neighborhood, explaining her idea. Visiting the butcher shop that same afternoon, she asked if she could leave some prized possessions of hers, including baseball memorabilia, in the corner of the butcher shop's basement so they'd be on hand when the time came to move in. In the event everyone had to remain in the shelter for an extended period, Goodwin would be able to entertain her fellow occupants by recreating nearly every recent Dodger game. The butcher shop owners had a better idea: Goodwin should keep her belongings in a suitcase under her bed, ready for removal when the time came.

"Now that I had formulated a reasonable plan for the evacuation that would allow me, my family, and our entire neighborhood not only to survive the bomb but to flourish intact in our subterranean shelter," Goodwin wrote, "I was ready to resume ordinary life."[3]

Goodwin's account encapsulates part of the paradox of life in 1950s America — a time succinctly characterized by one historian as an age of "affluence and anxiety." Everywhere one looked, Americans were endowed with unprecedented opulence.[4] Emerging triumphant from World War II, America was unscathed from the devastation other nations had suffered during the conflict, and helped allies and enemies to rebuild. Depression-era unemployment disappeared. The postwar economy wasn't without its setbacks, not everyone benefited from the economic boom, yet the durability of the era's prosperity struck some as astounding.

With $140 billion saved during the war, Americans indulged themselves buying new cars, household appliances, and television sets. America's car culture became a critical component in the rise of suburbia after the war. Not only did the car provide the means for suburbanites to commute to work, the car, along with the suburban home, became emblematic of the good life in America. The breadwinners living in these suburban dwellings had moved from blue-collar status to the white-collar world because of the G.I. Bill, which enabled them to attend college and become professionals, or, in the parlance of the time, "organization men."

Contributing to the ease and prosperity of the '50s were scientific and technological advances. The decade witnessed Jonas Salk's polio vaccine. Corporate America incessantly extolled the "free enterprise system" and the products it bestowed: "Progress is our most important product," proclaimed General Electric.[5]

Yet science had also contributed a grim reality, one that cast a dark shadow over this opulent scene: the continual possibility of nuclear war. It was an age characterized by dangerous and recurring international crises, radioactive fallout emanating from atmospheric nuclear weapons tests, and incessant scientific doomsday prophecies. No matter what they did to put it out of their minds, Americans of the time could never truly avoid a very harsh truth: a good portion of their country could be annihilated within a very short span of time.[6]

Even before the dawn of the atomic age, the public was acquainted with the notion that warfare might destroy civilization, possibly even annihilate mankind itself. Though atomic bombs were subjects of occasional prophecy, most people regarded them as either total fantasy or an issue too far in the future to be taken seriously. If there was to be another world war, the public believed it would wreak havoc with chemical weapons and poison gas — an idea extensively featured in popular journalism and stories, as well as in the motion picture *Things to Come*. During the 1930s such imagery may have slowed the acceptance of civil defense in the nation facing the greatest threat, Great Britain; such measures, many British asserted, would avail nothing. In the opinion of others, especially those on the Left, "Air Raid Precautions" would likely incite war, while other critics emphasized the social problems of a program where the only ones able to afford shelter would be the affluent. These objections elicited strong pro–civil defense arguments, particularly from the celebrated Communist scientist J.B.S. Haldane. The Munich crisis of 1938 silenced the doubts regarding civil defense: Every major European power hastened to augment civil defense preparations.[7]

Long before the nuclear age, the development of aerial warfare had affected a significant transformation in how wars were fought: civilians had joined soldiers as legitimate targets. The realization of this fact led to what became known as "civil defense." World War I, which witnessed German zeppelin attacks on England, marked the beginning of the American civil defense effort.[8] Almost until the time the nation entered the war, American mobilization appeared to reflect the overall lackadaisical national outlook. The principal adage of President Woodrow Wilson's reelection campaign in 1916 — "He kept us out of war" — ruled out any practical full-scale mobilization effort. Shortly after taking office for his second administration, though, Wilson requested and received a declaration of war. Even before then, Wilson had discreetly set up a Council of National Defense, the members of which belonged to Wilson's cabinet. Once the United States became a belligerent in 1917, each governor was asked to create a state council of defense. As there was evidently no clear direction as to what the exact goals and method of operation were to be for these councils, each state was left to formulate how these issues were to be handled. Over a year would pass before the matter of federal management was resolved when the Field Division of the Council of National Defense was created — and, even then, the latter's existence proved quite brief, as the entire civilian "defense" organization was disbanded shortly thereafter. Finding local volunteers was evidently never a major issue, as nearly everyone could receive the chance to "do his bit." It has been calculated that over one million volunteers served in these "civil defense" programs. While feeling that grouping these organizations within the civil defense category might be misleading as the lion's share of their efforts were concentrated on such activities as liberty gardens, scrap collection, and sweater knitting, one author conceded that they were the administrative forebears of subsequent agencies.[9]

Before America's entry into World War II, President Franklin D. Roosevelt established the Office of Civilian Defense (OCD). Initially led by Mayor Fiorella LaGuardia of New York, the OCD charged local councils with the responsibility of maintaining morale and training air-raid wardens and first-aid workers.[10] During the war, a recognizable aspect of life on the home front

> was the OCD air raid warden in his white helmet and armband and a bulky gas mask slung around your neck, who rapped on your door at night to inform you that a sliver of light was showing through your blackout curtains, who manned the sand piles and the first aid stations and the public air raid shelters during air raid drills and who stood lonely nocturnal watches on rooftops ready to sound the alarm at the first approach of enemy planes. He was a neighbor in all probability, and his wife might have signed on as a driver in an OCD motor pool or to help out one day a week in an OCD child care center for the children of working mothers, while his teenage youngsters did their patriotic stint as members of the OCD Junior Service Corps.[11]

When it came to Americans' view of civil defense, a pair of events — the bombing of Britain in 1940 and strongly sanguine government wartime propaganda — persuaded most of them that civil defense was a sensible endeavor. Average people believed they could take necessary measures to protect themselves. That civil defense did nothing to protect German and Japanese civilians from the air raids of 1944–1945 did virtually nothing to alter American thinking. Such an attitude began to change in the wake of the atomic attacks on Japan.[12]

By 1945, when President Harry S Truman terminated the OCD and the atomic bomb unleashed its fury on Japan, the targeting of civilians had already become an accepted aspect of total war. Both Allied and German commanders had ordered aerial attacks on those living in each other's cities. The Allies' bombing of Dresden, Hamburg, and Berlin had claimed tens of thousands of civilian lives, and, on the other side of the globe, one-quarter of Tokyo had been destroyed by a single American incendiary bombing attack — one that produced a firestorm, and killed an estimated 100,000 persons. Comparable air raids during the spring of 1945 yielded deaths far exceeding those at Hiroshima or Nagasaki. The fact was that, prior to the nuclear age, the deaths of a massive number of civilians had become an accepted component of modern war.[13]

During World War II, no one realistically believed that Americans would experience the occupations, invasions, and bombings other countries had suffered. The nuclear age, however, forced Americans to confront an unthinkable possibility: they and their homeland could now become targets of enemy attacks. Within a short time following World War II's conclusion, civil defense planners initiated plans to prepare Americans for World War III, plans that, by the late 1940s, included preparations for a Soviet nuclear attack against the United States. By 1950, the American policy of containing Soviet expansionism was wedded to nuclear deterrence. Should the Soviets rattle their saber in Europe, America would ensure the maintenance of peace, even if that meant unleashing nuclear weapons against the enemy's homeland. Nuclear deterrence depended on the Soviet belief that an attack on their part against Western Europe would trigger an American nuclear retaliatory response on Soviet territory. Such a policy, those who studied the early years of the Cold War have long emphasized, had, as its foundation, domestic requirements: the necessity to mobilize America and organize its institutions to maintain what President John F. Kennedy would characterize as "a long twilight struggle" to back a new idea of national security: the task of protecting America's interests in the age of nuclear weapons would be ceaseless in principle, exorbitant in ways previously unseen, and singularly perilous.

One aspect of Cold War mobilization hasn't received much attention: its moral underpinnings. Should the effort to maintain international tranquility by threatening to unsheathe the nuclear sword fail, igniting the conflict it was meant to avoid, it would be necessary for the American people to pay the price that would ultimately arise. Would they be prepared to do so should that become mandatory, provided the outcome wasn't that devastating to themselves? The answer to that question would determine their willingness to face and wage nuclear war.

Civil defense was the means selected to persuade Americans to accept such an outcome if it, indeed, became a necessary one. Americans would have to be shown that at a minimum, they would survive a nuclear conflagration and, after an acceptable period of reconstruction of their homeland, they could resume their accustomed prewar existence. Protecting Americans in a nuclear attack was not the purpose of civil defense as such protection was an impossibility. The real objective of civil defense was to prevent nuclear attack from occurring in the first place by occasioning the people's acceptance of deterrence — provided they would survive a nuclear attack should the deterrence strategy fail.[14]

The presentation of civil defense themes in popular culture — specifically film and television — during the period spanning the Cold War to the 9/11 era is the focus of this book. My interest in this subject is rooted in a pair of events. The more immediate event occurred in the summer of 2009, when I was viewing the original black-and-white version of George Romero's *Night of the Living Dead* on YouTube. The film's reference to the survivors of the zombies' attack seeking sanctuary at civil defense centers gave me the inspiration for doing this book. In planning this project, I had intended to include Romero's film but had to discard the idea when I failed to uncover any plausible references to civil defense to warrant such inclusion. The second inspiration goes back even further — to the early 1960s when I entered grade school. As a student at Garden City Elementary School in Roanoke, Virginia, my classmates and I marched out into the hallways, practicing evacuation drills. One classmate became so terrified that a bomb would be dropped on the school, he hysterically screamed to not remain there. During these same years, my parents and I visited neighbors across the street from where we lived. On one particular Saturday evening, the television set was tuned to *The Defenders*, a popular courtroom drama airing on CBS. When the preview of the following week's installment appeared on the screen, I wondered how that episode would air, as I believed a war would be occurring then. Cold War civil defense, along with the era's science-fiction films, sparked an interest in me for the 1950s that continues to this day.

An examination of how popular culture has treated civil defense reveals that such presentations have appeared in a wide range of genres: educational, informational, dramatic, exploitive, satirical, and comedic. The venues for the presentation of these themes ranged from school classrooms to movie theaters to living rooms. Especially during what might be termed the "Golden Age of Civil Defense," the 1950s and early 1960s, when Cold War tensions were quite pronounced, all three outlets were active in disseminating civil defense imagery to the public. Conceived as a means of mobilizing every American for a protracted Cold War, the civil defense effort utilized town meetings and public school educational programs and the mass media (television, radio, and, especially, motion pictures) to disseminate its message. The Federal Civil Defense Administration (FCDA) created a film library of short subjects covering nuclear destruction and civil defense; these films were seen nationwide in schools, churches, community halls, and motion picture theaters. The FCDA concluded in 1955 that "each picture will be seen by a minimum of 20,000,000 persons, giving an anticipated aggregate audience of more than half a billion for the civil defense film of 1955."[15] Furnishing motion pictures of the bomb for viewing by the American public was equally important for victory in the Cold War, as was producing the bomb for military utilization. Of great significance was the fact that the dissemination of atomic imagery depended on the concurrent censoring of images from the American atomic attacks on Japan in 1945. While they provided footage of these assaults, American authorities held back both detailed information concerning the bomb's effect on the human body and some firsthand accounts of the aftermath. In this way, Joseph Masco had noted, an immediate goal of the nuclear state was "to calibrate the image of atomic warfare for the American public through the mass circulation of certain images of the bomb" while censoring the remainder. "In this way, officials sought to mobilize the power of mass media to transform nuclear attack from an unthinkable apocalypse into an opportunity for psychological self-management, civic responsibility, and ultimately, governance."[16] Civil defense ultimately aimed to create an "atomic bomb proof" society — one where nuclear war was no more of a threat than any other hazard, "making public support for the Cold War sustainable."[17]

Hollywood films depicted civil defense and nuclear war themes that both exploited and reflected the tensions of the time. The same carried over into the new marvel of the age — television — which sought to inform and entertain viewers with public affairs programs and dramatic productions — the latter spanning the "Golden Age" of live television drama during commercial network television's formative years to the filmed programs that began to dominate the medium as the '50s drew to a close. Motion pictures and television also reflected the ugly everyman-for-himself impulse that arose from President Kennedy's push for fallout shelters during the 1961 Soviet-American confrontation over Berlin. The controversy over shelter ethics in the Kennedy era, the apex of Cold War civil defense activity, discredited the shelter boom.

As the crises that motivated that boom gave way, as the sixties unfolded, to Vietnam and the domestic turbulence brought on by the Southeast Asian conflict and racial discord at home, civil defense faded from the spotlight. As the sixties and the chaos it produced passed into history, a yearning for all things fifties took hold. Compared to the Vietnam-Watergate era, the fifties, a decade characterized by frightening Cold War tensions, now seemed tranquil and reassuring. Fifties nostalgia usually treated bomb shelters in a comedic vein — transforming nuclear hideaways into useful places for other, non-nuclear activities, such as making out with members of the opposite sex.

The fun, however, ended with the dawn of the Reagan era. Ronald Reagan's perceived image as a "nuclear cowboy" sparked renewed fears of nuclear war as well as a return of nuclear war themes in popular entertainment. The most controversial of these productions, The Day After, a 1983 made-for-television movie, sought to influence American public opinion in favor of the nuclear freeze movement.

The final years of the 20th century witnessed a resurgence of civil defense imagery in popular culture in a lighthearted guise, to be replaced, once more, by a darker hue inspired by the real-world events of September 11. The 2001 terrorist attacks on American soil called to mind earlier fears of threats to America's safety as symbolized by the "duck and cover" drills of half-a-century earlier. Movies once more produced images that recalled Cold War-era civil defense. The Cold War had been replaced by the War on Terrorism; "duck and cover" had given way to "duct and cover." The eras had changed, yet, in some ways, things hadn't really changed after all.

As was the case with my previous books, Photofest provided the illustrations appearing in this volume. Rick Worland, professor of cinema and television at Southern Methodist University in Dallas, Texas, reviewed a copy of my manuscript and provided kind words of praise as well as copies of an article he wrote that enhanced this book. Professor Allan M. Winker of Ohio's Miami University helped connect me with his former student, the Rev. Fred Small, senior minister of First Parish in Cambridge, Massachusetts, who gave me permission to use the lyrics of one of his songs in the chapter on *The Day After*. Film director Joe Dante was kind enough to answer questions regarding his film *Matinee*. And, as he's done before, Chris Hartness furnished his expertise in formatting the manuscript and photographs for CD.

1

Government Propaganda Films and Civil Defense

The opening scene shows an anthropomorphic turtle walking upright, his shell on his back, looking dapper in a bow tie, a helmet adorning his head. He is enjoying a carefree stroll down a tree-lined path in a black-and-white cartoon forest. All is calm until, suddenly, a stick of lighted dynamite attached to a string appears. The explosive is wielded by a monkey hanging from a tree limb. As the dynamite goes off, the turtle takes cover in his shell. Over this, a lively verse is heard:

> There was a turtle by the name of Bert
> And Bert the Turtle was very alert;
> When danger threatened, he never got hurt
> He knew just what to do...
> He'd duck and cover, duck and cover!
>
> He did what we all must learn to do...
> Duck and cover!

A narrator then explains that whenever danger looms, Bert protects himself in this manner: "Sometimes, it even saves his life."

Thus begins the most famous — or perhaps infamous — civil defense film in history, *Duck and Cover*. Produced for the FCDA, the film was aimed at school students and meant to teach its young audience that the best way to protect one's self against an atomic attack — with or without warning — was to do just what the film's title implies — duck and cover in the belief that such a strategy would protect students against injury, or even death from the bomb.

Having introduced Bert the Turtle, the film then contrasts the threat of the atomic bomb with such everyday hazards as fire and automobiles. "If you

Civil defense icon: The star of the classic government propaganda film ***Duck and Cover,*** Bert the Turtle taught fifties school children how to protect themselves in the event of an atomic attack (Photofest).

duck and cover like Bert, you will be much safer," the narrator explains. Compared to sunburn, the atomic bomb can burn one far worse, "especially where you're not covered." As people aren't equipped with shells to conceal themselves like Bert, "we have to cover up in our own way." School children are then shown diving under their desks, tightly covering the backs of their necks and faces. Should there be advance warning of an attack, heralded by the wailing of a siren, drop everything you're doing and seek shelter in a school or home — wherever one happens to be. In the event students are away from home, they should find cover at the nearest place, or ask an adult where to go. Should there be a surprise attack, duck and cover against a wall, under a table, in a doorway, away from windows. A family on a picnic is shown hiding from the blast under the cloth upon which their food was spread, while the father uses a newspaper he was stoking a fire with to shield himself. The next important action is to remain covered until the danger has passed.

The film then concludes with Bert the Turtle asking viewers, "What are you supposed to do when you see the flash?" The thunderous reply causes him to jump right back into his shell: "Duck and cover!"

Getting the Word Out: The FCDA and Public Education

America's children's experience in the Cold War had originated in an earlier conflict. World War II proved to be an era of rapid and great social change for children, millions of whom were relocated by their parents to war-boom towns and army posts nationwide. But wherever they settled, children had to contend with the anxieties the war produced. If a siren wailed during a blackout, they couldn't be sure if it was merely another drill or the real thing. These anxieties began on December 7, 1941, when children witnessed the emotional reactions — fear or anger — at the news of Pearl Harbor. The next day, at school, children talked about the war. "Fear of what was to come permeated the air," remembered a child of the time. As could be expected,

America's entry into the war elicited numerous questions on the youngsters' part: "Would the Japs come over here and bomb us next?" "Would they come *even before Christmas?*" "What are we going to do?" inquired a ten-year-old rural Indiana girl. "I am afraid."

Presently children began participating in school air-raid drills, which occasionally proved to be frightening experiences, as when a girl went with her fellow students to the basement during one such exercise and sat against the wall. "Right at that time," she recalled, "I heard an airplane and started to scream: I knew for sure we were going to be bombed." The fact that these drills were held during the daytime didn't make them any less frightening for some children as they were separated from their parents. "I was always afraid," one girl admitted, "that they would get bombed when I was at school and not at home with my family. That terror stuck with me for many, many years." Thus, when the "duck and cover" drills of the early Cold War period arrived, the children who had lived through the drills of World War II were already familiar with them. There were also similarities between the war games children played during the Second World War and the Cold War. The only difference between them was the kind of enemy they fought against: Where once they had played cowboys and Indians or cops and robbers, children now battled "Red Fascism." How they played the game continued as before: Boys enacted the part of valiant soldiers and pilots; girls enemy soldiers, POWs or, most frequently, nurses. Additionally, children chanted the same rhymes:

> Whistle while you work,
> Hitler is a jerk,
> Mussolini is a weeny,
> And Tojo is a jerk.[1]

Children's popular culture of the 1940s (radio, comic books, and movies) hardly changed after World War II — until the advent of television. The lion's share of American youngsters still tuned in to radio during the 1940s, where they followed the exploits of Superman, Captain Marvel, Jack Armstrong, and Don Winslow of the Navy. The main difference between radio and television was that the latter medium replaced the children's parents as the primary clarifier of what was happening in the world beyond the home. In the words of anthropologist Margaret Mead, "for the first time the young are seeing history made *before* it is censored by their elders."[2]

Just the same, the innocence of American childhood during the pre-television era wasn't all that innocuous. When listening to radio, children created their own visual images of what they heard; postwar research determined that radio was a more important stimulator of children's imaginations than television. Children also had entrée to outside visual images that lacked adults as intermediaries: war photographs, particularly those in *Life* magazine featuring war's barbarities — especially the Holocaust; newsreels ("a sort of *Life* magazine made animate" in the words of one journalist) that exposed children to combat footage; and Hollywood war films — which echoed the public's view that World War II was a righteous conflict against a vile enemy and confirmed the American Way of Life. These films continued to be made long after the actual fighting had ended, and found a most devoted audience in the boys of the veterans who had fought in the war.[3]

World War II also introduced the mixed blessing of the atomic bomb. While most American children accepted the fact that the bomb had been necessary to end the war and save American lives, the bomb also brought the frightening possibility of instant obliteration. One home-front boy remembered that "fear, bewilderment, and confusion swept the minds of grade schoolers when they heard the news."

"Every newsreel," a home-front girl wrote, "showed the mushroom cloud over and over," and *Life's* photographs were also "imprinted in my mind's eye forever." All of these images signified an inescapable reality: "There is no place to hide."[4]

Though children's fears gradually diminished, they never completely vanished. The immediate postwar years witnessed American atomic bomb tests, the Russians' acquisition of their own bomb, civil defense drills in cities and schools, the rise of Senator Joseph McCarthy and the outbreak of war in Korea — to be followed by fears over contamination from radioactive fallout, bomb shelters, and a parade of atomic-age monsters in such films as *Them!* (1954) and *It Came from Beneath the Sea* (1955). Given all those unsettling developments, nuclear fear became a primary cultural consideration — with children its greatest victims.[5] In summation, historian William M. Tuttle, Jr., has written:

> During the Second World War, America's children were patriotic to the core; in the years after 1945, they were ready — emotionally, cognitively, ideologically — to continue doing their duty during the Cold War. Yet in many ways the Cold War was a strange time to be a child. Children in postwar America were perplexed, and their lives were filled with a basic contradiction. In an era of permissive child rearing, their lives seemed especially precarious to their parents and to society generally, and yet, as the children themselves knew, they could be incinerated in a split second. This was a prescription if not for schizophrenia, then at least for deep ambivalence about life and the future.[6]

Bert the Turtle and the FCDA both owed their creation to the postwar rivalry between two erstwhile World War II allies, the United States and the Soviet Union. During the first stage of this competition, 1946–1948, the United States possessed an enormous advantage in its control over the atomic bomb — an asset that, in the words of Melvyn Leffler, constituted "a shield behind which the nation could pursue its diplomatic goals." Owing to America's sole possession of nuclear weapons, American officials shaped the international postwar recovery in line with their own objectives, to collaborate less and behave in such a way as "to do things they might otherwise have hesitated to do" had they felt their actions would result in armed conflict.

The Soviet acquisition of their own atomic bomb in 1949 completely altered this serene picture, causing a pair of grave concerns for the administration of President Harry S Truman. On the one hand, the president and his advisers were alarmed, not so much about the immediate atomic power now resting in Soviet Premier Joseph Stalin's hands, but by the diplomatic consequences arising from the Soviet atomic breakthrough; American concerns involved whether its European allies would continue collaborating with America's postwar objectives, and whether the Soviets would magnify their own postwar aspirations and undertake a more belligerent course to realize those aims. An added concern of the Americans involved the consequences that would be incurred should the Soviets now possess the means to annihilate or, at best, impair the American industrial core, which had been the foundation of the nation's might during and after the Second World War.

The solution the Truman administration decided upon was additional and larger nuclear weapons: Such a course would allow the United States to sustain both military and diplomatic advantage. Truman's successor, Dwight D. Eisenhower, continued this policy. Yet, as one historian has asserted, it "proceeded in confusing fits and starts" and shouldn't be considered a crystal-clear process. There existed serious disagreements throughout the security bureaucracy as to what was the best course of action to implement the containment of communism. These disagreements notwithstanding, there arose a national security state which sired numerous agencies — one of which was given over to civil defense.

The initial postwar civil defense agency was the National Security Resources Board (NSRB). As civil defense was but one of the Board's duties, it was at first shunted in favor of other matters. In 1948, a tiny NSRB staff took up the challenge of devising atomic-age civil defense, utilizing numerous military studies to aid them in their task. Each of these studies decided that, with modest adjustments, World War II–style civil defense procedures could furnish protection from the more advanced armaments of the nuclear age. Moreover, the studies urged President Truman to create a distinct agency, the sole purpose of which would be the development of a civil defense program. Owing to the American dominance in atomic weapons, and the absence of any current diplomatic menace, Truman merely threw his backing to "peacetime planning and preparation" for civil defense; his goal was "to minimize the program without completely abandoning it."

That all changed with the Soviet attainment of the bomb in 1949. Civil defense was now accelerated. All during the autumn of 1949, politicians, scientists, and citizens of every political persuasion pressed the administration for action beyond mere studies. These pressures intensified with the outbreak of hostilities in Korea the following year. The combination of the Soviet atomic bomb, China's absorption into the communist realm, and the Korean War were sufficient to lead to the establishment of a new agency solely committed to civil defense. NSRB head Stuart Symington, a former Democratic senator from Missouri and secretary of the Air Force, informed Truman that the time had passed when a military and civilian mobilization could be formulated "with relative leisure." In July 1950, he broadened the NSRB's civil defense planning staff and demanded that another recommendation be forwarded to the president by September. Bearing the formal designation "United States Civil Defense" (or the *Blue Book* as it was unofficially dubbed), the report recommended the enactment of civil defense legislation, the creation of a civil defense administration separate from the NSRB, and the designation of an administrator to run this new agency. Receiving presidential endorsement, the plan was sent to Congress for the latter's consideration, and as 1950 drew to a close, Congress, mindful of communist China's intervention in the Korean War, acted with comparative speed to approve what became known as the Federal Civil Defense Act. The new law shifted civil defense duties out of the NSRB's hands and into the new Federal Civil Defense Administration which was part of the executive branch. The law stipulated that the FCDA was to be placed under civilian management. To fill that post, Truman named Millard Caldwell, a former Democratic congressman and governor of Florida. Despite opposition to his appointment due to his support of segregation while holding political office, Caldwell was confirmed and began his duties as FCDA head in January 1951.[7]

From the start, the role of the FCDA was clarified as supervisory and inspirational in nature; state and local governments were to bear the burden of devising practical means of both putting civil defense measures into motion and underwriting them. Instead of earmarking federal resources to support civil defense projects, the FCDA produced educational and propaganda materials aimed at galvanizing state and local agencies and private citizens to invest their own resources to bring civil defense programs to fruition. Surveying the FCDA's activities during the Truman era, historian Allan Winkler observed that, while the agency's achievements bore scant fruit when it came to real content, its work nevertheless had major ramifications. Under Caldwell's watch, the FCDA busied itself convening conferences, authorizing studies, preparing intricate plans, and overall endowed civil defense with an essence of official activity. And, in Winkler's words, it did "a good deal of cajoling of the American public." During the early phase of its existence, the FCDA inundated the nation with 16 million copies of a brochure, *Survival Under Atomic Attack*; disseminated a motion picture bearing the same name, narrated by Edward R. Murrow; prepared Alert America, a civil defense exhibition that required ten tractor-trailer trucks to transport it for viewing nationwide; and, as a trial run of a planned national program, gave everyone living in Allentown, Pennsylvania, a metal identification tag.[8] Those attending the Alert America preview in Washington, D.C., came out "somber faced and noticeably lacking in small talk."[9]

In addition to these activities, the FCDA encouraged numerous professionals — educators, architects, morticians, hospital administrators, physicians — to climb aboard the civil defense bandwagon. Of these groups, educators evinced the greatest fervor for the civil defense effort. A huge percentage of FCDA publications was aimed at schoolchildren and, indirectly, their parents. Another federal agency, the Atomic Energy Commission (AEC), collaborated with the National Educational Association in issuing school materials. Civil defense provided educators a pair of advantages: it served as a means of sanctioning federal aid to education and provided a way of offsetting postwar condemnations of progressive education lodged by conservatives and anti–Communists, who complained of "reducation" or "why Johnny can't read."

Civil defense had been initiated in one-quarter of American schools before the end of 1951. The principal focus of civil defense measures on the part of educators was furnishing necklace identification tags and the establishment of air-raid drills — with the latter adopted by the school systems of numerous major cities by 1950. In Los Angeles, schools conducted surprise drills on a weekly basis in late 1950. Children were instructed to kneel with their backs facing the windows, their faces encased in their knees in fetal positions, eyes shut, their hands clasped behind their necks. In the words of a New York teacher reminiscing about this exercise during his childhood: "The teachers would tell every body to get under the desks. You could feel the tension in the air, fear. The kids are fidgety and jumpy ... then there would be absolute silence. You never knew if it was a drill — a test — or the real thing." Similarly, in the words of a Pennsylvania laborer: "And I can also recall the stupid instruction, if you can't get under the desk, then get in the doorway. I heard that Pittsburgh would be wiped off the map, and I said, 'Wow, so will we because we're not that far from Pittsburgh.'" And, in Minnesota, a clerk explained, students were led by teachers to the school basement for sanctuary during the drills. "It was kind of scary, but it was a different kind of frightening thing. It was not like somebody was going to come and get you, but if an attack actually did happen, it would be so terrible."[10]

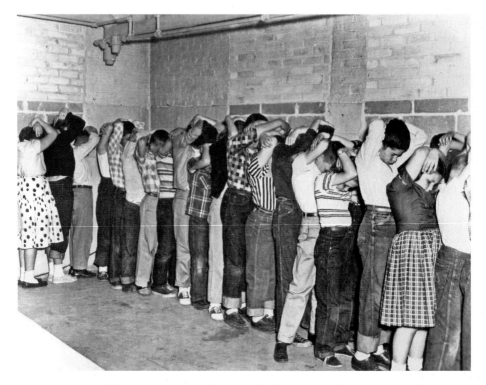

School children practice a civil defense drill in 1958 (Libra Films/Photofest).

Three types of drills were conducted by American schools in the 1950s. Of these, the most familiar — and most famous — was the "duck and cover" exercise, intended to provide protection against a surprise attack. Students either dropped to the floor or crowded under their desks when a teacher instructed them to and assumed what one educator dubbed "the atomic head clutch position": Backs facing the windows, faces hidden between the knees, hands clasped on the back of the neck, ears covered by the arms, and eyes shut (as a New York psychologist remembered). The purpose of the "atomic clutch" was to shield children from the bomb flash, flying glass, and falling timbers — what a civil defense advocate termed "life in a meatgrinder" and the National Educational Association cautioned teachers to have students assume the atomic clutch position instantly should a "sudden dazzling light" appear outside the school. The "atomic clutch," in the words of a Los Angeles school administrator, had received doctors' sanction as "it provides the desired protection for the back of the neck.... It compresses to some degree the organs of the abdomen, decreasing the effects of the blast on these organs."[11]

Advance warning drills, or "shelter drills," were based on the assumption that teachers and students had sufficient time to take cover in the school's basement, hallways, or other areas civil defense and school officials felt could endure an explosion. Once a school principal sounded the alarm signifying the start of the drill, teachers directed students to stand up, line up in a methodical fashion, and proceed to the designated shelter; once there, everyone sat near the walls, as the latter were thought to provide the greatest amount of protection. Occasionally students were directed to assume the atomic head clutch position for additional protection. To those who questioned the effectiveness of this method, Detroit educators, exhibiting a curious kind of reasoning, declared, "It is obvious that any particular building may be distant from any particular blast. Hence, any particular bomb may produce only light damage or no damage ... (though there is a significant chance it will destroy your area). *Hence, even light protection may yield appreciable security.*"[12]

The dispersal drill was also based on the theory of advance warning — this time the children had sufficient time to return home before the bomb fell. When the school day was over, teachers merely told students that an air-raid drill was about to start and asked them to go to their homes as quickly as they could. Only New York and a handful of eastern cities held these exercises, as school officials presently understood they had no control over the children in their charge and couldn't be certain that any warning would be enough to ensure their arrival at home before an attack.[13]

When it came to the ID tags, the New York City Schools expended $159,000 by early 1952 to furnish two million such tags for public, parochial, and private school children from kindergarten through fourth grade. A 1951 ad for Bead Chain Manufacturing Company appearing in the *School Executive* featured a child showing his dogtag to a soldier. In another ad, a mother was shown giving her son a dogtag necklace, with the accompanying caption saying in part: "From New York to Redwood, California, many cities ... are ordering Identification Necklaces as a safeguard for their school children." What went unsaid by the ad was the necklaces' true purpose: to allow more accurate identification of the dead — or of injured children who lived through an initial atomic explosion. In Chicago in 1950 city civil defense planners recommended a program "to tattoo its citizens with their blood types — underneath the armpits because arms might be blown off— in case radiation sickness called for quick transfusions."[14]

The educational film market provided the other option for the FCDA to get the civil defense message out. This option, in the words of Conelrad.com, an Internet website devoted to the study of Cold War–era civil defense, was "an ideal vehicle for the lessons of civil defense that utilized the genre of the training film that was perfected and widely used during World War II." With the coming of peace, training films were used in school systems, government, and private industry. Among the companies producing educational, or "mental hygiene," films were Coronet, Centron, and Encyclopædia Britannica Films. Early productions in the genre were *Dating: Do's and Don'ts* and *Are You Popular?*

Initially nine films, based on the number of subjects the FCDA wanted to cover, were to be produced. Some of the subjects were merely themes ("civil defense for schools," "the dangers of evacuating a target city"), while others had previously been the subjects of brochures published for the FCDA by the Government Printing Office ("Survival Under Atomic Attack," "Fire Fighting for Householders"). Presidential special assistant Dallas Halverstadt and the head of the FCDA's motion picture division, Howard R.H. Johnson, reached an agreement with several film distributors to have the films made in a speedy manner and with as little government direction as possible. Of the distributors entering into this arrangement with the government, Castle Films was the most important. The distributor would keep most of the profit while the studio that made the film obtained a small royalty for each print sold.

James M. Franey, president of United World Films, Inc., the owner of Castle Films, immediately got in touch with Archer Productions, Inc., vice president Leo M. Langlois about getting in on the project. Langlois later explained that Franey "suggested I look into it, that it might be something I'd be interested in and, you know, did a little job on me." Earlier, Langlois had informed Franey of Archer's desire to work on other projects besides commercials. Moreover, Archer had already notified the Defense Department that it wanted to produce training films.

Archer had initially been a sales "front" for Langlois's brother-in-law, Lars Calonius, an animator who had worked for the Disney Studios in Los Angeles. After World War II, encouraged by Langlois, Calonius came to New York to position himself for the anticipated explosion in television advertising. During this period, Langlois was an executive with the Campbell-Ewald ad agency. From there, he went to Cecil Pressbury, then joined Archer Productions as vice-president and executive producer.

Going to Washington to check out the offer Franey had passed on to him, Langlois gathered all the pertinent information, then reported back to a little executive meeting at Archer and acquired the go-ahead. The studio bid, successfully, to produce two of the nine civil defense films, when the truth of the matter was that Archer only wanted to do one film. Screenwriter Ray J. Mauer, who penned the script for *Duck and Cover*, explained, "I think we took the clunker in order to get 'Civil Defense for Schools' (the working title for *Duck and Cover*)."

Embarking upon the project, Archer fully realized that it wouldn't reap a financial gold mine in producing the film, yet, in Langlois's words, patriotic motivations also figured into the equation. The thought that the film would be seen in schools nationwide excited him. "I saw it not only as a good citizen and doing something for your country but also as a possibility of making some money at the same time," he recalled.

Once the contract to produce the two films was a done deal, Langlois enlisted the services of Mauer, an acquaintance from Campbell-Ewald, to write the scripts. A copywriter, Mauer was a novice when it came to writing dramatic material, and had to clear the assignment with his employer before accepting it.[15]

The government stipulated that "Civil Defense for Schools" receive the endorsement of the National Education Administration (NEA), most likely because the latter's approval would serve to deflect censure from the educational community. In Langlois's words, "Well, the NEA [requirement] was merely the civil defense administration protecting their rear end and making sure that they had endorsement from the union." During a two-day session in May 1951, NEA headquarters in Washington was the site of a brainstorming meeting involving Langlois, Mauer, FCDA and NEA officials, and 20 or more teachers from across the nation to formulate the best means of presenting the civil defense message to children — with Mauer recording notes for the outline of his script. One of the conferees, Helen Seth-Smith, a transplanted English woman, and the assistant headmistress of The Potomac School in McLean, Virginia, provided both the spark to the gathering and the phrase that would forever be associated with Cold War-era civil defense exercises in schools when she said, "We have duck and cover drills in our school." The words "duck and cover" registered, not only with Mauer and Langlois, but with the FCDA's Howard R.H. Johnson; the latter decided it would serve as the focus for the film.

Mauer set to work on the initial draft of what now was called *Duck and Cover*, while simultaneously penning the screenplay for the other film for which Archer contracted, *Our Cities Must Fight*. As Mauer tended to his screenwriting chores, Langlois brought a director on board for both films: Anthony Rizzo. The latter had relocated from Chicago to New York with a reference from suspense novelist Bill Ballenger. Ballenger himself was already acquainted with Langlois and Mauer, having worked with both at Campbell-Ewald. Before signing on to direct the Archer civil defense films, Rizzo had directed a TV drama series for ABC's Chicago affiliate from scripts Ballenger had penned. "Langlois recalled Rizzo was also hired on the basis of his confidence in being able to bring even more business to Archer."[16]

In Mauer's initial version of the *Duck and Cover* screenplay, the idea of Bert the Turtle was presented, but not in the cartoon format in which he eventually appeared. In conceiving the idea for the character, Mauer explained,

"I just thought of some way to illustrate that [the duck and cover drill] to kids. Little kids, big kids. I guess it worked." As to naming the character Bert, "I wanted a short and hopefully memorable name, so I resorted to euphony. BERT rhymed with TURT[le] which might have made Shakespeare retch, but ... it worked."

Lars Calonius's talents as an animator entered the picture after the second draft of Mauer's script — which presented Bert in animated form — was greenlighted. Calonius prepared little sketches and submitted them. The FCDA, in Langlois's words, was "very pleased and very happy" with how work on the project was coming along. In the new draft of Mauer's script, Bert's adversary was changed from a skunk to a monkey. As to why this change occurred, Mauer opined, "Sorry, I just don't remember. Maybe in those days, Sen. McCarthy's inquisition gave skunks an inferiority complex, rendering the little animals too bland for children." The change may also have been dictated by gender tastes: "The skunk appealed to boy students, but girls had daintier tastes. Apparently everyone prefers our simian relatives."[17]

Once the FCDA had approved the script and some demonstration sketches of Bert, filming on *Duck and Cover* began, with primary filming done at P.S. 152 in Astoria, Queens, which had been selected for the shoot by the superintendent of the New York City school system. Several real-life teachers and students appeared in the film, which was shot with a 35mm Mitchell silent camera. The only dialogue present in the film is that heard in the animated sequence. "Tony," the boy who jumps off his bike in the sequence and demonstrates what to do when the bomb explodes, was played by Langlois's son, Leo "Hitch" Langlois III; his appearance was due to budgetary reasons, according to his father, and because Hitch wanted to do it. The civil defense official who comes to Tony's aid in the same sequence was Ray J. Mauer himself.[18] Other talents who participated in the production of *Duck and Cover* were a pair of character actors, Robert Middleton and Carl Ritchey, who, respectively, provided the film's narration and Bert the Turtle's voice at the film's conclusion.

Leo Langlois himself lent his efforts to the writing of the film's theme song, collaborating with the commercial jingle team of Leo Carr and Leon Corday. This wasn't the trio's first songwriting effort, as they'd earlier teamed up on another commercial jingle, "See the U.S.A. in Your Chevrolet." In both instances, Carr and Corday received sole credit. In telling the latter pair what he wanted for the *Duck and Cover* project, Langlois was quite straightforward: "I told them, basically ... we have to write a song for Bert the Turtle. Here's the opening and closing. Here's what it does and this is what the lyrics will be about. And that was about the size of it. They were jotting down notes while I was talking." Langlois's other musical contribution to the film was the demo version of the song that Dave Lambert, Archer's primary music arranger, used to record the final version of the song that appeared in the film.

Almost as soon as Archer had completed *Duck and Cover*, the FCDA wanted to lay their hands on it and debut it as fast as possible. It was up to Milt Mohr, Archer's publicity man, to get the word out about the film and see to it that Archer was inseparably linked to it. In this task, he succeeded brilliantly: Of all the films produced on behalf of the civil defense campaign, Archer's contribution is the best known. Archer also had Burelle's clip service cull clippings citing the film from daily newspaper or trade publications which were sent to Langlois at the Archer offices.

Bert didn't have to wait for his film debut to get his image publicized. Before the film's release, he appeared in a 14-minute radio adaptation of the film, produced by the FCDA's Audio Visual Department, and a 16-page color booklet, drawn by Langlois and issued by the Government Printing Office, that was distributed to schools. Bert was also seen in a nationwide newspaper serialization.

Bert's film debut, along with that of *Our Cities Must Fight*, occurred January 7, 1952, in Washington, D.C., as part of the kick-off of the FCDA's Alert America effort. According to a letter to Bert's creator from FCDA chief Millard Caldwell, *Duck and Cover* was a smashing success: "The film was so well received at the Alert America Convoy Exhibit here in Washington last week that it was shown continuously during the entire week." Caldwell said nothing about how Archer's other film was received. *Duck and Cover* would also be part of the entire Alert America tour. The film's Washington debut was followed, on January 24, by a screening before educators at a preview theater in Manhattan. At this occasion, John C. Cocks, who represented the Board of Education on New York City's civil defense staff, stressed the film's "mental hygiene approach, its underlying qualities of cheerfulness and optimism." Page three of that day's *New York Post* proclaimed: "Pupils to See 'Bert Turtle' Duck A-Bomb."

Hollywood got in on the act as well as part of Milt Mohr's public relations campaign promoting *Duck and Cover*.[19] On February 5, 1952, with print and television journalists present, actress Maureen O'Sullivan, Jane of *Tarzan* film fame and the wife of film director John Farrow, held an atomic attack drill with her children at their home in Beverly Hills. Following the exercise, the kids were photographed with an enormous cardboard poster featuring Bert the Turtle's likeness. Appearing in newspapers the next day, the picture was accompanied with headlines such as "Alerted—Not Alarmed." One of the children photographed with Bert, seven-year-old Maria de Lourdes, would achieve Hollywood stardom as Mia Farrow.[20]

Duck and Cover's initial airing in the New York City television market occurred on February 23, 1952, with subsequent viewing as a "documentary" nationwide. The film then had its initial classroom viewing in the New York City area on March 6. The reaction of its young audience, summarized in the words of a pair of sixth graders — Marine Yull and Betty Ann Stackhouse — was that it was "very instructive," "not too frightening for children," "interesting and funny in spots," and "not too babyish" or "too grown up."

As part of the film's classroom debut, the FCDA issued a teaching guide declaring that *Duck and Cover* "demonstrates for school children the base principles of atomic self-protection." If the film "is carefully integrated with a study of civil defense," the guide added, "it can help your pupils acquire a quick and easy technique for self-protection from an atomic explosion as well as help them understand the need for civil defense." The guide sought to anticipate the questions that might arise from certain segments of the film ("Atomic flash may lead to questions about other effects of atomic explosions, additional uses of atomic energy"), as well as requesting teachers to "preview the film and analyze it" and consider "what scenes may arouse fear." Concerning the latter, the guide was silent as to what sort of "guidance" would help calm such anxieties but did suggest that teachers "provide each pupil with a copy of 'Bert the Turtle' [a pamphlet available through your State civil defense office]."[21]

Not everyone applauded *Duck and Cover*. In the view of certain groups — the Levittown (NY) Educational Association (LEA) and the Committee for the Study of War Tensions in Children — the film presented "terrifying concepts" and was an "actual disservice" to children. In most instances, the NEA's prior endorsement countered such criticisms. Defending the film against the LEA's strictures, Forrest Corson, a civil defense spokesman for Nassau County, accused the critics of "unwittingly following the Communist party line laid down in their official publications." Quoting the *Daily Worker* to back up his argument, Corson continued, "It is the Communist policy to deride Civil Defense wherever possible, to question and ridicule its necessity, and to 'abhor' the effect of air raid drills on tender impressionable young minds. I am sure that all thinking parents want their children to be prepared for catastrophe. It is exactly what Civil Defense is trying to do."[22]

In reality, *Duck and Cover*'s critics weren't far off the mark. The school air raid drills of the time did inflict trauma on the children who participated in them. Sociologist Todd Gitlin recalled what it was like to be a member of "the first American generation compelled from infancy to fear not only war but the end of days":

> Every so often, out of the blue, a teacher would pause in the middle of class and call out, "Take cover!" ... Sometimes the whole school was taken out into the halls, away from the windows, and instructed to crouch down, heads to the

walls, our eyes scrunched closed, until further notice…. Whether or not we believed that hiding under a school desk or in a hallway was going to protect us from the furies of an atomic blast, we could never quite take it for granted that the world we had been born into was destined to endure.

School civil defense drills were the greatest of all factors that subsequently stirred protests to civil defense programs across the country — and while mothers constituted the majority of protesters, on occasion students themselves rose up in outrage. During her days as a California high schooler in the mid–'50s, Joan Baez, later the queen of sixties protest music, committed her initial act of civil disobedience by refusing to comply with instructions during a school air raid drill. Consequently "the next day I was on the front page of the local paper, photograph and all, and for many days thereafter letters to the editor streamed in, some warning that Palo Alto had communist infiltrators in its school system." Another activist, Jackie Goldberg, a major figure in the free speech movement at the University of California in the early '60s, started her uprising at Berkeley by organizing fellow students to protest the presence of the university's bomb shelter. Looking back on his school drill days from the perspective of the late 1970s, a California cab driver explained, "If it happens, it happens. They drop it, then we are blown away, and that's it. Only the young, the naïve, and the school teachers were fooled by the drills."[23]

Anti-nuclear activist Charles Hansen felt his anxieties began on account of the "shapeless fears" occupying his mind since the civil defense drills held at the school he attended in Seattle: "I remember watching President Kennedy on television when he talked about the Cuban missile crisis. He said the Russian ship was in the bull's-eye, and that upset me." In connection with this, Landon Y. Jones has written: "It was no different after the Three Mile Island nuclear accident of 1979, when the first protestors to take to the streets were the same grownup kids who had marched through the air-raid drills a quarter-century earlier. Like the Japanese, they would never outgrow the feeling that they were all *Hibakusha*, survivors of the bomb."[24]

When it came to nuclear destruction, a generation of public school children were taught to regard it as nothing more than another problem of modern living. Of greater significance, observes historian JoAnne Brown, school civil defense programs sought to instruct American families "to equate emotional maturity with an attitude of calm acceptance toward nuclear war." In the summer of 1951, Dr. Jean A. Thompson, acting director of the New York Bureau of Child Guidance, noted the 12 psychiatrists employed by the New York Board of Education, who promised her that "well-adjusted," psychologically composed children displayed no evidence of nuclear fear. In support of this assertion, Dr. Thompson related the story of a 12-year-old boy: Hearing an explosion, he looked out the window of his home, and told his mother "no mushroom cloud" before "he returned to his homework, with a pleasant and reassuring smile at his mother."[25] Though numerous students recognized the fallaciousness of bomb-threat education, they kept their concerns about it private and found it hard, even embarrassing, to articulate such fears. "The Bomb," in the words of a New York social worker, "probably embarrassed my parents, and they sort of communicated it to me. Like sex, like death, like God, like certain things in my parents' past that they did not want to talk about."[26]

Where *Duck and Cover* was aimed at school children, *Our Cities Must Fight*, the "clunker" Archer agreed to do in order to get the former film, targeted adults—and took a hard line against those who dissented from its theme—the necessity of remaining in a city targeted for atomic attack.

As the film opens, an editor summons an acquaintance for help with a story he's preparing. The frustrated editor reads aloud a letter that sums up his sense of disappointment: "Dear Editor. Usually I agree with your editorials but your call for civil defense volunteers was nonsense. If this city is attacked, my plans are made and they don't include waiting around to get killed. I'm going to take my family to a place in the country where we'll be safe. I think I'm as patriotic as the next guy but I'd be pretty dumb to remain in the city when those bombs start falling."

"Another member of the 'take-to-the-hills' fraternity," observes the editor's friend. "Most of them are intelligent people, good citizens ... but they've made up their minds without thinking. They're letting fear push them."

"It's pushing them into something pretty close to treason," opines the editor. "Thank God most people don't feel that way. But enough of them do to make it a serious problem."

The film then explains why fleeing an enemy attack is inadvisable: "First of all, the highways would be about the most dangerous place you could be.... Second, mass evacuation of cities just doesn't work ... third ... if war comes, and we desert our cities, we've lost the war."

Picking up the argument, the editor observes, "The civil defense people are just being realistic in not planning mass evacuations. The roads have to be kept open for rescue and for fire-fighting equipment. That means every car which is not officially authorized will have to be stopped and moved out of the way." Here, the editor cites his experience in World War II when European refugees sought to flee their cities, only to "choke up the road so hardly anything could move. Even they couldn't get very far." The result would be that rescue operations would be halted. Likewise, transportation facilities must remain functional: "Every available kind of transportation will be needed for emergency work." Mass evacuation isn't allowable "if only for one reason ... the fact that every able-bodied person is needed in the city before as well as after an attack.... We must realize that, in modern warfare, city dwellers find themselves right in the front lines. After an attack, our first responsibly will be to keep our heads and get back to our jobs — for each of us has a job to do, and no matter what happens, the people of the city must be fed, clothed, supplied with electricity, heat. The city must be kept alive, and it will take everything the city has to do it."

Our Cities Must Fight goes on to downplay the hazards of remaining in a city in the aftermath of an atomic strike. Regarding the "danger of lingering radiation," the editor dismisses it as "not really very serious. After an atomic air burst, the danger of radiation and falling debris is over within a minute-and-a-half." More importantly, the experience of people in London, Berlin, and other European cities during World War II showed that they didn't want to vacate their cities; most who did soon returned. Certain individuals — small children, the elderly, and the infirm — should be evacuated, but voluntarily by their families before an attack. The able-bodied are duty bound to remain and help. Modern warfare is no respecter of civilians. To shirk such a responsibility is an act of desertion. For a civilian it would be treasonable, and would mean that one would have to live knowing that "in deserting your responsibility, you failed yourself, your family, your friends, your city." Deserting our cities would give the enemy a great, less expensive victory. It would relinquish "our most feared weapon — America's power to produce."

As the film concludes, the editor observes that an enemy attack on our cities would present dangers formerly limited to soldiers; this notwithstanding, "We've got to be able to take it and come back fighting. Everything we hope for, everything we believe in, everything America has fought for, will depend on us and what we do.... A lot of people behind the Iron Curtain are wondering whether we can take it if we're attacked. They're carefully measuring our courage, our capacity to fight, our capacity for sacrifice. They think they have the answers ... you and I and every American has to examine their minds and hearts and come up with a few answers of their own. The question is: Have Americans got the guts?"

The editor then turns and looks directly into the camera at the audience: "Have you got the guts?"

Our Cities Must Fight echoes many of the points set forth in an earlier civil defense publication, *How to Survive an Atomic Bomb,* published in 1950. Its author, Richard Gerstell, was a radiologist and an erstwhile researcher for the Pennsylvania State Game Commission, as well as an adviser with the Pentagon's office of civil defense planning. Gerstell's work had the posthumous sanction of Secretary of Defense James Forrestal, who committed suicide just before its issuance. For those residing "in an important city or a large seaport or manufacturing town," Gerstell wrote, "you ought to think about sending your children away to the country if we get into a big war." Urban dispersal was a "silly idea." As to leaving the city to avoid an attack, Gerstell asked: "Where are you going to end up? Who's going to take care of you? Who's going to keep you from running into worse radioactivity than you left?" The responsibility for such matters should rest with the authorities: "Your local government may decide to evacuate some people (That is, move them to a different place. It's pronounced 'ee-VAK-u-ate'). But if they do, they'll do it according to a plan." Shelters were a far more advantageous alternative. Every city "has *lots* of tall buildings which have deep, safe cellars.... So, you see, although there is more chance that big cities will be bombed, there is also more protection against bombings in big cities." In the event that it made appropriate preparations, a major city experiencing more than one atomic bomb "should be back to fairly regular life in one or two months.... Just keep *facts* in mind, and forget the fairy stories. Follow the safety rules. Avoid panic. And you'll come through all right."[27]

After producing *Duck and Cover* and *Our Cities Must Fight* for the FCDA, an event occurred that signaled the demise of Archer Productions. After becoming president of the company, Leo Langlois planned to move Archer into television production. That dream died when actor Raymond Massey, heeding his wife's counsel, backed out of appearing in *American Almanac*, an anthology series that was to be Archer's entry into network television programming. Massey's exit killed the production. Archer's income had been invested toward major television series production at the expense of the company's primary source of income. Film-development labs and other vendors lodged claims for unpaid bills. "I was there," Mauer explained, "when the sheriff came in and chewed everybody out." Shortly afterward Archer was dissolved and its assets auctioned to pay the company's debts. The government also wanted to buy both civil defense films the company had produced. A sale was orchestrated for $13,000. The combined sum Archer had invested in the productions — and never recovered — was approximately $25,000.

Archer's demise notwithstanding, almost everyone involved with the company went on to better days. Leo Langlois remained in the advertising field — penning a song for Lyndon Johnson's 1964 presidential campaign and personally providing LBJ a preview of the tune — as well as working in Hollywood as an assistant director on several TV productions, including *One Step Beyond*, *The Twilight Zone*, *The Monkees*, and *I Dream of Jeannie*. Yet his crowning achievement remained *Duck and Cover*, which his family replayed on the VCR at his wake in 2003.

For Ray J. Mauer, civil defense "was a good thing":

> I didn't know how effective it would be. I thought it was wise to make whatever preparations could be devised by the best minds. I had no idea whether that was

happening or not. But you know I was a writer for hire.... I would have written almost anything. It was fun and if it did some good that would make me feel good. And I guess it did. Thank heaven nobody ever had to put it into practice.

Continuing to work as a director and in the advertising field long after his association with Archer, Anthony Rizzo entered the real estate field; he died in 2004. Departing Archer before the company's demise, Lars E. Calonius established his own production company in New York and worked in animation until 1980. After his retirement, he painted portraits and still lifes. He died in 1995.

Bert the Turtle was introduced to a new generation with his appearance in the 1982 documentary film *The Atomic Café*. A dozen years later, Bert's claim to immortality was assured when *Duck and Cover* was chosen by the Library of Congress for inclusion in its National Film Registry.[28]

Other Government Propaganda Films

The *Duck and Cover* campaign illustrated one of the public relations challenges confronting the FCDA: balancing the paradoxes of nuclear preparedness. On the one hand, atomic secrets had to be kept under wraps while, at the same time, the public had to be sufficiently informed so that it would be eager to take part in the civil defense effort. Another public relations quandary for the FCDA mirrored, in Laura McEnaney's words, a "tension inherent in the paramilitary nature of preparedness itself: how to get people involved in civil defense without ordering them around like military grunts." Mindful that popular loathing of military rule precluded the use of a military figure as the public face of civil defense, civil defense planners sought the services of important and creditable civilians to advance their cause. Toward this end, planners utilized renowned scientists such as Ralph Lapp and Richard Gerstell, and show business celebrities. Among those in the latter category were George Burns and Gracie Allen, Groucho Marx, and Bing Crosby. Another spokesperson, photographer Ansel Adams, told the FCDA: "Pictures of schools, churches, individuals ... will stir the emotions, amplify morale and encourage greater service to civil defense."[29]

Also lending his services to the FCDA was CBS News commentator Edward R. Murrow, who narrated the film *Survival Under Atomic Attack*. Murrow's background as a war correspondent in Europe during World War II and the Korean War made him the perfect choice for this assignment and added to the film's credibility.[30] Produced by Castle Films, *Survival Under Atomic Attack* reportedly sold more copies than any previous government film had.[31]

"Let us face, without panic, the reality of our times," Murrow intones at the film's beginning, "the fact that atom bombs may someday be dropped on our cities. And let us prepare for survival, understanding the weapon that threatens us."

After explaining how the bomb "destroys or injures" through blast, heat, and radioactivity, the film reiterates the theme of *Our Cities Must Fight:* "If an emergency should come, our factories will be battle stations. Production must go on if we are to win. Our offices and homes will also be posts of duty — not to be deserted." The key to survival lies in the knowledge of what was learned from the bombings of Hiroshima and Nagasaki and, hence, making preparations.

Finding shelter space in one's home is the first step, with the cellar the "safest place to be. The lower" one gets, "the more barriers there are likely to be against" the bomb's principal dangers. Therefore, one should "select the basement wall nearest the probable target area of your city." Should the house be blown over, "it will most likely fall away from this wall." Should one have a work bench or strong table sufficiently large enough to get under, it is advisable to "move it into your shelter area near a wall or strong supporting column." In the event of an attack, one should "lie under the table." For those homes minus a basement, select a shelter area without windows on the ground floor, with an interior hallway the likeliest choice. In the event of an emergency, the "shelter area should be cleared of mirrors" and other potential injury-causing objects. Apartment dwellers will find rules for taking shelter posted in their building of residence. It is also advisable to find out the locations of public shelter facilities in places away from home.

Survival Under Atomic Attack urges its viewers to take proactive measures: arrange for trash disposal, stock up on canned food items, have a flashlight in the event lights go out, assemble a first aid kit, have plenty of bottled water, secure a radio, and fully equip the shelter area. Should the civil defense siren sound in the event of an actual attack or test drill, secure windows and drapes and switch off electrical appliances and gas or oil burners, close (but leave unlocked) outside doors, then take cover in your shelter. In the event of a surprise attack, duck into a doorway or fall to the ground. Home residents are instructed to get beneath a table or drop to the floor, turning your back to the window. An explosion near the ground or water would produce radioactive fallout: Take shelter indoors immediately, covering broken windows to prevent fallout from entering, and remain indoors until there's official word that it is safe to step outside. In the event of exposure to fallout, wash the exposed areas of the body — especially the hair and under the fingernails.

The film then concludes:

If the people of Hiroshima and Nagasaki had known what we know about civil defense, thousands of lives would have been saved.... The knowledge is ours and preparation can mean survival for you. So act now. Someday your life may depend on it.

Another FCDA film, this one produced by Reid H. Ray Film Industries, Inc., addressed a non-nuclear threat in *What You Should Know About Biological Warfare*. Biological warfare (or BW) can target people, homes, work places, food crops and livestock. Despite the safeguards we have to protect our health, crops, and food products, BW attacks can still be mounted using aerosols delivered by planes, submarines, germ-carrying bombs, or enemy agents. To forestall such assaults, one is advised to "keep yourself and your family clean," preventing germs from flourishing. "Enroll in a Red Cross home survival course" to treat illnesses should the latter occur. And report instances of any illness "promptly."

Should word come that a BW attack has occurred, don't succumb to fear; remember that the authorities are already on the job. Clean canned and bottled items before opening them. Most likely, packaged items in refrigerators and shelves are safe from contamination. Boil or cook all exposed food items and water before consuming them. Thoroughly wash all contaminated items of clothing. Cooperate with your doctor should the latter recommend hospitalization of a family member. Follow the directions of health authorities to contain the spread of disease. Provide a blood sample to help identify the cause of illness, if necessary. Participate in mass inoculations if the need arises. Most importantly, don't listen to scare talk or rumors; instead, obtain and study the civil defense pamphlet titled "What You Should Know About Biological Warfare." In conclusion: "Do your part, and we can successfully combat biological warfare."

Beginning in the latter stage of the Truman presidency, civil defense planning was based on several assumptions: propaganda should persuade Americans that nuclear weapons in no way differed from conventional armaments; the public should be instructed to see themselves as just "like trained soldiers under fire"—a disciplined force unflinchingly able to meet a nuclear attack and the challenges in the ensuing post-attack environment; the construction of a vast underground shelter program to ensure the continuity of the nation's governing elite; and a private shelter program to furnish the public the impression of security. The motto of this propaganda campaign, which carried over into the early Eisenhower era, was "Alert, Not Alarm!"

The unforeseen outcome of an American hydrogen bomb test in the Pacific on March 1, 1954, completely undermined this campaign. At 15 megatons, BRAVO (as the test was designated) was the largest H-bomb ever exploded by the United States. Detonated near Bikini Atoll in the Marshall

Islands, the bomb provided more of a punch than scientists had anticipated. In the aftermath of the test, radioactive fallout girded the world. BRAVO discredited the assertion that H-bombs weren't that much different from atomic bombs.[32]

The ultimate force of the explosion wasn't the sole unanticipated consequence of the test. Owing to unforeseen shifts in wind direction after the blast, 28 Americans stationed at a weather-and-observation station and 236 Marshall Island inhabitants suffered exposure to unsafe levels of radiation generated by fallout from the explosion. These weren't BRAVO's only casualties: The *Lucky Dragon*, a Japanese fishing vessel located some 85 miles east of Bikini Atoll, was caught in the fallout's path. By March 14, when the *Dragon* returned to its home port, the majority of the ship's crew had contracted radiation poisoning.[33] The funeral of one of the *Dragon's* crew members (who had uttered, "Please make sure that I am the last victim of the bomb") drew 400,000 attendees. At the same time, fishing boats in the Marshall Islands region brought more than 600 tons of contaminated fish to Japan. In the next six months, 30 million Japanese put their names to a petition advocating the cessation of nuclear testing.

AEC Chairman Lewis Strauss publicly refuted the extensive tainting of fish, speculated that some unknown chemicals in coral had caused the illness that befell the *Lucky Dragon's* crew, and privately proclaimed his conviction that the *Dragon* was actually a communist spy ship.[34] Presently, however, Strauss was forced to admit just how much destruction an H-bomb could wreak when he was questioned about this during an appearance at President Eisenhower's March 31 press conference:

> STRAUSS: Well, the nature of an H-bomb ... is that, in effect, it can be made as large as you wish, as large as the military requirement demands, that is to say, an H-bomb can be made as — large enough to take out a city.
> CHORUS: What?
> MERRIMAN SMITH (United Press): How big a city?
> STRAUSS: Any city.
> QUESTION: Any city, New York?
> STRAUSS: The metropolitan area, yes.

Prompted by this exchange, the following day's *New York Times* featured the blaring headline: "H-BOMB CAN WIPE OUT ANY CITY." The article went into detail: "A map of the New York area indicating incendiary damage from a thermonuclear attack on Manhattan covered a twenty-five-mile radius that extended to Scarsdale and Tarrytown in Westchester County, Hicksville on Long Island, and perilously close to Greenwich in Connecticut and Morristown and Plainfield in New Jersey."[35]

As a consequence of BRAVO, the exclusion area around future U.S. bomb tests in the Pacific was enlarged to include an expanse nearly comparable to 20 percent of the American mainland. Another consequence of the BRAVO test was that numerous enlightened Americans appreciated the fact that the greatest menace the H-bomb posed came, not from the blast itself, but rather from the fallout the explosion generated. To the AEC fell the burden of justifying the H-bomb and bomb testing, as the commission's leaders sought to conceal the fallout risk. This effort produced a significant public debate concerning the soundness of government secrecy and the credibility of AEC representatives. Still, the most unusual assurance the public received that fallout wasn't all that dangerous came, not from the AEC, but from the "father of the H-bomb," Edward Teller, who declared that since the likelihood of birth defects is diminished by keeping sperm cool, the best way to lessen deformities lay, not in halting bomb tests, but in forcing men to wear kilts!

Just the same, the reality of thermonuclear war was now worldwide knowledge. Such a conflict could virtually destroy Americans and Russians alike and, depending on the dispersal of radioactive fallout, millions of others elsewhere. Hundreds of thousands, perhaps millions of people in Western Europe could die from the fallout resulting from an American attack on the Soviet Union.[36]

The hydrogen bomb also impacted school civil defense programs in that it more clearly illustrated that "duck and cover" exercises were less than adequate protection against nuclear attack, prompting some schools to establish their own shelter zones and having children seek sanctuary there. "To many youths," Alice L. George has written, "these events seemed like little more than charades in which adults tried to mislead children and make them feel safe in a world plagued by dangers too horrible to face."[37]

2

Fifties Cinema and Civil Defense

Where government propaganda films sought to educate Americans about the dangers of nuclear war and ways to prepare for it, Hollywood filmmakers exploited nuclear fears as a way to entertain audiences in films covering a wide range of genres: comedy (*Living It Up*), melodrama (*Split Second*), monster movies (*Them!*), pseudo-documentaries (*The Beginning or the End?*), science fiction (*The Day the Earth Stood Still*), and end-of-the-world epics (*On the Beach*).[1] Yet very few films in the 1950s directly presented a nuclear attack on the United States.[2] One of the earliest films to do so was the 1952 Poverty Row "quickie," *Invasion U.S.A.* Produced by Albert Zugsmith and Robert Smith, written by Robert Smith from a story by Smith and Franz Spencer, and directed by Alfred E. Green, the film has been characterized as a "Right Wing cautionary tale," warning that the best deterrence against foreign aggression is a strong national defense.[3]

Invasion U.S.A. belonged to a category of motion pictures, the Red Scare film, that reflected America's fears of communist militarism. Badly directed, these films were inhabited by B actors who couldn't find employment in top-flight films. Howard Hughes, the man behind many of these films, had taken over RKO Pictures (and its theater chain) in 1948 for the sum of $9 million. Once in charge, Hughes demanded that everyone on the studio's payroll sign loyalty oaths — an edict that prompted most everyone there to leave. Those remaining found themselves toiling on a wave of Hughes-produced anti-communist films, the most famous of which was likely 1950's *I Married a Communist.*[4]

Albert Zugsmith, the man behind *Invasion U.S.A.*, was a former newspaperman who relocated to Los Angeles, aspiring to embark upon a career in movies. Zugsmith approached Hughes with a proposition to make three very low-budget pictures at prices which Howard Hughes was reported to have said: "It can't be done." They were $100,000 each. Under strictly union conditions, IATSE conditions, and on the old RKO-Pathé lot, now called the Culver City Studios, which were the old Selznick studios. So we made them with our own money, but Hughes reimbursed us, up to $100,000— no more than that!— on each picture.[5]

Zugsmith's interest in apocalyptic films was rooted in financial considerations: Such productions, he recognized, were invariably box-office winners. That he was footing the bill for his films out of his own pocket was tantamount to an interest-free loan to Hughes and the studio, thus Zugsmith had to make certain he earned back the money he invested in them. As he explained:

We made these three pictures for RKO and, of course, we were forced to use people we didn't want to take as actors, so the pictures weren't that great. The first one was a look into the future, which we called *3000 A.D.* RKO, possibly on Mr. Hughes's orders, changed the title to *Captive Women* [1952]. It was a look at what would happen to places like New York after the atomic bomb fell, and so forth. Something like *Beneath the Planet of the Apes* [1970]. So I was determined then to make a picture of my own and I made *Invasion U.S.A...*, which was my first big sleeper. I made that for $127,000 cash and about $60,000 deferred.... And while it's far from perfect, for $127,000, for a film shot in seven days, I feel it's a good job. Of course, full of heartaches and headaches, but worth it. And I suppose the public responded, because the net profits on the film were close to $1,000,000.[6]

Zugsmith's editing of World War II combat footage into scenes featuring the film's cast helped offset the production's shoestring nature. The way he intermixed his stock footage with his actors conveyed the idea that the scenes of devastation presented in the film showed that American, not foreign cities, had been attacked. The enemy soldiers are Russian in all but name only. In what was then an innovative move, Zugsmith, an independent producer, persuaded a major Hollywood studio, Columbia Pictures, to release his film to make a quick buck "as sensationalized advertising" generated a buzz about the film "that purported to warn Americans what might be about to happen."[7] The trailer promoting *Invasion U.S.A.* featured such taglines as "SEE! New York Disappear! SEE! Seattle Blasted! SEE! San Francisco in Flames!" A contemporary reviewer of the film from the *New York Times* felt that "all the actors in it, especially the leads ... are dismal in their roles."[8] Long afterward, calling *Invasion U.S.A.* "a film that could have been made by Senator Joe McCarthy himself," film historian Bill Warren goes on to label it a "wonderfully evocative picture," one that recalls the age of "the anticommunist witch hunts and nervousness about any international development (not that that has changed much)."⁹

The film opens in a Manhattan bar where the patrons are enjoying themselves while a televised newscast brings the day's events. Another newscaster, Vince Potter (Gerald Mohr), enters and begins questioning the patrons for a survey he's doing for his broadcast: "Are you for or against the universal draft? ... drafting soldiers for the army, factories for war work, labor for factories, the whole business." Ed Mulbury (Erik Blythe), a cattle raiser from Arizona, feels there's already too much government in business; he complains about how price controls have affected the size of the herd he had raised that year. Added to that are hefty income taxes.

Another businessman, George Sylvester (Robert Bice), a tractor manufacturer from San Francisco, calls drafting factories "communism," then relates how he laid down the law to an Army major who had asked him to produce tank parts, then stood up to the major when the latter told him that if he didn't willingly manufacture the components, the "day may come when we'll be forced to take over your plant without asking your permission." He defends his actions, saying, "Just because he was wearing a major's uniform, he thought he could threaten me but I sure told him off." When it comes to drafting women in addition to men for war work, Sylvester's girlfriend, Carla Sanford (Peggie Castle), recalls that when she worked in a factory during World War II, it ruined her hands, prompting her to quit. Arthur V. Holloway (Wade Crosby), a visiting congressman from Illinois, joins the discussion; based on the letters he received from his constituents, he explains that the people want communism destroyed "wherever it rears it ugly head.... They don't like war at all" as well as high taxes — "Sending all that money to Europe ... what my constituents want are lower taxes."

Another bar patron adds his voice — Mr. Ohman (Dan O'Herlihy): "I think America wants new leadership ... a wizard, like Merlin, who could kill his enemies by wishing them dead. That's the way we like to beat communism now — by wishing it dead. A manufacturer wants more war orders — and lower taxes. Labor wants more consumer products — and a 30 hour week. A college boy wants a stronger army — and a deferment for himself. The businessman wants a bigger air force — and a new Cadillac. The housewife wants security — and an electric dishwasher. Everybody wants a stronger America — and we all want the same man to pay for it. George — let George do it."

"I disagree with you," Sylvester chimes in. "I don't want to let George do it.... I'm George!"

"Everyone wants George to do it," observes Potter.

"Except George," says Carla, picking up the line.

"A very good joke," Ohman says, "but wars are not won by making jokes.

Long before the events of 9/11, New York City was vaporized on screen when enemy planes dropped an atomic bomb on the Big Apple in the 1952 film *Invasion USA* (Columbia/Photofest).

To win a war," he continues, picking up his drink glass, swirling its contents, "a nation must concentrate." Potter and the others stare at Ohman's glass, as though hypnotized by it. Setting down the glass, Ohman then takes his leave. Just then, the bartender notices that the televised newscast has taken on an urgent tone and turns up the volume. Word has come that hundreds of unidentified aircraft are flying across Alaska. Once Alaska had fallen into their hands, the enemy uses it as a staging ground from which to attack the continental United States.

Washington State, San Francisco, and several other West Coast cities are captured. Another shattering blow is inflicted when Boulder Dam is leveled by an atomic bomb, followed by the sinking of the American carrier *Crown Point* by an atomic torpedo — a development that threatens the entire American Navy. Then enemy bombers are detected approaching New York City. Despite intense anti-aircraft fire, the bombers drop an atomic bomb on the Big Apple. Disguised as American soldiers, enemy troops parachute into

Recruiting drive: The press book for *Invasion USA* urged theaters to stage recruiting drives for civil defense workers (such as the one here for the Civil Air Patrol) as part of the film's promotion campaign (Columbia/Photofest).

Washington D.C., where they storm Capitol Hill, gunning down members of Congress. Simultaneously, they invade New York. Potter's radio station is cut off, and Potter and Carla are taken prisoner. Potter is shot trying to protect Carla, who then jumps to her death when one of the enemy soldiers tries to have his way with her.

The film then returns to the bar, where we find Potter, Carla, Sylvester, Mulbury, and Holloway still together, alive and well. It turns out that Ohman is a hypnotist who put them all into a trance to provide them a glimpse of the future they face unless they all change their ways. "If you want to change what you will become," Ohman tells them, "first change what you are." The film's concluding scene features the words of George Washington: "To be prepared for war is one of the most effectual means of preserving peace."

In the best Hollywood tradition, the pressbook for *Invasion U.S.A.* laid it on thick, urging theaters to go all-out in promoting the film: "Get the full defense set-up of your community behind your screening of the film! Put your theatre and lobby to work! Tackle the radio stations, television and the newspapers for full co-operation! 'Invasion U.S.A.' is the year's shock drama ... sell it big!" When it came to hyping civil defense in connection with the film, the pressbook declared: "*Invasion U.S.A., ...* will inspire awareness of civilian defense in everyone," after which the pressbook urged theater owners to "contact civilian defense authorities for the following":

RECRUITING: Set up a Civilian Defense recruiting booth in your lobby starting opening day. Publicize booth in local newspapers and on the air. Plant photo of a prominent person signing up for Civilian Defense in your lobby.

HERALDS: Arrange for members of the local Civilian Defense Corps to distribute heralds throughout your city in advance of playdate. Too, ask key members to spread news of your engagement of "Invasion U.S.A." by word of mouth at every Civilian Defense meeting.

PARADE: If feasible, set a parade of Civilian Defense men and women to your theatre opening day. Accompanied by appropriately bannered trucks, with music supplied by a local military or veterans' contingent, the parade can and should be one of the biggest items in your campaign.

SIREN: Work out, if possible, a "siren" opening of your film — a test "alert" for civilian defense workers. This practice drill, called in conjunction with "Invasion U.S.A.," should be an invaluable promotion idea.

POSTERS: Distribute posters, for use in all public buildings throughout your city, boosting civilian defense and your showing of "Invasion U.S.A." Sample poster copy: "*Learn What Will Happen If the Bombs Start Falling! Join the Civilian Defense Corps.... See Columbia's 'Invasion U S.A.' State Theatre Friday.*"

The pressbook went on to urge "a parade of servicemen" to be present at the theater on opening day, a "color guard of servicemen out front opening night," a "joint armed services recruiting booth" in the theater lobby during the film's run there, and finally, a "special exhibit of new techniques of warfare that are off the secret list, but are not too generally known. Display photos, and, if possible, weapons themselves."[10] Such ballyhoo may seem, in retrospect, extravagant and, in the case of staging parades of civil defense and military personnel an unwarranted misuse of official resources intended for a serious and valuable purpose — national defense — but at the time it (like civil defense) was taken quite seriously.

Taking note of the fact that official discussions of the atomic bomb sought to present it as nothing more than another, albeit larger, conventional explosive, film historian Cyndy Hendershot categorizes the nuclear war fought in *Invasion U.S.A.* as more conventional in nature — specifically resembling World War II, with enemy forces resembling Nazi, Soviet, and Japanese warriors. The enemy commanders wear SS-style uniforms. The enemy's atomic bomb assaults on the United States are equated with Pearl Harbor and being "like a modern kamikaze attack." The enemy soldier who gets drunk and tries to rape Carla conforms to the World War II stereotypes of Russian soldiers as rapists. The focus of the enemy's atomic attacks on military targets as the initial phase of their assault on America are depicted as an aspect of a conventional military attack, instead of part of the Second World War sired idea of total warfare. Furthermore, the targeting of military locations buttresses the American assertion that Hiroshima and Nagasaki were both military targets — when the truth was they were civilian targets. The reason military targets in the film suffer the wrath of the enemy's initial blow is that such was the American course of action in World War II. What makes the enemy of *Invasion U.S.A.* far more monstrous than America is the fact that, in the film, the aggressor provides no advance warning of his intentions and eventually turns his fire on civilian targets.

    Invasion U.S.A. ridicules the strength of the enemy's atomic arsenal and uses actual footage of conventional bombing to represent atomic attack and its aftermath — with no evidence of the aftermath of radiation apparent. When conventional bombs rain down on New York, Potter describes it as "like London in the Blitz." Both Potter and Carla then escape unscathed when a building near them collapses from the enemy's atomic bomb strike on the Big Apple — making it seem that, even when people are outside in the midst of an atomic attack and in close proximity to Ground Zero, survival is still possible. Moreover, the film makes it appear that radiation from a nuclear war will be non-existent, as when enemy paratroopers descend upon Puget Sound in the wake of an A-bomb drop there — an incident paralleling the real-life intentional exposure of American soldiers to dangerous levels of radiation in the above-ground nuclear tests in Nevada. The fact that all of the principal characters in the film die, not from the atomic bomb, but from more conventional means of extermination, signifies what Hendershot describes as the film's inability to depict death as resulting from the A-bomb. Sylvester is shot when enemy forces capture his plant and he tries to escape; Mulbury drowns in the flood waters unleashed by the destruction of Boulder Dam; Congressman Holloway is shot in the enemy's assault on Congress; Potter, likewise, is felled by an enemy bullet; and Carla chooses suicide over submitting to the Russian soldier's advances. The scorched-earth strategy Americans employ to prevent vital facilities from falling into enemy hands indicates that the paramount issue for the film's characters isn't nuclear war but invasion — a notion illustrated by a general in Washington's query, "Could the bombing of New York have been a diversion?" revealing just how insignificant the atomizing of America's most populous city was to government officials.

    In all of this, *Invasion U.S.A.* transforms nuclear war into merely another version of World War II.[11]

    Another fifties-era film dealing with a Russian nuclear attack on the United States, *Rocket Attack U.S.A.,* was exploitation filmmaker Barry Mahon's attempt to make a topical film — one rooted in the panic occasioned by the Russians' launching of *Sputnik,* the world's first artificial satellite, into space in October 1957. Made at a time when film reviews apparently feared upsetting studios by rendering negative judgments on their offerings, *Rocket Attack U.S.A.* drew laudatory notices. Long afterward, film director Joe Dante offered a more objective critique: "Sexploitation king Barry Mahon ... turns his heavy hand to Big Themes with defeatist spy-fi minibudget melodramatics.... Lacks the verve of your cousin's bar mitzvah movies and isn't as well acted." Calling it "possibly the cheapest film" among those covered in his massive study of 1950s science-fiction films, Bill Warren cut right to the chase in his assessment: "The slow pace, vapid content and wretched production values make it almost unwatchable today."[12]

Just the same, *Rocket Attack U.S.A.* did finally earn a place of distinction: It became one of the films lampooned by television's *Mystery Science Theater 3000.*

Like *Invasion U.S.A.* before it, *Rocket Attack U.S.A.* is a cautionary tale about what the lack of preparedness on Americans' part could mean for the future of the country and how it would spell the difference between life and death for the United States. Beginning with *Sputnik*'s launch, the film explains that in accomplishing this feat, the Soviet Union "changed the entire concept of modern warfare." What the viewer is about to witness "would be inevitable should the wrong people gain control of that government."

The success of *Sputnik* galvanizes the federal government — especially the Central Intelligence Group (CIG) of the Defense Department — to ascertain the true objective of the Soviet space shot. The West Berlin office of the CIG is directed to send an agent to Moscow. Landing at a small, vacant pasture in Soviet territory, Marston, the American agent, makes his way to Moscow, where rumors are rampant that the military might seize control of the Russian government. Marston learns that a split in the Soviet Presidium has occurred: The military is pushing for a showdown to attack the U.S. while the latter lacks the capacity to retaliate. The leader of the war hawks advocates a strike at New York that would deliver the United States to the Soviets.

The American missile program, now fully backed by the government, proceeds with the development of an American ICBM. However, the program suffers a setback when, owing to shortcuts meant to expedite the program, a test missile explodes in flight shortly after liftoff. The sole option left to the United States to forestall a Russian assault is a failure on the part of the Russian missile program or sabotaging the latter. Reaching the missile's launch site, Marston joins Tonya, his Russian contact, in proceeding to sabotage the missile. Tonya is shot by a Russian guard; Marston manages to attach an explosive device to the side of the missile but is subsequently shot dead, and the device he planted is removed.

The film now shifts to a morning in America where, despite the war scare and other recent international tensions, things seem calmer. A newscaster reports that the new Kremlin leadership seems more concerned with peace and ending the Cold War than their predecessors. As evidence of this, an important meeting in the Kremlin is scheduled to begin very shortly. When the meeting convenes, the Russian marshal gives the order to fire the missile. Once the latter is detected approaching the eastern seaboard of the United States, the alert is sounded: Civil defense sirens sound — only there have been so many alerts, no one takes this one seriously.

"That's not another of those things?" one woman asks another as they are walking in the street.

"I think they're stupid," her companion replies. The two of them continue on their way, ignoring the alert.

Breaking in with word that this is no false alarm, the newscaster tells listeners to tune in to civil defense channels on radio for instructions, while police cars advise those in the street to take cover immediately. Parents hustle their children indoors, businesses close up shop. People enter public air-raid shelters.

American Nike missiles are launched in a desperate attempt to knock the inbound Russian missile out of the sky before it reaches New York. In scenes recalling the war footage used in *Invasion U.S.A.*, B-52 bombers are shown taking to the air. Other scenes show New York City streets deserted against the wail of air raid sirens. The Nikes fail to destroy the enemy missile which imparts its target, vaporizing New York in a mushroom cloud.

"The suburban areas were spared," intones the film's offscreen narrator, "but metropolitan New York City was almost completely destroyed — with a death toll of well over three million. Regardless of possible disagreements over conference tables, in spite of the selfish interests of political factions or special interest groups, WE CANNOT LET THIS BE — THE END."

Numerous plot elements in *Rocket Attack U.S.A.* parallel actual events of the late 1950s. The film's theme of "the wrong people" ascending to power in the Soviet government may very well have been inspired by the attempted ouster of Nikita Khrushchev from office in 1957 by rivals angry at the reforms he had instituted in the wake of Stalin's death.[13] Russia's success in the film in firing an intercontinental missile at the United States was an extension of a real-life debate over what was known as the "missile gap."

In April 1957, President Eisenhower named a committee to advise him on the necessity for an enhanced shelter program. Called the Gaither Committee after its chairman, H. Rowan Gaither, the committee, whose members were scientific and technical authorities, nuclear strategists and business people, eventually enlarged the scope of its original mission. This enhanced study was largely due to one of the committee members — Paul Nitze — whose main worry was that the Soviets might employ military supremacy as a means for nuclear blackmail.

To meet the perceived mounting danger of Russian military capabilities, the Gaither Committee advocated an immense military buildup. Taking note of the Strategic Air Command's (SAC) vulnerability to annihilation on the ground by a Soviet attack, the Gaither Report proposed an enormous boost in both America's intercontinental missiles and conventional military forces — costing $19 billion over the ensuing five years. When it came to civil defense, the committee members concurred that it would not only save lives, but would enhance America's deterrent power by, first, discouraging an attempted enemy attack "on what otherwise might seem ... a temptingly unprepared target," and, second, by "reinforcing [the enemy's] belief in our readiness to use, if necessary, our strategic retaliatory power." Civil defense would show the Russians America's willingness, if need be, to utilize nuclear weapons and denote to the American public the seriousness of the nuclear menace posed by the Soviet Union. The Gaither Report advocated a $25 billion program intended solely for those people outside important target areas who could survive a nuclear attack and go to a fallout shelter, where they would remain for two weeks. "The political and nuclear strategists who devised the Gaither Report," Dee Garrison has written, assembled the kind of civil defense, the main purpose of which wasn't to preserve life, but "to pretend to save lives and to show Americans that their government was concerned about their safety."

The Gaither Committee warned that by 1959 or 1960, Russian ICBMs would be capable of destroying SAC with the kind of first-strike blow that would forestall an American retaliatory response. The committee urged that America make preparations for waging a limited war and greatly boost the defense budget. This marked the start of the fictitious "missile gap" that the Democrats, as well as numerous conservative Republicans, employed as a means to undermine Eisenhower's reduced military budgets and to help restore the Democrats to power in 1960.

Shocked by the Gaither Committee's recommendations to boost the defense budget by more than $40 billion a year, Eisenhower rejected such proposals and demanded that the Gaither Report not be publicized. However, some of the report's authors leaked it to the press. What followed was a public-relations campaign, mounted by what Eisenhower would term the "military industrial complex" to sanction more spending for nuclear and conventional arms. The military establishment, particularly the air force, denounced the caps on defense spending, while corporations and groups of organized labor, contractors, scientists, and technicians involved in the production of weapons urged additional funding. Important newspapers played up the dangers of the presumed missile gap.

Though Eisenhower did yield somewhat during the remainder of his term to advocate a bigger defense budget and numerous additional American missiles, when it came to weapons or civil defense, he remained steadfast in opposing greatly enhanced outlays in these areas.[14] Rejecting the recommendations for a substantial shelter program, the president, as was his predilection, sought to persuade the people to take voluntary measures. The National Shelter Policy, which he unveiled in May 1958, functioned on the notion that protection was primarily the duty of every American, and stressed private shelter building by homeowners. The federal government's activities in this area would be limited mainly to leadership, direction, and counsel, with scant funding. In August, following a bureaucratic reorganization that established a new Office of Civil and Defense Mobilization (OCDM), Eisenhower signed an additional measure, one that sanctioned federal financial aid for state projects. Yet again, the monetary element was restricted, as the funding earmarked for this program was nominal: "Civil-defense requests for the last half of the decade averaged a mere $102.7 million annually; appropriations averaged an even more minuscule $60 million."[15]

Eisenhower's opposition to increased spending for weapons and civil defense stemmed from two factors. First, the U-2 spy flights over Russia demonstrated that (the opinions of numerous members of the Gaither Committee notwithstanding) the Soviets weren't manufacturing ICBMs in any significant number. Second, Eisenhower privately worried that military-related disbursements would, in Garrison's words, "strengthen the tendency of the nation toward becoming a garrison state. He refused to give in to what seemed to be widespread and growing hysteria, at least" on the media's part. Thanking the Gaither Committee for its work, Eisenhower reminded the committee members that, for him, all-out nuclear war wasn't an alternative. "You can't have this kind of war," he explained. "There just aren't enough bulldozers to scrape the bodies off the streets." Garrison has concluded: "Eisenhower's opposition to the calls for large increases in weapons and civil defense in 1957 saved billions of dollars and perhaps even a war."[16]

One final aspect of *Rocket Attack U.S.A.* that mirrored reality involves the two female pedestrians who ignore the air raid sirens, mistaking them as merely another civil defense exercise. Obviously, these women were either unfamiliar with, or failed to read, the emphatic caveat of one early-fifties civil defense pamphlet: "WHEN THE ENEMY ATTACK IS BELIEVED TO BE IMMINENT, THE SIRENS WILL BLOW A RISING AND FALLING SIGNAL FOR THREE MINUTES. This is the only warning you will receive and you must act immediately.... The Air Raid warning does not necessarily mean that your city is the target, but remember, the undulating siren means TROUBLE somewhere near. TAKE COVER. Unless announced in advance as a TEST, the AIR RAID SIREN MEANS BUSINESS."[17]

In reality, people *did* ignore civil defense warnings, as the *Saturday Evening Post* noted in its edition of May 25, 1957. That issue reported the findings of the National Research Council's Committee on Disaster Studies. The committee's task had been "to determine the probable behavior of the American people during and after a thermonuclear assault." The committee's members analyzed disasters to determine how the American people would react to them. The committee's findings were, in the *Post*'s words, "far from reassuring," as the committee had discovered that Americans persisted in disregarding the dangerous reality of the atomic age: "One thing the committee had learned is that most Americans won't listen to warnings. They just won't admit to themselves that something awful may befall them." The *Post* concentrated on this heedlessness to warnings, even to "the threat of nuclear attack itself," by presenting a real-life example:

> One morning in May 1955, a flight of unidentified bombers was spotted approaching the California coast. The Air Force was so alarmed that it ordered a "warning yellow" — attack imminent — in the Oakland area. Sirens wailed throughout the city. Fortunately, it turned out to be a false alarm — the planes were actually SAC bombers. The residents of Oakland can be thankful they were. For a team of Survey Research Center interviewers later learned, to their dismay, that a mere three out of every twenty people had believed the sirens.

A similar scare subsequently occurred in Schenectady, New York, when, early in the morning of July 22, 1957, the air-raid sirens erroneously sounded: Only one Schenectady resident responded to the "alert" by evacuating his family. Everyone else, civil defense officials among them, reacted the same way as the mayor did: "He had rolled over and gone back to sleep." The committee connected this "ignoring of danger to another major psychological reaction to disaster: losing 'contact with reality' and existing 'in a state of dazed indifference.'"[18]

Other Americans deliberately chose to disregard real-life civil defense exercises as an act of civil disobedience. A pair of events — the development of large H-bombs and the swift headway in guided missile research — persuaded many that civil defense was an impractical measure should nuclear war come. As the '50s unfolded, more and more Americans advocated an international prohibition on nuclear testing as the best way to ensure national survival. Initially, such people were a minority and were viewed by the status quo as communists, socialists, misinformed, or crazy. Yet in the mid-fifties, as bombs became larger and the dangers of nuclear testing became more obvious, the peace movement began winning more adherents and notice, especially "when its leaders came to include" some of America's — and the world's — foremost "scientists and thinkers in other fields."[19]

In the aftermath of the Hiroshima bombing, newly organized groups of atomic scientists and world federalists had advocated global sanctions against nuclear war — only to give way to the burgeoning anti-communist Cold War ideology that arose in the wake of the Soviet atomic bomb and the start of the Korean War — leaving only two factions of the significant organizations within the prewar peace movement to endure into the early fifties.

One of these factions, which appealed to primarily liberal pacifists, comprised the American Friends Service Committee (AFSC), created in 1917, and the Women's International League for Peace and Freedom (WILPF), created two years later. In addition to opposing Cold War hawkishness, nationalism, and assaults on civil liberties, both groups tried to enlighten the public about the necessity for peace, yet had little immediate interest in staging a mass-protest movement, opting instead to writing politicians, holding conferences, and issuing materials favoring disarmament and conciliation.

Radical pacifists, who comprised the other important peace group, were far smaller in number, and included numerous Second World War conscientious objectors among their adherents. They preferred peaceful direct action as their tactic and took a "third camp position": opposition to capitalist and communist forms of nationalism. Adhering to an explicit manner of living, many radical pacifists frequently lived in groups and forswore the acquisition of material wealth. New York City was the primary residence for this group of peace activists, who were to be found in the War Resisters League (WRL), the Catholic Workers (CW), and the Fellowship of Reconciliation (FOR). At a time of muzzled but mounting revolt, radical pacifists were greatly discouraged by their failure to rouse the public to the hazards arising from the Cold War-inspired arms race and Senator Joseph McCarthy. By mid-decade, numerous leaders in the radical pacifist movement had concluded that an accelerated program of peaceful civil disobedience was necessary. In taking this course, they would play a leading role in re-energizing the American anti-nuclear movement.

"Because radical pacifists in New York City were beleaguered, isolated, and fully committed to social change," Dee Garrison has written, "they knew each other well and communicated frequently." In 1955 these groups joined forces in New York City to oppose Operation Alert, a federally supported, national civil defense exercise. Along with the bus boycott in Montgomery, Alabama, that same year, the Operation Alert protest marked the start of the Gandhi-influenced, peaceful, mass civil disobedience movement in America — one that became a pivotal organizing principle of both the civil rights and ensuing anti-war movements.

Operation Alert, which involved the collaboration of federal and state civil defense agencies and the mass media, involved the execution of an imaginary nuclear attack on the United States during the summer in more than 60 major American cities. During this exercise, urban dwellers were required to take shelter for 15 minutes while the simulated nuclear attack occurred. The entire drill was a full-scale dress rehearsal in which local civil defense officials practiced preparations for nuclear war, and the nation's leaders were evacuated to secret hideaways. The purpose of Operation Alert was to show that, even in the midst of an extreme emergency like nuclear war, the American government and people could still function smoothly, calmly, and orderly during and after a nuclear conflict.

The truth was that most people either paid no attention to Operation Alert, or, if they did, scorned it. Some cities went so far as to decline participating in the exercise, Peoria, Illinois, being one of the earliest of the dissenting locales. In this instance, a popular witticism, "If it won't play in Peoria...," held great truth.

In 1954, federal officials conducted a trial run of Operation Alert to make certain that both the shelters designated for occupancy by political and military leaders, and the P.R. plan to convince the American people that such sanctuaries were a necessity, worked. The initial Operation Alert involving public participation was slated for June 15, 1955.[20]

Among those in the radical pacifist camp who were ready to take more direct means to challenge the dangers of the nuclear age was Catholic Workers founder Dorothy Day. Her conversion to direct action was expedited by a visit she received in 1954 from an FBI agent who wanted to know more about one of Dorothy's friend. During the interview, the G-Man brandished his gun in front of her. What was meant to be an act of intimidation instead persuaded Day that a new effort was needed to confront "J. Edgar Hoover's political police." The last straw was provided when she learned that participation in the Operation Alert exercise would be legally mandated by New York state in 1955, with penalties involving a fine of $500 and a year in prison. Day and a fellow member of the Catholic Workers, Ammon Hennacy (who was also affiliated with the WRL), helped organize a tiny band of dissidents who would defy the legal requirement compelling participation in the 1955 Operation Alert drill. They informed the FBI, city authorities, and the media of their plans.

In New York City, on D-Day, the protestors lunched at a local church and received final instructions in how to conduct themselves. When the big moment came, they held their ground, quietly praying and meditating on park benches in City Hall Park, and, in the presence of journalists, presented their case for noncompliance with the drill. Some 27 pacifists — and a shoeshine man who was taken into custody by mistake — were arrested. Facing Judge Louis Kaplan that evening, the protestors were branded murderers by His Honor, who held them responsible for the simulated deaths of nearly three million New Yorkers killed during the exercise, according to government-announced statistics of the presumed casualties. Bail for each protestor was set at $1,500. Following stormy words with actress Judith Malina, the judge precipitated a small-scale courtroom disturbance by sentencing her to psychiatric observation at Bellevue Hospital, where she remained for several days. During the same Operation Alert exercise, Boston, Philadelphia, Chicago, and other communities witnessed anti-civil defense protests which were ignored by civil defense officials.

At the subsequent trial of the New York City civil defense protestors, a hostile judge, Hyman Bushel, asked if the defendants' attorneys intended to summon Soviet official V. M. Molotov to testify on their behalf; he also inquired of veteran pacifist leader A. J. Muste if he'd ever read Marx. Dismissing the case of two defendants — one who was pregnant and another whose arrest had been made in error — Bushel found the remainder guilty, but handed down suspended sentences on the grounds that he had no desire to turn the defendants into martyrs. To columnist Murray Kempton, the convicted individuals represented a "collective threat to our insanity."

The limited attention the national news media accorded the protest and trial was, on the whole, factual and supportive. *Harper's* and a number of progressive national periodicals wrote highly salutary stories on the case. New York newspapers and CBS television were fair in their coverage, including the report that police paid no attention to anti-civil defense activities in Boston, Chicago, and Philadelphia, while people in numerous cities totally disregarded the Operation Alert exercise. Save for *Commonweal,* important Catholic periodicals condemned the Catholic Workers' defiance of authority. The FBI added new information to its dossiers, and bureau chief J. Edgar Hoover unsuccessfully tried to convince the Justice Department to bring sedition charges against the Catholic Workers movement.[21]

The 1955 protest was only the beginning. In the years to come, there were further protests against Operation Alert. A new element eventually entered the protests when angry mothers appeared with their children at the demonstrations — a development that won public support for the anti-civil defense movement.[22] On May 3, the scheduled date for the 1960 exercise an ad hoc Civil Defense Protest Committee drew a multitude numbering more than 600 backers, among them Dwight MacDonald and Norman Mailer, to City Hall Park. The throng, in the words of a *Village Voice* correspondent, comprised "members of the Catholic Worker organization, the War Resisters League, Quakers, as well as mothers of young children, pacifists, Socialists, and a large scattering of rugged individualists."[23] Asked why he had come, Mailer explained, "Politics is like sex: you've got to go all the way."[24] When the civil defense sirens wailed their alert, the protesters held their ground, prompting a police official to issue a command for them to disband. The response from the demonstrators was pleasant boos and guffaws, followed by cheers when the policeman shouted, "Are you Americans?" When the police officer finally informed the crowd that they were all under arrest, several people began singing "We Shall Not Be Moved." A total of 26 people, none of whom were pacifist leaders, were arrested. When one of the protest leaders, Dave McReynolds, declared that the civil defense drill was dead, the throng broke up. Simultaneous acts of noncompliance with the drill had been staged by college students at CCNY, Brooklyn College, Queens College, and Columbia University and numerous New York City high school students.

It was the conviction of the civil defense protesters that they were acting logically, while civil defense advocates were the "ideologues." What rationale was there in hiding in the subway or under a school desk when knowledgeable people understood that one H-bomb would instantly destroy New York and a substantial chunk of Northern New Jersey. Speaking to a *New York Post* correspondent, a defiant student at New York City's High School of Music and Art who had been suspended for refusing to take shelter said:

> [The teacher] stood in the corridor and told us were confusing the issue and that what we were doing was mixing up the other students and making the school unorganized. We said it was the only way we knew to let the kids know that hiding under a desk was not the way to avoid getting killed.[25]

Only a few years short years before, such acts of noncompliance would have been judged as proof of probable insanity, were now considered displays of sound reason. In the words of Murray Kempton: "We seem to be approaching a condition of sanity where within a year or so there'll be more people defying than complying with the Civil Defense drill."[26] A pair of considerations — a shift in the political climate that allowed more and more Americans to refuse to let the government tell them what was right and what was wrong and, according to one newsletter, the fact that "many students are now aware of and responding to an atmosphere of action resulting from the Southern sit-ins" explains the growing display of resistance to civil defense exercises.[27] After the 1961 Operation Alert exercises, no further drills were held.[28]

Civil Defense Themes in Fifties Science Fiction Films

If any film genre benefited the most from fifties Cold War and nuclear anxieties, it was science fiction. To be certain, sci-fi had existed previously in American cinema — mainly as serials (*Buck Rogers, Flash Gordon*), with the significant exception of the feature-length production *Things to Come* (1936), which was inspired by H. G. Wells's novel.[29] But it was in the 1950s that the genre mushroomed into a major Hollywood category. One reason for this involved popular attitudes toward sci-fi: As no one paid heed to "that Buck Rogers stuff," science fiction afforded a perfect medium for advancing what were considered to be subversive political ideas.[30] Other explanations for the fifties sci-fi explosion were nuclear fears that were magnified by the Russian acquisition of the bomb in 1949; the great popularity in the early fifties of sci-fi literature as represented by the likes of authors Robert Heinlen and Ray Bradbury and editor John W. Campbell, Jr., and the box-office success of science-fiction films in the early years of the decade, which generated the production of additional films in this genre. The successful reissuing in 1952 of the 1930s monster classic *King Kong* was additional evidence of the public's yearning for science fiction — and may have influenced fifties science fiction in the direction of mutant and monster themes. The sci-fi films resulting from all this have remained quite popular and influential long afterward.[31]

Alien invasion films of the era (*The War of the Worlds. Earth vs. the Flying Saucers*) depicted the authorities ordering evacuations of those metropolitan areas threatened by extraterrestrial attack — complete with wailing air-raid sirens and fleeing multitudes — all suggesting civil defense measures. When *The Beast from 20,000 Fathoms* stormed into New York City in the 1953 movie of the same name, civil defense workers and shelters were mobilized to meet the crisis occasioned by the monster's rampage.

A recurring theme in nuclear war films was that of the post-apocalyptic world — a theme derived from popular rhetoric and sci-fi literature. When it came to the former, one film historian observed that Cold War rhetoric entailed images of mass obliteration, with America surviving the devastation comparatively unscathed to start fresh again. Stories of nuclear survival appearing in the era's popular media reaffirmed America's faith in its invincible supremacy. A common theme in the majority of postnuclear films is the nation's undying impregnability and its prevailing against all efforts to destroy it. Normally, these films operated on the assumption that all someone had to do to emerge triumphant from the effects of nuclear war was to briefly take refuge in a shelter to await the dissipation of the fallout and communism's demise through nuclear annihilation. Once these inconveniences were past, a reborn America would rise from the rubble of war to resume its daily activities.

Sci-fi's contribution to the post-apocalyptic film genre lay in the timeworn theme of the "myth of the heroic survivors"— those individuals who, in the aftermath of the cataclysm, set out to construct a new and better society from the debris of the preceding one. The post-holocaust environment tested whether the time-honored principles of self-reliance and simple living were still relevant, demonstrating that American institutions and values were abiding and an inherent aspect of humanity. While the use of nuclear power hadn't established the "atomic utopia" that had been promised, it had allowed the emergence of a new and improved America.

The blueprint for the post-apocalyptic film was established in the 1951 feature *Five*. According to Joyce A. Evans:

> The formula introduces survivors in a postatomic world who are saved through some accident and then set out to make it in the new world. The survivors are confronted in some way with the old prejudices or social mores of the preholocaust civilization, which they then address and usually resolve before the final scene. There is never any attempt to confront the horror of the overall situation; the reality of the nuclear destruction is not allowed to interfere with the mostly illogical contrivances. For example, the dead populations have conveniently disappeared and are only fleetingly referred to. The lingering effects of radiation are not realistically depicted; in these movies, the effects of the blast and the fallout last only a few days, and then normality returns to the Earth's ecosystem. Environmentally, the planet suffers only a minor inconvenience; nuclear war is like a cloth that wipes away the accumulated ravages of history and allows a clean, fresh world to be reborn.[32]

One of the films that conformed to this template was the 1955 release *Day the World Ended*. The film's producer and director, Roger Corman, explained, "I'm very much interested in the concept of nuclear holocaust. I think the possibility of it happening is there. Personally, I don't think its going to occur, but I think that, through film, we should keep on cautioning and warning people that it might."[33] *Day the World Ended* was Corman's initial nuclear apocalypse film, followed by *Teenage Caveman* and *The Last Woman on Earth*.[34]

After showing scenes of the nuclear war that has ravaged the world, leaving it enveloped in a deadly radioactive haze, *Day the World Ended* introduces viewers to a cross section of survivors — a gangster named Tony; his stripper girlfriend, Ruby; Rick, a geologist; Radick, who is mutating into a nuclear-age creature; and Pete, a prospector, and his mule, Diablo. All of them converge on a home in a valley. The house is the residence of Jim Madison, a former Navy captain who, having foreseen the calamity, has transformed the residence into an above-ground bomb shelter, equipping it with provisions for himself; his daughter, Louise, and her boyfriend — the latter now presumably killed in the bomb blast. Consequently, he mutates into the creature that menaces Louise all through the film.[35] In addition to the supplies Jim has stocked, the house is surrounded by hills rich in lead-bearing ore which shields it against radiation. The winds also deflect radioactive contamination.

Initially, Jim is reluctant to let the other survivors into the dwelling, feeling that such a large number of people will diminish the limited supplies available, only to relent when Louise admits the others into the house.

As the weeks pass, Radick begins venturing forth at night and returning at dawn, forsaking normal food. During one of his excursions, he kills a rabbit and is about to eat it when a mysterious creature appears, chasing him off, taking Radick's meal for himself. Rick believes that Radick survived enough radiation contamination to the point where he is now eating raw meat — a fate that may befall the others as well. This isn't the only unsettling development: Louise begins hearing a mysterious sound as though an unseen presence is calling to her.

The mysterious creature eventually comes closer to the house, killing Radick when the latter tries to dine on Pete's mule. Devastated by the animal's death, Pete tries to leave the house, knocking Jim out when he tries to follow him. In trying to save Pete, Jim is exposed to the radioactive vapor, receiving a fatal dose. Death comes sooner to Ruby: Coming to Louise's aid when Tony pulls a knife on her, Ruby is stabbed to death by Tony, who then throws her body off a cliff.

Ultimately lured out of the house by the creature's call, Louise falls into the monster's clutches. Carried to the waterfall by the creature, Louise seeks safety in the water, discovering that the monster is verse to it. When Rick, who has set off in pursuit of Louise, finds that bullets are useless against the monster, he, too, dives into the water for protection. Just then, a thunderstorm breaks; the rain, now free of radioactive contamination, proves fatal to the creature, which could only exist in a radiation-contaminated environment. Trying to shoot Rick, Tony himself is felled by shots fired by Jim, who then dies after telling Rick and Louise that he picked up someone on the radio, meaning that there are other survivors. Leaving the house, Rick and Louise set out to find the new world waiting for them.

One analysis of *Day the World Ended* labels it "naive and simplistic," yet considers it one of the few post-apocalyptic films "to suggest that some sort of society other than the one" we're presently acquainted with "or an adaptation of it might" emerge in the aftermath of the nuclear holocaust.[36] In that sense, the film corresponds to the aim of civil defense: Should a nuclear war be unavoidable, the people would survive to rebuild their land and themselves and resume their pre-war lives.

The origins of another fifties science fiction film with civil defense elements began when two men, producer William Alland and screenwriter Martin Berkeley, paid a visit to the Los Angeles Museum of Science and Industry in 1956, searching for an inspiration for a new monster film. They found it in a praying mantis exhibit at the museum. Berkeley then prepared a "formula sheet" for their new project, one that also had its roots in the film that became the template for all the atomic mutation films of the fifties — Warner Bros. 1954 hit, *Them.* In this thriller, giant ants, mutated by radiation resulting from the test explosion of the first atomic bomb at Alamogordo, New Mexico, in 1945, emerge from the New Mexican desert, ultimately migrating to the sewer system of Los Angeles, where they established a colony. The mutation films were cautionary tales concerning the development of atomic energy. The monsters in these films were an example of nature's vengeance against man's exploitation of atomic energy and the latter's employment in the service of harmful ends, lest man disappear and the beasts take his place as the reigning life form on Earth. Mutation films afforded Hollywood producers a safe means of exploiting the public's growing awareness and concern about the nuclear fallout issue. Owing to the continual media coverage of the latter and the commercial success of *Them!*, the number of mutation films emanating from Hollywood studios burgeoned. Movie theaters were inundated with swarms of giant insects in *The Black Scorpion* (1957), *Tarantula* (1955), mutated wasps in *The Monster from Green Hell* (1957), monstrous grasshoppers in *Beginning of the End* (1957), and a creature that, while gigantic in size, was never identified as an atomic (or, for that matter, any other sort of mutation): the monster inspired by William Alland's and Martin Berkeley's visit to the Los Angeles Museum of Science and Industry — *The Deadly Mantis* (1957).[37]

If ever a 1950s science fiction film makes it clear that it was a metaphor for the Cold War, it is *The Deadly Mantis* — an analogy the film makes evident right from the start with its description of the radar defense networks stretching from the U.S.–Canadian border to the North Pole that guard against enemy attack. The farthest of these networks is the Distant Early Warning System (the DEW Line) — ready to sound the first alarm in the event of an enemy sneak attack across the Pole. It is a distant outpost of the DEW Line that is destroyed by a mysterious force which subsequently destroys a C-47 transport plane, terrorizes an Eskimo village, and, finally, attacks an Air Force installation — a giant, prehistoric praying mantis released from its icy hibernation after millions of years. Leaving the Arctic, it heads south, along the Gulf Stream, for a warmer climate.

To locate the winged terror, the 400,000 members of the Civilian Ground Observer Corps are summoned to a meeting of the Continental Air Defense Command. They are instructed to listen "for a loud droning sound, much like that of a squadron of heavy bombers flying in formation.... If the mantis is sighted, the procedure will be the same as though an enemy aircraft had been spotted. Take no chances. Report any unusual flying object." Footage is then shown of spotters scanning the sky for the monster. When the mantis is sighted, carrier-based interceptor aircraft are scrambled but fail to down the intruder.

The mantis makes its way to the Washington, D.C., area where all military, civil defense, police, and fire department personnel are summoned to duty. Ground batteries open fire on the mantis and, this time, the Air Force downs the creature, driving it into a tunnel in New York where it waits, mortally wounded, before being finally destroyed by mines wielded by a team of armed men.

Films like *The Deadly Mantis* treated nuclear war symbolically instead of realistically.[38] To Joyce A. Evans, the "threat from the invading creature and the idea of a communist first strike against the United States are virtually interchangeable."[39] Similarly, Spencer R. Weart notes that the mantis is treated "exactly as if it were an approaching Russian bomber, tracked by radar and Air Force interceptors." The nuclear war simile was even more applicable to the film *Rodan* (1956) produced by the only nation in history to actually experience atomic attack — Japan. *Rodan* presented aerial monsters that have been given life by bomb tests. In the film, people watch the skies for evidence of the threat, then, when air raid sirens sound the alarm, they scramble for cover.[40]

The metaphorical war waged in *The Deadly Mantis* was fought, in part, with the help of a real-life civil defense organization — the Ground Observer Corps (GOC), the cooperation of which is acknowledged in the film's final credits. Originating in World War II, the GOC numbered more than a million civilian volunteers who staffed 14,000 observation posts along the coasts of the United States. In February 1950, General Ennis Whitehead of the Continental Air Command recommended that the GOC be revived with 160,000 volunteers running 8,000 observation posts in those areas where breaks between radar network locations existed.[41] These "blind spots," explained a 1952 civil defense handbook, resulted from "the topography of the terrain. Only those points designated will take part in the Ground Observer Corps." The same publication went on to explain how the GOC operated:

> The Corps provide information to our Air Defense Control Centers via a very simple system. First, a civilian volunteer reports by telephone from his assigned observation post, all the aircraft he sees or hears. Secondly, a Filter Center takes the information from the observers, establishes the speed and direction of the airplanes, which means that they have established a track, and passes the information on to the Air Defense Control Center.

These Filter Centers, staffed by civilian volunteers, were situated in those cities "best equipped" to immediately receive reports phoned in by observers.[42]

"Operation SKYWATCH," as the reanimated GOC was dubbed, was initiated on July 14, 1952. Before its conclusion in 1959, the new GOC would, at its apex, utilize in excess of 800,000 civilian volunteers of all ages who kept an eye out for an aerial assault at some 16,000 observation posts nationwide. The purpose of the GOC was the subject of a pamphlet, "One Call: The Ground Observer Corps," issued in the early 1950s, and which, upon closer reading, seems like a blueprint for *The Deadly Mantis*:

> *The Threat*
> In the event of World War III, we must assume that the Soviet Union will strike first — and hard!
> The Reds will try to knock us out in a single blow.

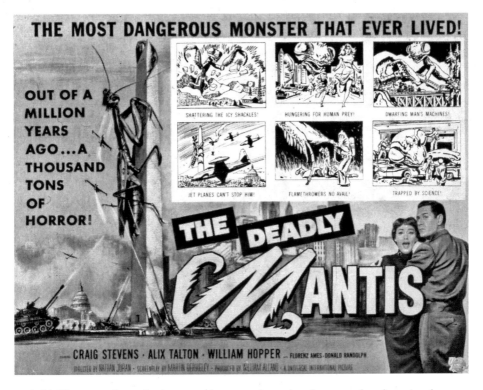

Cold War metaphor: A giant praying mantis replaced enemy bombers in the skies above America in *The Deadly Mantis* (1957), which featured a real-life civil defense organization, the Ground Observer Corps (Universal International Pictures/ Photofest).

If we are to survive — prevent a surprise atom bomb attack — we must have warning!

You can be an important figure in our warning system.

THE FACTS

TODAY

... the Soviet Union has more than 1,000 long-range bombers in the Red Air Force. *For what purpose?*

TODAY

... the Reds have enough bombs to inflict a devastating blow against the most vital targets in the United States in a single day. No part of the nation is safe from the threat of these bombs-dropped by accident or by design.

IF WE ARE TO SURVIVE
WE MUST HAVE WARNING
WE MUST HAVE WARNING
IF WE ARE TO SURVIVE

Are We the Target?
TODAY
The Soviet Union has polar bases from which their long-range bombers could
fly to any part of the United States in a matter of hours. These bases are useful
to the Red Air Force only for an attack against us!

One Call then emphasized that, while radar was in operation around the
clock, there still remained "dangerous, unavoidable gaps in our present system
through which low-flying enemy aircraft could sneak undetected." The key
to rectifying these blind spots was the volunteer plane spotter, but "there are
too few of them at the present time to do the job adequately. The thousands
of patriotic citizens now in the Ground Observer Corps need and deserve
your help in the defense of our country." Stressing the important difference
one GOC spotter could make, the pamphlet declared: "*With one* telephone
call, the spotter could start the warning that might save a city. *You* could be
the one to make that call":

> ONE CALL
> **One call** from a civilian plane spotter could sound the alarm that would give
> our interceptor pilots in the Air Defense Command more time to challenge the
> invaders in *the sky before they reached their targets.*
> **One call** could alert the Army Anti-Aircraft batteries in time to swing into
> action.
> **One call** might save our long-range bombers in the Strategic Air Command
> from possible destruction on the ground — give them a chance to strike back at
> the enemy in his own territory.
> **One call** could give local Civil Defense organizations more time to sound the
> air raid warning.
> **You** could make that one all-important call as a Civilian Plane Spotter if the
> Red bombers ever come.

One needn't be an authority at recognizing aircraft to be a plane spotter:
"Any intelligent person with normal sight or hearing can learn to be an important figure in our warning system after two or three simple lessons":

> You are only asked to report the flight of aircraft in your area of observation —
> their approximate number — approximate height — and approximate direction of
> flight.
> A typical call to your nearest Civil Defense Filter Center goes like this: "Air-
> craft Flash!" When you are connected with the Filter Center, you identify your
> observation post by some code name such as "Gopher reporting — two multimo-
> tored planes — flying very low-direction South," etc.
> You are asked to work only two hours a week with other volunteers in an
> observation post near your home.
> The job of the observer is not easy — it is not exciting — but some day it
> could be the most important job of your whole life.[43]

Reading the aforementioned pamphlet, one sees parallels between it and the plot elements of *The Deadly Mantis*: The placement of Red Air Force bases in the polar regions from which to strike at the United States was the real-life equivalent of the mantis thawing out of the Arctic ice and, from there, taking flight to wreak havoc on the continental U.S.; the vital role of the GOC plant spotters in locating and sounding the alarm against enemy bombers in the pamphlet — and the mantis in the film.

Ground-based defenses against attack from the air also figure into *The Deadly Mantis*. Starting in 1957, thousands of nuclear antiaircraft arms were dispersed nationwide as defense against attacking Soviet bombers. By early 1961, the Army's Nike-Hercules and Air Force's BOMARC surface-to-surface air missiles and Genie and Falcon air-to-air projectiles made up approximately one-fifth of America's nuclear arsenal. Such weapons were intended to solve the problems of defense confronting American officials at the start of the jet-bomber era. National leaders were concerned about another "Pearl Harbor" but faced serious technological problems supposedly inherent in finding ways to offset a surprise air attack. It was calculated that Soviet aircraft enjoyed the advantages derived from postwar improvements in propulsion and aeronautic design, permitting the transport of heavier loads at greater distances, higher altitudes, and greater speeds. Such advancements made it almost impossible to knock down such aircraft with antiaircraft artillery firing explosive shells on a ballistic trajectory. Further complicating the problem was the assumption that attackers would be armed with nuclear weapons.

Just the same, planners conjectured that a weapon producing an aerial nuclear blast could annihilate numerous adjacent incoming bombers and the weapons they carried, even without scoring a direct hit. Such a weapon, in addition to overcoming the restrictions already present in existing anti-aircraft technology, eliminated the likelihood stemming from conventional armaments that the nuclear payloads aboard a downed enemy aircraft would remain intact, hence still producing a nuclear blast.

In the early fifties, specialized publications and the popular press speculated that the military was weighing the possibility of atomic antiaircraft weapons — an idea that also received notice in some official statements about nuclear tests in Nevada and the Pacific. Such speculation was silenced by a Pentagon news release in February 1957 that it "has begun deployment of nuclear weapons within the United States for air defense purposes." The Pentagon's announcement added that "elaborate precautions have been taken in the design and handling of these air defense weapons to minimize harmful effects resulting from accidents either on the ground or in the air. Atomic Weapons tests conducted by the Atomic Energy Commission have confirmed that the possibility of any nuclear explosion occurring as a result of an accident involving either impact or fire is virtually non-existent."[44] Subsequent news coverage reported that "atomic rockets for blasting enemy bombers out of the skies are now being distributed to jet interceptor planes in the United States" and discussed the Pentagon's safety guarantees. The *Washington Post and Times-Herald* opined that "from a defense standpoint the plan makes sense," though it voiced some distress about the likelihood of an accident.[45]

In a September 1957 interview with *U. S. News and World Report*, Gen. Earle E. Partridge, commander in chief of the newly created North American Air Defense Command, announced that the Army was about to install nuclear armed surface-to-air antiaircraft missiles around numerous American cities. Beginning three years earlier, more than 100 underground concrete magazines and missile-launching facilities had been built near municipal areas for housing similar conventional Nike-Ajax weapons. While the latter's design was in the process of finalization, the Army began developing a larger version that could accommodate a two or 22-kiloton nuclear warhead. The decision to replace the Ajax with Nike-Hercules, as the new missile was called, around various American cities was a significant news event for its time, as evidenced by a January 1958 page-one story in the *New York Times*, quoting an Army announcement that the "atomic capability" of the Hercules meant that it could "destroy whole formations of planes." A Washington paper reported: "It can neutralize a nuclear bomb carried by the enemy plane so it would not explode as the bomber is destroyed." In ads it took out at the same time, Douglas Aircraft, the manufacturer of the new weapon, proclaimed that the "U. S. Army's Atomic Nike Hercules" was about "to guard America's skies," protecting "the Free World against supersonic enemy attack."[46] Eventually, 123 Nike-Hercules sites (86 converted from the Nike-Ajax and 34 newly constructed) were located around 26 cities and ten Strategic Air Command bases in 25 states in the continental U.S.—accompanied by marked local newspaper coverage of the building and operation of these installations. Attempts aimed at fostering close ties between those living in the cities that the missiles guarded, and the troops assigned to the missile batteries, were undertaken.[47]

One aspect of life at the Nike-Hercules sites involving base security was the theme of an episode of the popular television series *Lassie*. The press took note of the guard dogs that accompanied soldiers on guard duty at those areas of the base where the nuclear missiles were stored. Subsequently disclosing that it required "more than 1,000 German shepard dogs" for base security, the army implored those with canines to get in touch with the quarter-master general's office. Evidently learning of the army's request, Lassie Television, Inc., acquired permission from the Pentagon to film an installment of the series at a Los Angeles-area Nike installation in 1960. In the episode "The Patriot," broadcast February 12, 1961, Timmy Martin, Lassie's owner, comes to understand just how significant a Nike base is to American defense after visiting such a facility, and decides to train a stag dog for army duty. "Maybe they'll have a visitors' day," Timmy tells Lassie. "Then we could get inside and really see what a Nike base is like." Shortly thereafter, the boy and his dog are conveyed through the installation while a Nike is hoisted from its underground magazine.

"Look down there! ... Is that a missile?" Timmy inquires.

"It's called the Nike Hercules," the sergeant accompanying him explains. "It's one of the most effective weapons in America's defense arsenal."[48]

Earlier, Capt. Joe Griffith, the fictional commander of a missile battery, was the subject of an army film, *The Nike-Hercules Story*, which explained that the missile yields "an atomic punch" meant to devastate "a whole fleet of planes at a blow."[49] The Nike-Hercules also lent its presence to a series of trading cards and plastic scale-model kits aimed at young hobbyists.[50]

By the early 1960s, public interest in atomic antiaircraft weapons had dwindled. The displacement of bombs by Soviet ICBMs as the perceived principle threat to the United States was one explanation. Another was the Vietnam War and the collapse of the Cold War consensus that had prevailed in America since the end of World War II. Owing to growing uncertainties about Soviet international aims and intentions toward the United States, the public was far less apt to accept the idea of numerous nuclear antiaircraft weapons spread out across America.

The emergence of the ICBM and U.S. policy makers' acceptance of the mutual assured destruction (MAD) concept signaled the demise of American air defense weapons — the majority of which were decommissioned by 1974. But to many people, television viewers and hobby enthusiasts among them, "U.S. atomic antiaircraft weapons formed part of the American cultural tableau in the early Cold War."[51]

1959: *The Mouse That Roared* and *On the Beach*

By substituting a monster in place of the Russians, films like *The Deadly Mantis* could well be considered satiric or a science-fiction take on the threat of nuclear war. Two years after *The Deadly Mantis'* appearance in theaters, there appeared a genuinely satirical film send-up of the grim Cold War climate of the 1950s.

In the summer of 1958, Julius Epstein, who had co-authored *Casablanca*, informed his friend Jack Arnold of a film-directing opportunity in England. Columbia publicist Walter Shenson had purchased the film rights to the Leonard Wibberly novel *The Mouse That Roared*, which had been serialized in *The Saturday Evening Post*. Shenson had spent approximately five years attempting to get the story produced before approaching Carl Foreman, whose company, High Road Productions, had wrapped up one project, *The Key*, and was now involved in the pre-production of another, *The Guns of Navarone*. What was required was a production to which office expenses could be charged; a low-cost comedy film like *Mouse* would be just the thing to fill this requirement. Foreman wanted a "fresh talent" to direct *Mouse*. Arnold accepted the offer, and production commenced.[52]

Jack Arnold had made his name directing science-fiction films *(Creature from the Black Lagoon, Tarantula, The Incredible Shrinking Man*, etc.).[53] One of Arnold's sci-fi epics, *It Came from Outer Space* (1953), belonged to a class of science-fiction films that presented aliens as peaceful, having come to Earth to warn mankind of the dangers of the arms race, promoting peaceful coexistence between the superpowers, or revealing the lunacy of McCarthyism. Other films in this subgenre are *Stranger from Venus* (a.k.a. *Immediate Disaster*) (1954), *The Cosmic Man* (1959), and, the most significant of them all, *The Day Earth Stood Still* (1951). Co-written by producer William Alland (a former member of the Communist party) and Ray Bradbury, *It Came from Outer Space* reproached McCarthy-era America's dread of the Other in its story of alien space travelers forced down on Earth who face the enmity of the inhabitants of a small-town, and are protected from the mob by a non-conformist astronomer, John Putnam (Richard Carlson). In its presentation of sections of the United States "as narrow-minded and virtually barbarous," writes Tony Shaw, the film "also suggests that the 'civilized' West might have more to learn from the Other Side — terrestrial and extraterrestrial — than prevailing discourse would allow."[54] For his part, Alland subsequently maintained that *It Came from Outer Space* featured FDR's declaration that the only thing humanity had to fear was "fear itself.... If you fear the Communists, we destroy ourselves." Jack Arnold declared: "I think science fiction films are a marvelous medium for telling a story, creating a mood and delivering whatever kind of social message should be delivered. If ten percent of the audience grasped it, then I was very successful."[55]

The genesis of *The Mouse That Roared* was an old joke about a small nation that intentionally loses a war with the United States. The reason behind this curious strategy was that the vanquished nation could then enjoy the benefits of American beneficence. The story was given a modern twist by becoming a satire on the arms race, and nuclear war in particular.[56]

The independent, 15th-century style duchy of Grand Fenwick occupies a mere three-quarter square miles of the French Alps. The sole European nation where English is the national language (owing to the fact that its founder was an Englishman "who took a fancy to the neighborhood and moved in"), Grand Fenwick is ruled by Duchess Gloriana XII (Peter Sellers), who spends her time puttering around in her old car, waving to her subjects. Grand Fenwick's hereditary prime minister is Count Rupert of Montjoy (Peter Sellers). The national weapon of Grand Fenwick's armed forces is the longbow. The armed forces are led by Tully Bascombe (Peter Sellers), who, in addition to his duties as the hereditary forest ranger, is the army's hereditary field marshal and grand constable. Grand Fenwick's economic well-being is solely dependent on its export of Pinot Grand Fenwick, a wine popular mainly in the United States.

This perfect state of affairs is shattered when a California wine grower produces a less expensive imitation version of Grand Fenwick's principal export that surpasses the original in sales in America, throwing Grand Fenwick into economic turmoil. Count Rupert comes up with a solution: Grand Fenwick must declare war on the United States. There is a logic to his proposal: While acknowledging that Grand Fenwick could never be victorious in such a conflict, it can, nevertheless, win the peace that would follow: "You must remember, the Americans are a very strange people. Whereas other countries rarely forgive anything, the Americans forgive everything. There isn't a more profitable undertaking for any country than to declare war on the United States and be defeated.... No sooner is the aggressor defeated than the Americans pour in food, machinery, clothing, technical aid, and lots and lots of money for the relief of its former enemies ... we declare war on Monday, we are defeated on Tuesday and, by Friday, we will be rehabilitated beyond our wildest dreams." While conceding that such a course isn't really honest, the prime minister, nonetheless, calls it "terribly practical and infallible.... It will solve all out problems."

To implement his scheme, Count Rupert proposes sending the tiny Fenwickian army, under the command of Tully Bascombe, to New York, where they'll be arrested for not having visas. The Parliament of Grand Fenwick approves the prime minister's proposal, and a declaration of war is promptly mailed to the United States. Led by Tully Bascombe, Grand Fenwick's army, clad in medieval helmets and chain-mail armor, sets out on foot and by sea for their objective, taking their assignment quite seriously; Tully, by contrast, suffers interminable seasickness during the voyage. The Fenwickian Army sails into New York harbor, only to find it seemingly deserted ("Doesn't seem to be anyone around we can surrender to," says Tully). Unknown to them is the fact that New York, along with the rest of the East Coast, is participating in a presidentially mandated air-raid drill, during which time all American ports in the affected area will be closed to all ships. The alert is being held in connection with the development of the new Q-bomb, which supposedly renders the H-bomb "a firecracker." The initial signs of life the invaders discover is a group of people jiving to dance music on a radio in an underground public air-raid shelter. "Hey, you down there," one of the soldiers asks the shelter dwellers, Why don't you come up and fight?" (The scene of the jitter-buggers in the shelter suggests that life in a shelter has its advantages, and can even be fun! Such a lighthearted attitude may be necessary for one's sanity in the event of waiting out a nuclear attack. Yet, in a subsequent scene, when the shelter occupants hear a radio newscast that men from Mars have landed, they all panic; apparently space aliens are a far graver menace than nuclear war.)

Upon reading a newspaper account of the drill, Bascombe decides to proceed to an arsenal by way of Central Park. Along the way, he and his fellow soldiers find a truck belonging to the civil defense decontamination squad and decide to appropriate it for the remainder of the trip to the arsenal — but not before they and the truck's original occupants (the latter attired in radi-ation-proof clothing) catch sight of each other; both Fenwickians and the civil defense men think the other are men from outer space who've disem-barked from a flying saucer.

Reaching what they think is the arsenal, the Fenwickian Army discovers that they've actually arrived at the New York Institute of Advanced Physics, the facility where the Q-bomb has been perfected by its inventor, Dr. Alfred Kokintz (David Kossoff). Entering the building, Bascombe and his men meet the scientist and his daughter, Helen (Jean Seberg), and decide to take both them and the doctor's creation to provide Grand Fenwick a better bargaining position with America.

Bascombe and his men, their "POWs" and the Q-bomb in tow, return in triumph to Grand Fenwick. The latter's possession of the ultimate weapon precipitates an international crisis, with the duchy's European neighbors jock-eying for position to remain in Grand Fenwick's good graces. The United States sends a high-ranking diplomat to make peace with Grand Fenwick — only to discover that he's been preceded by representatives of other nations — the Soviet Union among them. To pass the time while waiting to be admitted into the duchy, the diplomats play a variation of Monopoly called Diplomacy; the Soviet representative gets to bomb Philadelphia when its his move, while the American delegate gets Saudi Arabia when his turn comes up.

Aided by Count Rupert and a member of the loyal opposition of the Fenwickian Parliament, Dr. Kokintz's daughter, along with an American gen-eral and several members of the New York City police department who were captured by Bascombe's army along with the Kokintzes, try to flee the duchy with the Q-bomb. When the car they're riding in is unable to make it up a hill, Helen Kokintz and the policemen get out and try to push it; with the general seated inside, the Q-bomb in his hands, the car rolls on down the road, finally crashing into a haystack. The collision activates the bomb, prompting the general to toss it into the air. Catching it, the policemen then hurl it to the Russian diplomat who, in turn, passes it to his fellow diplomats. The last to catch it, the American, gives it to Tully Bascombe. The latter, having fallen in love with Helen Kokintz, has chased after the car in which she had been riding. Exhausted by his pursuit, Tully collapses to the ground, placing the football-shaped bomb to the ground as if he has scored a touchdown — just as the bomb fizzles out without exploding.

Now Grand Fenwick's new prime minister, Tully negotiates a treaty with the United States, stipulating that the California wine that started this mess in the first place be removed from the market with the resumption of the import of Grand Fenwick's product; financial and technical aid to the duchy; and both Dr. Kokintz and the Q-bomb to remain in Grand Fenwick: Dr. Kokintz is to develop a chewing gum for export to America, and the bomb to remain under Fenwickian control, so that the duchy and its kindred neutral nations can maintain world peace on the theory they can do a better job of it than the superpowers.

Such an idea would have been abhorrent to Eisenhower's secretary of state, John Foster Dulles, who died the same year *The Mouse That Roared* was released. A devout Presbyterian as well as a devout anti-communist, Dulles, unlike his boss, viewed compromise and conciliation in foreign policy as the vilest of iniquities. Visiting Egypt's President Mohammed Naguib in 1953, he presented the Egyptian leader with a gift from Eisenhower: a nickel-plated automatic pistol, a symbolic reminder, in William Manchester's words, to "statesmen in the uncommitted nations that militant vigilance against designing Communists was the price of American friendship." On the other hand, neutral leaders like India's Nehru believed it was important to oppose colonialism and communism. Dulles, who viewed neutralism as an abomination, supplied weapons to Pakistan, thereby forfeiting India's friendship.[57]

Giving the Q-bomb one last inspection, Dr. Kokintz, Helen, and Tully discover it's nothing more than a dud; for everyone's sake, they all agree to keep this fact a secret. However, after they leave the room where the bomb is kept under guard, the reason for the mechanism's failure is revealed in the film's concluding scene: A white mouse climbs out of the bomb, reactivating it!

Critics raved when *The Mouse That Roared* debuted in America in October 1959. Calling it a "rambunctious satiric comedy," the *New York Times* extended kudos, not only to Arnold, but also to screenwriters Roger MacDougall and Stanley Mann, and "to all the people who play in this lively jape. They whip up a lot of cheerful nonsense that makes wild fun of the awesome instruments of war and does so in terms of social burlesque and sheer Mack Sennett farce." Commenting on how he took all of this, Jack Arnold said:

The interesting part, for me anyway, was when the film opened in New York it got sensational reviews — but they gave credit to the British! One said, "When the British put their best effort into satire no one can top them." Even the *Motion Picture Herald* said, "Only the British could be so funny." Of course both Walter Shenson and I are American. We had a little laugh at that.

It did very, very well indeed, and, as I said, it is my favorite film for many reasons.[58]

Considering that political satire of whatever sort was a rarity in the 1950s (possibly owing to the repressive, McCarthyite-inspired mood of the time), *Mouse* was quite unusual cinematic fare — a fact noted by *Saturday Review* in its critique of the film:

> Funny though the film may be — and some of its sequences are downright hilarious — there is no doubt that its makers are kidding in earnest.... Topical comedy is too rare upon the screen today for us to demand of this one a fully practicable answer to questions beyond the grasp of even our most astute politicians. It is enough that *The Mouse* restores to comedy its tonic purpose of puncturing political and militaristic shibboleths, and exposing to healthy laughter some of the more ridiculous aspects of these overcautious times.[59]

In making *Mouse* a satire on a very serious subject, director Arnold explained:

> It was a way of making a social comment I felt was important ... the most effective way to make a social comment is to do it by satire and comedy.... Those who were sophisticated enough to get the meaning we were putting into the film got it, and those who enjoyed the slapstick comedy-visual comedy, enjoyed that aspect of the film. If you're going to say something that means something and has a message, I think you should do it satirically and do it in a way that audiences will get it even though they're not aware of it, that they're getting it.... You have to do it through comedy, a satirical, soft touch. A whole spectrum of audiences have found *Mouse* enjoyable ... this was proved by its reception.[60]

Arnold further explained:

> *Mouse* is my favorite film because I was able to make use of what I proudly call my sense of humor.... I had definite opinions.... I thought I expressed them in that film in a way that is acceptable to a mass audience. I'm anti-war ... and I think what governments do — I'll say it kindly — is childish. I thought we should show the idiocy of what we adults make of our government, besides having a lot of fun doing it, making people laugh and maybe think a little bit, too. So, not only because it's essentially satirical and gave free reign to whatever comedic talents I may have, it also was a vehicle for me to express my own opinion.[61]

Arnold felt the film "was a little before its time.... The basic premise ... plot ... thrust of the film is as pertinent today as it was in the late fifties when we made it, even more so, perhaps. So, it hasn't been hurt by time, it may have been aided by time. My personal opinion is that it would have been a much larger success if it had been made and released ten years later.... It would have gotten a much wider audience than it did in art houses because they're small houses and you can only do so much business in them...."[62]

More somber in its tone was the first American film to take issue with the notion that a nuclear war could be survived. Released shortly after *The Mouse That Roared*, Stanley Kramer's *On the Beach*, the film adaptation of Nevil Shute's 1957 novel, focused on the crew of an American atomic submarine, the *Sawfish*, who, along with the inhabitants of Melbourne, Australia, await the arrival of a cloud of radioactive fallout heading their way in the aftermath of a nuclear war that has wiped out everyone in the Northern Hemisphere. Unlike most military-themed films of its time, which benefited from the Pentagon's logistical assistance and presented atomic weapons as a defender of democracy, *On the Beach* raised the possibility of total global destruction from nuclear weapons, and won kudos as an anti-nuclear arms film and was credited as the catalyst for a public debate concerning the bomb's merits.

Kramer, who specialized in making socially relevant films, could not have made *On the Beach* had the traditional Hollywood studio system not folded during the 1950s — a development that began in the late 1940s when the Supreme Court severed the link between the film studios and their theatre chains to further equitable competition within the motion picture industry. Because the High Court's decision left the studios in an even more precarious situation in regard to television competition, the studios slashed in-house production and remade themselves into conglomerates that stressed distribution and the subsidizing of contracted independents. This, in turn, facilitated the advent of a larger number of independent producers who felt greater freedom from both the old studio hierarchies and the Production Code Administration's (PCA) dictates. Accompanying these developments were surveys suggesting that the postwar baby boom was fostering a younger, more open-minded audience that desired more experimental motion pictures. Finally, by the late fifties the House Un-American Activities Committee's (HUAC) hold on the film industry had loosened and blacklisting was falling into disuse. The fusion of these considerations made possible the appearance of more socially conscious and artistically inventive moviemakers like Stanley Kramer. In 1954, Kramer established a new company which released films through United Artists. Given Kramer's political slant — he was neither an anti-nuclear activist nor a staunch nuclear unilateralist — *On the Beach* was a surprising movie for him to make. His motive for so doing was "to attempt to get people to think about the arms race," declaring it would be "a concept of hope on celluloid ... to reach out to the hearts of people everywhere that they might feel compassion — for themselves."[63] It would also be a film that would attract the scrutiny of officials of the Eisenhower administration who were concerned about its potential impact on American civil defense.

Initially, the prospects for the film's success were considered dismal, with *Variety* opining that its bleak story ("heavy as a leaden shroud") would adversely dampen it appeal to moviegoers. Its chances for success, in *Variety's* judgment, hinged on its star power (the film featured such big-name Hollywood talents as Gregory Peck, Ava Gardner, Fred Astaire, and Tony Perkins) and how effective it would be in attracting "the non-movie-going moviegoer" by being touted as a "status symbol," meaning "something to be seen despite its grim nature."[64]

As it turned out, *On the Beach* did quite well, yielding $6.2 million in domestic rentals by year's end — ranking it in eighth place among 1959's top moneymakers, surpassing *The Big Fisherman* and *The Story of Ruth* by more than $3 million. Expressing surprise at how well audiences had received *On the Beach*, Robert Hatch, film critic of *The Nation*, wrote: "As the last flicker of life disappeared off the face of the earth, the audience applauded. That is unusual movie-house behavior and I wondered what they were applauding. Had they 'enjoyed' the picture or were they glad to be alive?"[65]

The controversy it spawned notwithstanding, *On the Beach* was a reflection of the anti-nuclear sentiment of its day. Shute's novel sold 100,000 copies during its first six weeks of publication in America, and had subsequently been serialized by approximately 40 newspapers with a circulation of eight million. A poll conducted by the American Institute of Public Opinion in March 1958 revealed that 70 percent of Americans supported the establishment of an international organization that, through regular inspections, would guarantee that no country — Russia and America included — was manufacturing atomic and hydrogen bombs and missiles.

"Kramer," film historian Tony Shaw has written, "had a habit of leavening the political content of his movies by focusing on individual lives and romance"; thus *On the Beach* featured the romance between the American submarine commander (Gregory Peck) and the Australian woman (Ava Gardner). Moreover, Kramer moderated the novel's grimness. Nuclear explosions, dead bodies, and the effects of radiation sickness are absent, and the concluding sequence — showing the now lifeless Melbourne and a Salvation Army banner's declaration, "THERE IS STILL TIME ... BROTHER" — offered a glimmer of hope. Another departure from the novel, which had the final conflict begin with China and Russia deliberately attacking each other, was that in the film Armageddon arose from both technical failures and human shortcomings, hinting that the elimination of all nuclear weapons was the sole realistic answer to the dilemma with which mankind was confronted. As one of the film's

Melbourne, Australia, stands lifeless in the wake of a nuclear war in *On the Beach* (1959), a film that unsettled members of the Eisenhower administration due to its potential impact on the American civil defense program and military spending (Artists/Photofest).

characters, Julian Osborne, a nuclear physicist played by Fred Astaire, explains: "Everybody had an atomic bomb and counter bombs and counter counter-bombs. The devices outgrew us. We couldn't control them." Attempts by the Defense Department and the navy to change this and depict the Russians as the instigators of the conflict were unsuccessful.

Another point of contention between Kramer and civil defense experts was the magnitude of the nuclear conflict. Where Kramer contended that nuclear weapons could destroy the entire planet, the authorities asserted that the number of such weapons then available were incapable of global annihilation. When Kramer refused to change his screenplay on this point, the Pentagon refused his request for a nuclear submarine. Just the same, Kramer's willingness to openly contest the armed services' close ties with Hollywood and the latter's backing of nuclear deterrence during the 1950s was of great importance, for, as Lawrence Suid has noted: "*On the Beach*, not the Vietnam

War, marked the real beginning, albeit in a small way, of a greater scrutiny of the U.S. military establishment by the mass media and the cultural community."[66]

When Kramer finally submitted his script for PCA approval, PCA chief Geoffrey Shurlock was particularly disturbed by the screenplay's treatment of scenes involving government distribution of suicide pills to victims of radiation poisoning; misgivings that prompted Shurlock to ask his assistant, Jack Vizzard, to take up the matter. Discussions between Vizzard and Kramer won the latter's consent to add extra dialogue, stressing the immorality of suicide. Vizzard informed his boss that Kramer had sufficiently altered the initial screenplay to "somewhat counter-balance the manner in which the suggestion of euthanasia is proposed in this script," but "we told him frankly that there was still doubt in our minds whether it would be sufficient to satisfy the Legion of Decency" (LOD).[67]

The LOD was indeed less than satisfied when its officials viewed a rough cut of *On the Beach* prior to the film's public debut, saying that the screenplay was a "condonation of race suicide." When Kramer protested, Legion Director Msgr. Thomas F. Little, decided, in the face of opposition from several of his own reviewers, to change his appraisal of the film, calling it "morally unobjectionable for adults." Lest potentially embarrassing objections arise from conservative priests, Msgr. Little appended his ruling:

> There are certain moral issues in the development of this story which superficially seem to involve a condonation of race suicide. These dramatic elements, however, are intended to be a challenging symbol to argue the central theme of the film, namely, that nuclear warfare *is* race suicide.[68]

Little's explanation of the LOD's ruling failed to pacify numerous Church leaders, one of whom, Cardinal McIntyre of Los Angeles, took the extraordinary step of asking the FBI for an "investigation of the personnel and circumstances concerning the preparation and the production of *On the Beach*." Agreeing to McIntyre's entreaty, the bureau lodged a confidential request for assistance with the CIA. The two agencies failure to uncover "information to support [the contention] that *On the Beach* is a communistic vehicle of propaganda" failed to appease McIntyre, who wrote to Bishop McNulty that he well understood that "this information is not traceable by the FBI," yet that in his view "this would not diminish its likelihood. We are living in strange days, and communist propaganda finds expression in unexpected channels."[69]

Official interest in *On the Beach* extended as high as the White House itself. Presidential concern arose on November 6, 1959, when OCDM head Karl Harr was asked to report on OCDM's progress in developing prototypes for fallout shelters. In the midst of this discussion, Secretary of State Christian

Herter mentioned that the American Red Cross had been requested to sponsor the premiere of *On the Beach*—a request that distressed Herter because, in his opinion, the movie was "extremist, ban-the-bomb propaganda." He explained that in light of "the unprecedented publicity given this film, the President has asked me to add a discussion of the film to the next Cabinet meeting."[70]

Herter believed that a favorable reaction to Kramer's film would represent a "serious obstacle" to national security. Should moviegoers accept the film's "extremist" message, it could have "tremendous impact," weakening public backing for the government's civil defense program and military outlay. Concurring with this assessment, Harr criticized *On the Beach* for making his fallout shelter program seem "utterly hopeless."[71]

Earlier, an OCDM-sponsored opinion survey revealed that 78 percent of Americans who had "heard of fallout" were convinced that, in the event of a global conflict, the H-bomb would be employed against America. What troubled the OCDM was that (notwithstanding an optimistic publicity effort stressing minimal safeguards were all that were needed to meet the fallout hazard), merely 18 percent of the American population were convinced they had excellent chances to survive, even if they took refuge in a fully provisioned shelter. Furthermore, by 1959, only 2 percent of the American population had built a shelter, with most people saying they just didn't want to invest the money in such an effort.

Based on their analysis of these poll findings, government psychologists decided that what seemed mere indifference was indeed evidence of the public's psychological inability to "think about the unthinkable" without feeling completely helpless — a feeling psychologists contended was the most serious danger to civil defense. In light of this, Secretary of Defense Robert Anderson concluded, "Given the film's undeniable emotional power, it's a tricky problem." Herter decided that the best course of action was "to turn this emotional response into support of our own quest" for heightened military spending and civil defense.

Adding to White House worries was a December 17 announcement that *On the Beach* would simultaneously open in 18 major world capitals, Moscow among them. Kramer characterized these openings as "an invitation to the world's leaders to share a collective moment of reflection on the dangers of nuclear war." The press went so far as to render the premiere a significant occasion. Disturbed, Eisenhower told Herter that "given the unprecedented publicity being given this film," it warranted further Cabinet discussion. Taking note that Cabinet members were asked to attend the film's Washington premiere, one memo recommended that it would be helpful to "develop guidance for members of the government, as well as for USIA and our missions overseas."[72] Cabinet members were also asked to come to a private showing of *On the Beach* at the White House, to be held before the December 7 Cabinet meeting.[73] In the wake of that screening, OCDM's Harr restated his position that the film was very dangerous. Conceding that it posed a difficult challenge for the government, Harr observed that "we cannot try to suppress or even criticize the film, because it is undeniably an emotionally moving film." Secretary McCane proposed that Defense Secretary Anderson make a national television statement challenging the film and Shute's novel, in particular utilizing his affiliations with religious leaders to capitalize on Catholic distress regarding the film's presentation of mass suicide. Herter voiced his misgivings about such strategies, worried they would confer additional publicity upon Kramer's production. Concurring with this view, Labor Secretary James P. Mitchell expressed his hope that the film "doesn't get advertised as 'discussed at Cabinet!'" The Cabinet ultimately agreed with Information Director Abbot Washburn's judgment that "while we can show no signs of approval, it is a tricky situation, and we're stuck with it. We must not give the appearance of an American government boycott of an anti-war film."[74]

The strategy agreed upon was to have the White House prepare a confidential report on the movie for use by members of the State Department and the Pentagon in answering questions about their opinion of *On the Beach*. Though counseling that no comment should be made about the film, the edict nonetheless acknowledged that "we hardly can refuse comment on the question of whether or not the situation portrayed in the picture has scientific validity," and provided a question-and-answer sheet, six pages in length, which furnished guidance in how to answer questions:

Q. Do you have any comment on the film, *On the Beach*?

A. I am not a movie critic, and am not particularly qualified to discuss the film's dramatic qualities or the performance of the actors.

Q. But do you think that the film portrays a situation which could actually occur?

A. No. I don't think this could happen. Let's assume a hypothetical nuclear war involving the detonation of somewhat more than 1400 megatons in the U.S. and another 2500 megatons elsewhere in the Northern Hemisphere. Under these conditions, it is estimated that about 30 percent of the U.S. population would be killed. This would be terrible but not anywhere near total destruction.... After all, unprecedented destruction is not the same as unlimited destruction.[75]

Important military and civil defense officials drew upon this paper when making public statements refuting *On the Beach* in nationwide presentations. Accompanying most newspaper reviews of the film were stories regarding local civil defense officials' complaints about it. Frequently, quotes from the government document appeared in negative appraisals of the film. The document, furthermore, was supplied to elected officials to provide a means of answering any questions their constituents might raise. Members of Congress were urged to provide noncommittal replies to questions and then provide a specially prepared OCDM information sheet. Another element of the official strategy to refute *On the Beach* involved classified information guides about the film the U.S. Information Agency dispatched to all American embassies, with a cover letter bearing Herter's signature. Cautioning that the film's emotional call for the abolition of nuclear weapons could persuade audiences "to think in terms of radical solutions to the problem," Herter's missive continued that "to a limited extent, it may offer opportunities to turn this emotional response into intellectual support for our quest for safeguarded disarmament":

> Our attitude should be one of matter-of-fact interest, showing no special concern. We should refrain from public criticism of the film, which would be counter-productive. We should, however, be ready to discuss the film in private conversation with opinion leaders. In this connection ... special points should be noted.
>
> The greatest impact of the film for thinking people should be to underline ... the vital importance for the U.S. and its allies to maintain armed strength to deter aggression and for self-protection.
>
> War itself is the real evil, not any particular weapon. Conventional weapons kill just as effectively as nuclear weapons; morally there is no distinction. It will be unfortunate if the scientific inaccuracies of the film mislead and drive them to pressure for ban-the-bomb-type solutions.[76]

It didn't take long for Herter's directive to find its way to journalists. "In a secret six-page cable," *Newsweek* reported, "American military VIPs around the world were ordered to stay away from premieres of the movie *On the Beach*."[77] There was one exception: Moscow. Desiring to open the Soviet film market, Hollywood was agreeable to allow Moscow to score some propaganda successes at the West's expense if such a compromise would enhance free trade. Of this "trade-off," G. Tom Poe has written: "The Soviets used their endorsement of the film" to show everyone "that the USSR was as 'peace-loving' as the United States; while the American film industry got its foot into the film market behind the Iron Curtain."[78] To make the arrangement even better, the star of *On the Beach*, Gregory Peck, made an unofficial visit to the Soviet Union for the film's Moscow premiere — a trip that worked to Hollywood's advantage by intimating that the American movie capital was succeeding where governments were failing by saving the world from nuclear Armageddon. Kramer and United Artists took full advantage of Linus Pauling's comment: "It may be that some years from now we can look back and say that *On the Beach* is the movie that saved the world."[79]

The truth was that the Moscow debut of *On the Beach* made only a scant contribution to opening the Soviet market. Hollywood's hopes that the film would be publicly shown in Moscow were dashed, when directly after the film's debut, Soviet Minister of Culture Alexander Charkovskii informed *Pravda* that *On the Beach* was "obviously objectionable and unacceptable to Soviet audiences"[80]— the reason being that Soviet functionaries, like their American counterparts, found the film too hopeless and depressing for the public to see. Just the same, such a downbeat situation was construed by the Soviets as further evidence of Western shortcomings. *On the Beach*, in Charkovskii's characterization, indicated "the atomic psychosis ... being kept up recently in ... the United States."[81]

For their part, the White House and the Pentagon were insufficiently prepared to keep up with the serviceable buzz surrounding *On the Beach* emanating from the studio. Indeed, newspaper accounts pointed out that official efforts to discredit the film merely worked to the film's advantage. Nonetheless, outside the biggest urban markets, the film was a commercial disappointment, especially in those regions such as the Midwest and South where, according to surveys, indifference and unfamiliarity with nuclear issues remained astonishingly strong. The apathy and feeling of despair the government feared the film would produce apparently had the opposite effect of dissuading "regular movie-goers"— mainly adolescents and blue-collar adults — from seeing it to begin with. "Ironically," Poe has written, contemporary public opinion surveys "suggested that most Americans found the film realistic and accurate in its depiction of the real threat of nuclear war" to avoid seeing it.[82] Adding that "the film made no difference to the average American's commitment to civil defense preparedness," Poe feels that *Science* magazine's assessment was likely on target when it noted that "the viewer leaves the theatre ... moved more by what he has brought to the film than by what the performance itself accomplished."[83]

Beyond its initial release, *On the Beach* continued exerting an influence, becoming part of the propaganda arsenal of anti-nuclear groups from New Zealand to Britain during the early 1960s, before being eclipsed by Stanley Kubrick's *Dr. Strangelove or: How I Learned to Stop Worrying and Love the Bomb* (1964) and Peter Watkins's *The War Game* (1967). The reemergence of nuclear escalation as an issue in the 1980s brought Kramer's film once more to the forefront of the anti-nuclear ranks.[84]

3

Early Television and Civil Defense

The "Golden Age of Civil Defense" corresponded with another "golden age": the flourishing of commercial network television broadcasting during the post–World War II era. Virtually from television's beginning, concerns about nuclear war made themselves part of the new medium. Powerlessness and fear permeated depictions of nuclear war, pushing the nuclear threat into the background of everyday living where it stayed as a perpetual menace. Even before they learned to read, children comprehended the meaning of nuclear war. Televised tests of civil defense broadcast frequencies, airing on home TV sets, accustomed children to nuclear war as a regular aspect of family life. As Alice George writes, "Like people living for generations near a long-dormant volcano, Americans proceeded from day to day with the realization that tomorrow their world might melt away."[1]

The children's mothers were especially targeted for the civil defense message. The FCDA was already spreading its message via advertising during radio soap operas because, as one official put it, "these programs pack a terrific wallop on the gals who follow them." With the advent of television, the FCDA coproduced programs with the major networks. One such collaboration occurred in February 1951, when the agency and CBS produced a two-week informational program focusing on women and civil defense that earned praise from the *New York Times* as an "admirable new television series for the housewife" that allowed her "to become versed in the needs of civilian defense without leaving her home." The FCDA made certain that it received such laudatory press coverage by offering renowned female journalists positions on its Women's Advisory Committee and by currying the favor of organizations such as American Women in Radio and Television, whose female professionals furnished "an invaluable opportunity for a direct and effective contact with the woman at home."[2]

Civil Defense and Public Affairs Programming

The year 1951 witnessed the aforementioned collaboration between the FCDA and CBS marking the beginning of the FCDA's campaign to reach the public via the print and broadcast media. Regarding the latter, the agency concentrated its efforts on producing radio and television programs and films. In the case of the television networks, seeking to prove that they were as patriotic as everyone else during the McCarthy era, they eagerly cooperated with the government in getting the word out by airing thousands of hours of programming devoted to civil defense.

The collaboration between the media and the FCDA had the unsettling impact of clouding the boundary between government-sanctioned propaganda and a free press. So effective was the FCDA's information blitz and so absolute was the press's concurrence in this campaign that citizens were essentially incapable of telling the difference between the FCDA's take on the facts and independent journalism. "The mainstream news media was both victim and perpetrator of this process," Laura McEnaney has observed. "The government's shroud of secrecy made thorough investigative reporting essentially impossible, but the media nevertheless acted as more partner than adversary to the civil defense establishment." During the preparation of a civil defense broadcast, an ABC emissary told the FCDA: "We hope this program will help your cause ... our cause." Naturally this collaboration between what the government wanted and what the press wanted didn't worry FCDA planners, whose main goal was to make it seem that press coverage and complete disclosure were one and the same.[3]

Virtually from its inception, the Eisenhower administration stressed that the primary frontline for civil defense was the American home. As Washington had excluded a publicly financed civil defense program, the American civil defense effort was to be mainly a private undertaking that relied on traditional American values — self-determination, personal responsibility, and voluntary collaboration — to succeed. These values, it was thought, were grounded in the framework where they were mainly fostered and implemented — the family, which made the home the moral basis of civil defense. The latter, in President Eisenhower's words, was based in the "moral structure" of the family and the "spiritual strength" of American home life. Hence, national security, in Guy Oakes's words, was linked to "the character of family life, and civil defense ... to family values."[4]

Writing to Allan Wilson of the Advertising Council in February 1953, FCDA Executive Assistant Administrator J. M. Chambers explained the Eisenhower administration's goals in the civil defense realm and stressed the significant part advertising could play in achieving them. Owing to nuclear weapons and the international crisis the Cold War had occasioned, national security now entailed "total security," necessitating both a strong military establishment and civil defense. As total security required the merging of civil defense into daily living, it was vital to formulate a marketing plan to make civil defense "a permanent part of our way of life in the atomic age" — a plan that would succeed only if the American people could be persuaded that civil defense was absolutely necessary to their personal safety. In Chambers's words, "Not enough people as yet visualize civil defense as something which intimately affects them as individuals, and in their families and communities." While the FCDA would continue recruiting volunteers for work in specialized cadres — the Alert America program of the preceding administration — the agency's future endeavors would be more and more directed to an "action program" for local communities, the purpose of which would be to emphasize the significance of civil defense preparations in the home itself. At least one family member would receive first-aid training, and each family would learn "the principles of fire-safe housekeeping" and how to fight household fires. "The list could go on," Chambers wrote, "but I am sure you get the pitch."

Speaking on the connection between home safety and national security, Eisenhower's FCDA administrator Val Peterson declared that the primary objective of "a determined mass attack" on the Soviets' part would be "*our people — our human resources at home*" — a drastic "depletion" of which could result in the collapse of the home front and "the end of our nation as we know it." This explained why the Cold War home front "actually exists in our homes, right in our living rooms," and why national security necessitated a family civil defense program. The failure to combine civil defense and the home, in Peterson's view, would be unpatriotic at worst, even treasonous and equivalent to a "'fifth column' action which undermines our national defense."

Therefore, Peterson called for the transformation of every household into a home-grown civil defense unit — a move that would stymie the Soviets' nuclear war capability by preventing them from achieving their immediate goal of the collapse of American morale that would cripple the home front as well as persuade the Soviets that a nuclear offensive simply wasn't a worthwhile undertaking; in this way, civil defense would sustain peace by rendering nuclear war less of a likelihood. Should deterrence fail and nuclear war occur, one could survive a nuclear attack wherever one lived — provided the family had received complete instruction in "civil defense housekeeping." Whatever the circumstances, Americans could sustain both the morale of their soldiers and the home front by training families. Civil defense training for the home would endow Americans with the confidence that no matter what the enemy did, they could take the necessary actions to look after themselves. The key to managing the far greater challenges nuclear war would present nationally was to master the challenges civil defense provided within a far smaller framework — the family.[5]

Television's emergence as the primary means of reaching the home rendered television programs and made-for-television films the favored method of disseminating the techniques of household care in the nuclear age. Appearing in the film *This Is Your Civil Defense*, OCDM head Leo Hoegh declared that the "forces of communism" were deployed against the "forces of freedom." While civil defense was intended as a deterrent, the United States had to make preparations against the chance that the deterrence strategy might be unsuccessful. Americans were advised to prepare for a nuclear conflict where "only the self-sufficient will survive." Survival would be "a starkly personal matter," meaning that the family would have to utilize its own resources — technical, moral, and emotional — to make it through the ordeal. The same film presents a white, middle-class family riding out the aftermath of a nuclear attack in a well-stocked, comfortable fallout shelter — implying that life in a post-attack environment was roughly the same as that of the pre-war world.

A more detailed explanation of how a family could safeguard its dwelling from radioactive defilement was provided by an FCDA film, *Facts About Fallout*, which also tied family civil defense to the Cold War. This film stressed that civil defense meant to offset a nuclear attack on American soil was just as important as military might in meeting the Soviet aim of global mastery. In describing the dangers of fallout, the film presented a grim picture: "Fallout could hurt you, might even kill you." One nuclear explosion yielded fallout that could be harmful for quite some time. Not only human life, but all other life, even the earth itself, could be harmed by fallout. When it came to the home, fallout could befoul lawns, cars, even the water supply — all of which would remain dangerous until decontaminated, or the radiation had diminished to an "acceptable level." Nonetheless, the "knowledge of a few simple rules and precautions" could preserve life. The solution to the fallout problem was to be found in procedures easily grasped by the ordinary householder. All one needed to effectively "cope" with fallout was to understand the pertinent facts and implement some basic safeguards.

When it came to protecting an ample, well-maintained, two-story residence with a huge yard, *Facts About Fallout* argued that weather forecasters would be capable of plotting the direction and makeup of the "fallout pattern" — which gave viewers the impression that the site of the "fallout area," as distinguished from the "actual bomb zone," could be correctly forecast. Families with advance notice of fallout were the same as those confronting natural disasters such as blizzards or hurricanes. Within the fallout area, the individual had an exceptional likelihood of surviving by taking appropriate shelter. By merely staying indoors, one could lessen the risk of contamination by half, though the favored means of survival was an underground shelter. Ideally, such a sanctuary should be built away from the family home to protect it against the possibility that the residence would collapse or burn. Moreover, the shelter should be covered with at least three feet of earth — the latter to act as a shield against radioactivity. The film featured a sanctuary of this type which would house a family of five for an extended stay. A separate underground shelter was built on the assumption that the family for which it was intended had both the property and money to accommodate such a dwelling. In the event that such a shelter was beyond one's resources, a basement shelter was advised; if one lacked a basement, you were advised to close the windows and remain on the first floor.

When it came to removing fallout in the wake of a nuclear attack, *Facts About Fallout* advised sweeping the roof and hosing down the residence — assuming that the city water supply had been spared the effects of such an attack. The effects of the runoff from the water used for such decontamination procedures on the lawn and on those individuals who trod on it went unmentioned. Contaminated apparel should be left outside and not cleaned "until radiation decays." Once more assuming that an unspoiled source of water was available, the film counseled those watching it to take an invigorating post-attack shower with soap and water. The film concluded with the declaration that the techniques it presented for fallout protection were dependable and beyond doubt — that they were "the facts that should reassure and encourage you — and families all across America."[6]

What has been called the "most sophisticated attempt by the civil defense community to conceptualize fallout as a problem of nuclear housekeeping" was *Retrospect*. Produced by CBS News and sponsored by the OCDM, *Retrospect* was a series of 15-minute television programs, hosted by Douglas Edwards, whose credentials as the man who read the CBS evening news enhanced *Retrospect's* credibility in much the same way as Edward R. Murrow's background as a war correspondent added to the believability of the FCDA film *Survival Under Atomic Attack*.

Each episode of *Retrospect* featured three five-minute segments. Utilizing film and commentary by Edwards, the first segment covered 20th-century history. From there, the broadcast focused on the government's civil defense program, and the final piece resumed coverage of 20th-century history, usually highlighting the entertainment or sports fields. *Retrospect* had two goals: First, to provide its viewers the "facts" about the necessity of home preparedness in view of the hazards of nuclear war; and second, to furnish reliable information to families to enable them to be self-sufficient in a nuclear attack. The civil defense segment of *Retrospect* featured a mock fallout shelter, complete with bunk beds and equipment recommended by the FCDA home-protection literature.

Retrospect, in Edwards's words, was a "film excursion" into past events that had greatly affected modern life. In this way, *Retrospect* aimed to link important past crises and the failure to take proactive measures toward them to the hazards of the Cold War and the importance of home-front preparedness. One such historical segment linked the nuclear threat posed by the Soviet Union to the attack on Pearl Harbor. Were the United States to be caught unawares by a nuclear Pearl Harbor, the stakes would be far graver. The obvious lesson was that, no matter how strong the military might of a country was, it couldn't be a substitute for preparedness.

Edwards went on to say, "Today we realize that preparedness is our first line of defense." When it came to what preparedness implied for the American family in the age of the H-bomb, it primarily entailed home measures to provide fallout protection to families. "The links between national security and the danger of fallout and the translation of this danger into a household problem that could be managed by family self-protection," Oakes has written, "were the major themes" of *Retrospect*'s civil defense segments.

During one such segment, Edwards, entering the CBS fallout shelter, noted that the crux of all the serious problems confronting the American people was survival — "yours, mine, the survival of the entire free world." The Soviet Union sought global domination; toward that end, Soviet leaders were ready to employ any method, including the use of nuclear weapons. Americans must face the fact that the Soviets were waging "total war" against the United States. In such a conflict, total defense was necessary. Military forces alone were an inadequate means of meeting the Soviet threat: "This is why every American must prepare his home and family against possible attack."

Given the dangers of fallout, could one actually survive a nuclear war? Appearing on *Retrospect,* Paul McGrath, the director of Intelligence and National Security Affairs for the OCDM, declared that, such a danger notwithstanding, the survival of the American family in a nuclear attack was "substantiated by facts." The home shelter provided the "one sensible answer" to the fallout problem. "Recent studies" had "proved" that merely adding a shelter to the home would lessen American casualties in a nuclear conflict by 75 percent. In fact, McGrath asserted that a sanctuary patterned after the CBS model would furnish "excellent protection against radiation."

"We've learned the facts," Edwards said. "Now we must do something about it" [sic]. Edwards then recapitulated the segment's essential theme, which was "the importance of the fact that simple, inexpensive home shelters can save millions of lives in case of nuclear war." In case anyone missed this salient point, the CBS announcer said at the broadcast's conclusion:

> Survival in the nuclear age is a personal responsibility touching every American family. Make sure you take part. Learn the facts about civil defense home preparedness. Start your home preparedness program today. A prepared family builds a prepared nation. Civil defense is an American tradition.

Another guest on *Retrospect,* Charles Schaeffer, the director of Radiological Defense Plans for the OCDM, addressed the issue of decontaminating food so that normal family dining could continue in the wake of a nuclear attack. Schaeffer contended that food that had been stored in a refrigerator or on kitchen shelves and survived such an attack could be decontaminated by various simple means. He "contaminated" a banana with a "radioactive solution," then, after running a Geiger counter over it to prove it was despoiled, peeled it, checked the peeled banana to show it was safe to eat, and ate the banana. He stored the peel in a plastic bag for "later disposal," but didn't demonstrate this for *Retrospect* viewers. Shaeffer went on to say that what he had just done to make the banana safe for dining could also be applied to any thick-skinned fruit or vegetable, such as an orange, grapefruit, or melon. Shaeffer then proceeded to show how to decontaminate a head of lettuce and a can of Spam. Hence, "The radiation picture is not all black. In fact, if you do the proper things, it becomes quite manageable."

Retrospect also examined the challenges that would confront a family living in a fallout shelter for an extended period of time by having the Browns, a Topeka, Kansas, family who, along with their eight children, spent a whole week inside the CBS shelter, experiencing what Edwards termed a "personal survival test." The head of the family, Mr. Brown, himself a commercial builder of shelters, wanted to have his family experience life under a nuclear attack. Mrs. Brown admitted that shelter life wasn't entirely "homey," but compensated for that by decorating the refuge, transforming it into a place for living, not merely surviving. The key to the success of the Browns' experiment in shelter living had been intricate advance planning, precise scheduling, and the close systematizing of shelter life. "We had regular times for everything that we did, and we did it together," Mrs. Brown explained. The Browns kept their children in line with organized play times, using toys and games — all under the control of what Edwards called "police work." "We controlled their play," said Mrs. Brown of her brood, and "we did it all together so that everybody was working with each other." The lesson of the Browns' story for the American people was that civil defense was something average people with big families could do to shield themselves from fallout and, in so doing, learn something about themselves and have fun at the same time. In exhorting American families to follow the Browns' example, Edwards concluded, "The Browns are helping to ensure survival in this nuclear age. What about you?"

In his analysis of *Retrospect*, Guy Oakes calls the series "an ideal vehicle for marketing civil defense home protection":

> Because it was produced by the Public Affairs Division of CBS News, "Retrospect" was able to take advantage of the conceptual and institutional separation between the press and the state, supposedly a fundamental principle of the American polity. CBS News was not a government news agency, but an independent news organization that could be trusted to provide a reliable account of civil defense. Edwards was not an employee of OCDM or a minion of the civil defense community, but a news correspondent, committed by the ethics of his profession to maintain an uncompromising political neutrality. The format of "Retrospect" was drawn from the repertoire of familiar radio and television news programs. A journalist-narrator recites facts to an audience and tells a story the public needs to know. By the end of the program, the public has "the real facts" and knows "the whole story." Thus the warrant for the claims made on behalf of family civil defense was not the potentially partisan political requirements of national security policy, but the allegedly objective standards of reportage.
>
> "Retrospect" also skillfully exploited the historical themes and the metahistorical assumptions built into the program. The positions on civil defense taken in "Retrospect" were represented as inescapable lessons of history. Because historical events have already happened and cannot be changed, they do not seem to be open to political debate. Civil defense was not a matter of policy — an unresolved set of issues about which there could be more than one legitimate opinion — but a historical fact.... In the monistic philosophy of history to which "Retrospect" was committed, there was only one valid account of historical events and only one true interpretation of history. Any interpretation that diverged from the privileged story could not be regarded as an alternative account, possibly legitimate if judged on its own premises. To the extent that it departed from the one true story, it was in error. It followed that there was only one valid account of the origins of the Cold War, the development of the American national security crisis, and the place of civil defense in American life. Any other version of this history was false and had to be rejected precisely for this reason. As a result, civil defense was insulated from criticism and protected from competing alternative views of the domestic requirements of American security. Because civil defense was as essential part of the current chapter in the one true history of the Cold War, there were no such alternatives.
>
> Finally, "Retrospect" possessed a formidable public relations asset in the person of Edwards himself, who was known to the television audience as the broadcaster who had read the news every weekday night since 1948 on "Douglas Edwards with the News." Edwards was cast as a narrator of impeccable reliability. He simply related information, read factual reports, or posed questions to expert interviewees and summarized their answers in an untendentious fashion. In fact, the civil defense community employed Edwards as an advocate of its

own policies and an accomplished publicist who assisted OCDM officials in presenting questionable and controversial positions as if they were incontestable facts, guaranteed by the authority of science or history.

All of these elements, in Oakes's judgment "made 'Retrospect' a remarkably well designed instrument in the program to sell family civil defense."[7]

In presenting an indiscriminate combination of canards and realities concerning the Cold War to credulous viewers nationwide, public affairs programming greatly contributed to disseminating social and political anxieties of the day. The mingling of fact and fiction was a component of civil defense programming which, as we have seen, was produced in collaboration with the federal government. Appearing on a 1951 CBS series, *The Facts We Face,* AEC officials clarified atomic warfare and how to survive such a conflict. Another production, *Prepare to Survive,* which aired monthly on Pittsburgh's WDTV, was produced in cooperation with the FCDA. Another 1951 series, *Survival,* which aired on NBC that summer, proved to be such a success that the FCDA requested kinescopes of the series for training civil defense volunteers.

Informational broadcasts such as these undoubtedly aired on network and local radio, which likely enjoyed a larger audience, as just a tiny share of American homes — 58 percent — were equipped to pick up television broadcasts in early 1951. Just the same, television's ability to present, visual images of the nuclear threat enhanced the compelling nature of the message civil defense programming sought to convey. Such imagery was part of *Survival Under Atomic Attack.* Airing on Louisville station WHAS-TV in December 1950, this series addressed what should be done in the event of a Russian A-bomb attack on Kentucky. The series' visual content augmented the theme it sought to present, which had been announced on the initial episode: "This is just a program, but there could be a bomber carrying the equivalent of 20,000 tons of TNT on its way to Louisville right now."

Instead of reproaching government policy, which had already precipitated a superpower arms race, television justified such a course: American hawkishness was nothing more than a sensible response to Soviet Russia's communistic ambitions. Should the American campaign to curb Russian aspirations produce nuclear war and destruction on the home front, it was worth it, as such destruction was survivable. This theme was presented to New York City residents in a locally produced broadcast, *You and the Atom Bomb.* Presented on WOR-TV, September 21, 1951, the program provided its audience an explanation of fission and the kinds of atomic explosion — water, land, and air — to expect. For a dime, viewers would receive an instructional brochure "so you'll know what to do in the event of an atomic attack." The announcer gave the television audience the notion that they could survive a nuclear attack with a few simple precautions:

I hope that we have been able to remove some of the fears and misconceptions that have surrounded the atomic bomb. I hope that you realize now that there's nothing mysterious about radiation, and that the atomic bomb will not create a race of monsters. And that terrible as the atomic bomb is, it does not mean the end of our large cities or country or of our population. You are not helpless if you know your atom.[8]

When it came to atomic energy, especially the likelihood of nuclear war, fifties television rarely ignored the opportunity to capitalize upon its dramatic and propagandistic elements. Such was the case with *Three, Two, One-Zero!* a 1954 NBC documentary presentation, produced by the network's *Project XX* unit, that presented its subject within a partisan political framework. Human-regulated atomic power was presented as the brainchild of American science. Atomic energy was extolled as the "maximum expression" of "a free society." Such energy "belongs to the citizens of the United States," and was nothing less than the "industrial genius of America," which had "come into full potential." Atomic weaponry was lauded as "it guards the freedom of the West today."

Three, Two, One-Zero! explained Russian industrial development from nothing in 1917 to the present as the result of "generations of slave labor ... sacrificed to this end. The means are of no consequence. The end is all important." Quoting American airmen, narrator Alexander Scourby intoned words of caution: "If the Russians go to war, they won't have a country to come back to."

As was characteristic of most television broadcasts dealing with the subject of nuclear war and how to survive it, this one presented terrifying imagery and implored its audience to accept increasing hawkishness on America's part. "How many bombs do the Russians have?" Scourby asks. "The exact number is not known, does not matter," yet "they have enough, if delivered on target, to inflict incredible damage on the United States, on the West." The appropriate answer to the Russian challenge was "defense against aggression"—a course the footage illustrated by showing film of Air Force jets and bombers. Scourby continued:

> On the airfields of North America the intercontinental bombers are constantly fueled, constantly tuned, constantly ready—twenty-four hours a day, day in and day out. The planes and their crews are always on the alert, their targets picked, their courses long since set. Somebody might blow the whistle tomorrow morning.[9]

Televised Nuclear War

As important as public affairs programs about atomic energy and civil defense were, in no way could they equal the dramatic force of the numerous simulated nuclear attacks on American cities that were a recurrent feature of entertainment and nonfiction television during the fifties. CBS repeatedly offered such fare. New York was "attacked" on the June 29, 1952, edition of Edward R. Murrow's *See It Now* series. Four years later, the Big Apple, along with other American cities, fell under the gun in the debut installment of *Air Power*. Portland, Oregon's civil defense program was the subject of yet another CBS presentation, *The Day Called "X,"* which aired December 8, 1957.[10]

Produced in cooperation with the FCDA, and narrated by film actor Glenn Ford, *The Day Called "X"* opens with Ford telling the viewer, "There are no actors in this story, but there are a lot of people — the people of the city of Portland, Oregon — and what happened to them, or could happen to them on a day that we'll call 'X.'"

The day begins like any other — a housewife turns to the women's section of the paper, ignoring the front page "scare headlines"; a child is born in the hospital; a church service is held; people work their jobs; children are in their kindergarten class; the city council and other municipal functions are operating. Then this peaceful routine is interrupted by word that enemy planes have crossed the Poles, heading toward Portland. Informed of the situation, the mayor calmly directs the city council to reassemble at the emergency operations center.

The wail of the civil defense siren alerts the residents of Portland to the crisis. The fire and police departments hasten to their duties, seemingly unconcerned about the gravity of the impending nuclear attack. Similarly, the kindergarten students calmly follow their teacher to shelter; elsewhere, Portlanders evacuate "according to a well thought-out plan. The question is ... 'Will it work?' Quietly, without panic, the city organizes."

Hospital patients, school students, office workers, and families relocate to safety, seemingly without congestion or traffic jams. The city government relocates to a blast- and radiation-proof operations center in a hill outside town where it can still function and oversee the evacuation of Portland and the latter's reorganization if necessary.

Emergency kitchens are set up in local public buildings. The police report that Portland is about 65 percent evacuated, while state and county police roadblocks have guaranteed that all lanes can be used for outbound traffic. All indications are that Portland's evacuation plan is operating smoothly. As zero hour approaches, there's time to relax and rest. The city streets are deserted. As the impending attack draws closer, the signal to take cover sounds. All Portlanders can do now is wait. Silence envelops the emergency operations center as everyone waits for the bomb to explode.

The program then concludes with Ford's final summation:

What happened after that moment, we leave you to contemplate. But one thing is certain: Portland has a plan for the survival of its people and the continuity of its government ... actually the survival of this entire nation depends upon the ability of federal, state, and local governments to carry out their responsibilities in the event of a massive nuclear attack. Each new scientific development in the weapons of war presents a new challenge. And the people of Portland, through working together — they're ready if there really were a day called "X." How about you?

The residents of Portland who appear in *The Day Called "X"* are apparently nothing more than white, middle-class types who meet the impending crisis with serenity. City officials and civil defense workers are well dressed. Sweeping and detailed preparations are the heart of Portland's evacuation. Civil defense measures have become a routine aspect of life there, thus making nuclear war itself seem routine. When the day called "X" does come, everything functions with clockwork precision: Everyone knows what's expected of him and her and does so flawlessly. Because the federal government is unwilling to support civil defense measures to protect Portlanders, the latter must assume that task themselves. Civil defense is ultimately a local obligation. "Like any other community problem, it can be handled by native pragmatism, quiet courage, and selfless devotion to the common good." Because Portlanders know precisely what their duties are, the Portland model can be applied elsewhere. In this way, the final outcome of a nuclear war was never in doubt, even before the bombs fell. "Nuclear war was envisioned as won even before it had begun."[11]

Such broadcasts, even when featuring renowned network journalists, were accurately identified as "fictionalized documentaries." Footage of atomic explosions, on the other hand, were genuine. From the first bomb tests at Eniwetok-Bikini in the South Pacific in 1946, the Pentagon provided free footage of its atomic and hydrogen tests to local and network television. February 6, 1951, marked the beginning of television coverage of domestic bomb tests at Yucca Flat, Nevada, when KTLA and KTTV, both in Los Angeles, broadcast and recorded on kinescope a test explosion.[12] On that date, what historian Thomas Doherty has called "a select but no doubt attentive local audience" viewed the first live images of an atomic explosion to be aired on television. The cameras, located atop Mount Wilson, approximately 250 miles distant from the site of the detonation, the Las Vegas Proving Ground, presented "the flash of eerie white light" which the blast produced. KTLA reporter Gil Martin covered the event from Las Vegas and interviewed spectators. The mushroom cloud was plainly visible from atop Las Vegas hotels and casinos.[13]

Another televised atomic blast, this time from Yucca Flat, Nevada, on April 22, 1952, reflected TV's technical progression by being present live from coast to coast. "The home audience heard the call of 'bomb away' and listened to the counting of the seconds and saw a flash that, for a few seconds, blackened TV screens with a dark penumbra around the control point of light that was the blast," observed the trade publication *Broadcasting/Telecasting*. Viewers tried to make out a small white pinhole they saw that occurred as the blinding light of the bomb detonation caused orthicon tubes in the pickup camera to break-down. Though the announcer marveled at the "beautiful, tremendous, and angry spectacle," numerous television viewers were upset about the less than perfect audio and visual quality of the telecast. *Variety* dismissed the proceedings in its characteristic fashion: "A-Bomb in TV Fluff Fizzles Fission Vision."[14]

More successful was another live broadcast from Yucca Flat this one on March 17, 1953. The purpose of the test was to replicate an atomic blast's effect on an average home. Toward that end, "Doom Town," a two-household community, complete with upright mannequins, was constructed for use in the test — the latter receiving intense coverage in all its aspects by the three major television networks. Because commercial advertisers (in the words of *Washington Post* television critic Sonia Stein), "did not feel eager to associate their products with the horrors of war exemplified by atomic bombing," the broadcast aired as an unsponsored public service presentation.

Under the gaze of television cameras, trucks were shown unloading Army troops to within 3,500 feet of ground zero. A long shot framed a floodlit, tall, slender tower from which the bomb would be set off. When the detonation occurred, "The tremendous atomic burst over Doom Town in Nevada sent TV screens across the nation into 'wobbles,' and a brief blackout at the instant of the blast," noted a wire service reporter. "But then the picture returned and tense watchers at their TV sets got their clearest look yet at what an atomic explosion is." A thin cloud "like a tall thin mushroom" surged upward, then altered its form "into something approaching an irregular upside down 'L.'" Correspondents near ground zero — Walter Cronkite, Morgan Beatty, and Chet Huntley — spoke of ground tremors and of getting dust in their eyes. Viewers unable to see live coverage of the blast saw kinescopes of it that evening. Imagine, cautioned civil defense authorities, if "one of the homes belonged to *you* and *your* family was inside."[15]

The armed forces' PR operations evidently benefited from such coverage of bomb tests. During the 1952 test, Marine Corps helicopters installed commercial television-relay equipment at critical points between Los Angeles and ground zero in Nevada. When Operation Smokey was held in 1957, 1,140 soldiers were ordered into the blast area two hours after the bomb had been set off. The exercise was filmed by the Army, and aired on commercial television stations as part of the Army's *Big Picture* series. Conceding that it exposed soldiers to radiation hazards such as this, the Army justified it in part "to portray to the public the Army at its best employing [its new Pentomic] organ-ization in operations under atomic warfare conditions."[16]

Four months before the Yucca Flat test of March 17, 1953, the United States had set off the infinitely more powerful hydrogen bomb on the Pacific island of Eniwetok in the Marshall Islands. Over a year later, on April 1, 1954, 35mm black-and-white film of the detonation was finally released for public viewing on newsreel and television screens, with narrator Ed Herlihy announc-ing "the second era — the thermonuclear era — of the atomic age." To provide prospective on the enormity of the blast, the latter was superimposed on the skyline of New York. As the fireball from the "awful destructive power of the H-bomb" expands across the screen, the "heart of the metropolis would be instantaneously transformed into an inferno while shock waves devastated the rest of the city." (This unsettling image was followed by "Hollywood Fashion Holiday," in which "starlets Mamie Van Doren, Ruth Hampsen and other lovelies model an eye-appealing array of summer styles, ranging from travel suits to swim wear, a lovely picture.")[17]

The H-bomb's impact was greater still with the television audience. The small screen was already pushing theatrical newsreels aside as the primary source of news. Produced by the Defense Department and the AEC, *Operation Ivy* recounted the story of the initial hydrogen bomb blast, with actor Reed Hadley, the star of CBS's *Racket Squad,* serving as narrator. Speaking from a U.S. Navy cruiser on a station for the nuclear fireworks, Hadley tells the audi-ence that "we'll soon see the largest explosion ever set off on the face of the earth — that is, the largest that we know about." While the success of the bomb test is a bit uncertain, "The uneasy state of the world puts everything on a gambling basis." Because remote television cameras are present to film the occasion, "You have a grandstand seat here to one of the most momentous moments in the history of science," Hadley gushes. "In less than a minute you will see the most powerful explosion ever witnessed by human eyes."

Gesturing to the left, Hadley indicates that "the blast will come out of the horizon just about there. And this is the first full-scale test of a hydrogen device. If the reaction goes, we're in the thermonuclear era." He pauses. "For the sake of all of us, and for the sake of our country, I know that you join me in wishing this expedition well." The time has now come to put on goggles and turn away from the direction the explosion will come.

When the big moment does arrive, the image on the screen is that of a gigantic fireball. As was done in the newsreels, stateside reference points were utilized to illustrate the scope of the blast. The fireball itself would envelop one-quarter of Manhattan Island. With the Capitol dome in Washington, D.C., as ground zero, everything within an area of three miles would experience "complete annihilation."

The day of the film's release, April 1, 1954, CBS beat its rivals in airing it first on *The Morning Show,* ABC presented the film in its entirety once that morning, followed by a second airing in prime time; while NBC showed it at 8:00 A.M., 7:00 P.M., and 11:15 P.M. "Sold commercially at $28 a print and widely distributed in the secondary school system, *Operation Ivy* had a long half-life as an educational tool in science and civics classes, not to mention the nightmares of impressionable baby boomers."[18]

Because bomb tests were subject to such factors as the weather, inadequate visibility, winds blowing in the wrong direction, etc., there could be brief delays before the detonations could be set off; hence, financial losses could be incurred in providing live coverage of the tests. Such was the case in the spring of 1955, when CBS and NBC dispatched a group of 95 technicians, announcers, engineers, and photographers to Yucca Flat in what was intended to be what *TV Guide* called a significant television event, featuring "not only the blast, but the split second reaction of people hunched in a trench less than two miles from the 500-foot steel tower that held the bomb."[19]

The blast, designated as "Apple II," involved numerous federal agencies and private-sector industries, who participated in the event with the AEC and the Defense Department. Their efforts were organized and managed by the FCDA. The civil defense aspect of the test received the label Operation Cue. A total of 48 of the 65 experiments that were conducted as part of "Apple II" related to civil defense.[20] The purpose of Operation Cue was to test how residences, shelter designs, utilities, mobile housing, vehicles, warning systems, and various domestic items stood up under an atomic explosion. Moreover, the FCDA conducted several post-blast exercises involving rescue operations, fire control, plane evacuations, communication and sanitation efforts, and mass feeding.[21]

To cover the event, over 500 newspaper and broadcast journalists (the latter comprising both television and radio correspondents) were present. "The world's most expensive premiere will be unfolded out on the Nevada desert, and nothing that Hollywood has ever produced will be able to equal it," offered one journalist. Two days before D-day was slated to occur, network television provided its audience with a look inside what government spokesmen called "Survival City," and the troops participating in the test dubbed the community constructed for the test Doom Town. Television crews filmed the interior of a yellow frame house, representative of the residence of a "typical American family." Big name network journalists such as Dave Garroway, John Cameron Swayze, Walter Cronkite, and John Charles Daly were slated to cover live what a fellow reporter called "the greatest horror program ever produced."[22]

As part of its civil-effects experiments, the FCDA intended to subject a wide range of items to the consequences produced by the "Apple II" blast.

Doom Town featured ten full-scale homes, the reinforced structures of which were devised by an architect who had studied the damage inflicted on Japanese residences after the atomic bomb attacks there. Many of the Doom Town homes were equipped with the latest appliances as well as carports or garages, housing late-model automobiles. What truly made the test iconic was the presence in the atomic community of fully clothed dime-store mannequins in the role of the town's inhabitants. The use of the mannequins, in the words of Harold Goodwin, was a "deliberate attempt to get attention." Characterized as a "very imaginative public-information type, concerned with the public impact," Goodwin, the FCDA's civil-effects-tests director during Operation Cue, added, "We wanted to really dress up the set, so we used mannequins. It was for the TV cameras and the movies. The newsmen wanted drama — not reality."[23]

All was in readiness for the big event when the weather upset the scheduled fireworks. Ten days of false starts and postponements followed. Garroway, Cronkite, Daly, and Swayze stuck it out. "To build up the suspense," in the words of *Newsweek*, "on-the-air coverage began on D-day-2." Beginning April 24, television shows such as *Youth Wants to Know* and *The Today Show* presented special broadcasts tied to the anticipated atomic spectacular. Coverage would continue all during the delays, costing the networks huge sums. As part of their reporting, newscasters descended on Doom Town, holding "interviews" with a mannequin "family," the Darlings. The latter's cupboard and refrigerator was scrutinized by the food editor of the television program *Home;* the editor ruminated on what effect the bomb blast would have on baby food, dishwashers, and children's pajamas.

By the time "Apple II" was finally exploded on May 5, 1955, the national media, especially the big-name television reporters, had already packed their bags and left, due to soaring expenses.[24] Only those correspondents from wire services and "picket-fence dallies" remained. It had been a losing experience for the television networks and the government public relations people who had counted on televised coverage of the "Apple II" shot to make a hit on prime time.[25] Commenting on the fiasco, a news magazine observed:

> Last week, TV's biggest bomb finally went off with a bang and a whimper. The bang came from the 500-foot tower on Yucca Flat, Nevada, where a 35-kiloton nuclear device was detonated. The whimper came from the networks. After spending an estimated $200,000, they were left with only skeleton crews on hand when the bomb was finally triggered.[26]

The *Home* show aired five minutes' worth of film "between a lesson in meringue whipping and a promo for Mother's Day."[27]

"An elephant has just given birth to a mouse," remarked Dave Garroway.[28]

Just the same, by airing nuclear weapons tests, network television did fulfill a significant PR function, one that gave confidence to Americans in the wake of the Soviets' acquisition of the atomic and, then, the hydrogen bombs that their nation would not accept parity with its communist adversary, but would move forward with each test to attain nuclear superiority.[29]

Civil Defense and Entertainment Programming: From Live Drama to Episodic Television

For most people, television signified entertainment, a diversion from the trials and hardships of everyday life. The early years of the medium have been called the Golden Age of Television, mainly because most families couldn't afford to buy television sets owing to the high cost of such receivers. Those people who bought TVs during this period were educated, relatively prosperous, and refined in their tastes, thus the networks presented programs that appealed to such upper-class types. The format that most typified the Golden Age, live drama, dominated television schedules, simply because they gave the networks something with which to fill their schedules. This need arose out of Hollywood's refusal to let the networks show old films due to the film industry's fear of competition from television.[30]

Unlike programs that featured continuing characters, anthology dramas such as *Playhouse 90, Studio One,* and *Kraft Television Theater* presented different stories each week. The people involved in these programs presented a worldview that generally was at variance with the notion of a united, harmonious America featured in Hollywood films. Live television also afforded an outlet for some blacklisted Hollywood writers to continue to ply their trade. What linked these scribes with other television writers (who avoided blacklisting by never having been affiliated with "subversive" organizations) was that they all shared an analogous belief system. The writers living in New York City — among them Paddy Chayefsky, Rod Serling, Gore Vidal, Horton Foote, and Reginald Rose — dealt with such, for their time, "abnormal" behavior as homosexuality, teenage pregnancy, alcoholism, juvenile delinquency, and mental illness, as well as challenging the Cold War by advocating pacifism, censuring McCarthyism, and impugning the nuclear arms race. In so doing, they voiced dissenting views and presented unconventional universes for the television audience at a time when the prevailing political climate limited the expression of these ideas and themes elsewhere.

Though they drew inspiration from various sources, the paramount experience the anthology writers shared was World War II, which instilled in them a particular appreciation for universalism — a concept they, like Hollywood progressives, believed could take the place of fascism and militarism. Before they became television writers, Rod Serling, Paddy Chayefsky, Robert Alan Aurthur, Gore Vidal, Reginald Rose, Tad Mosel, and others had served their country in the military — and, as they embarked upon their TV writing careers, these writers' progressive worldviews would be expressed as part of television content.

Other veterans — Marc Daniels, Martin Ritt, Franklin Schaffner, Fielder Cook, Paul Bogart, George Roy Hill, and John Frankenheimer — made their mark on television as significant directors. To many of them the medium provided a way to merge creative freedom, progressive activism, and first-rate salaries. Television, in Martin Ritt's words, was "very interesting, it was exciting, and it was live."[31] These qualities attracted him greatly as he had worked with the *March of Time* war documentaries that stressed realism (and drew congressional attention). Where Hollywood and Broadway seemed limited for sundry reasons, Ritt, a blacklist victim, felt that he could do practically anything he wanted to in television. Working in New York City for Americans United for World Government in 1946, Franklin Schaffner, seeking a different career path, obtained employment as a radio producer before entering the television realm. John Frankenheimer found "an ideal existence" as the assistant director on a number of programs. "In subsequent years this partnership of progressive talents in television would," in Andrew J. Falk's words, "only grow more influential as they would challenge the views of doctrinaire Cold Warriors."[32]

The chaotic nature of early television promoted experimentation. Many in television drew upon their experiences in radio, stage, print media, and advertising for guidance. Rod Serling remembered, "There was a sense of bewilderment on the part of everyone"; live television's trailblazers were "feeling their way around," seeking "some reason for being, and some set of techniques."[33] "The ensuing disorder," Falk continues, "facilitated an environment where writers and directors could audition experimental themes as well." Such an ambience permitted "an intense debate over industry development and television content. Changing Cold War mentalities would play an important part in how those debates were resolved and what content would be produced over time."[34]

The television audience — as viewed by sponsors, networks, and writers — was also a factor in television's rise, the acceptance of controversial programs, and why programming changed over time. Paramount among the reasons for television's success in postwar America was expanding prosperity, suburbanization, and the readiness on the part of average people to embrace novel programming. In addition to making television a popular and available medium, these considerations fashioned the kind of environment where progressive themes could flourish. Just the same, "some of "the very same institutional forces that initially welcomed controversial themes" would subsequently levy a restricting hand on them, fostering "the Cold War consensus ideology of anticommunism, unfettered capitalism, and a national image of exceptionalism."[35]

One reason for television's popularity, aside from the medium's sheer novelty or the status owning a TV set conferred upon its owner was that viewers welcomed programming unavailable elsewhere, including Hollywood, which, in order to pacify Cold War zealots, had dropped the production of films containing controversial themes, replacing them with fare that, in all likelihood, satisfied those on the House Un-American Activities Committee more than the lion's share of movie-goers. The American public hadn't blindly or totally converted to the era's Cold War consensus. Television's weekly anthology dramas had picked up the baton Hollywood had dropped under pressure from the Cold Warriors. Live television plays, in Paddy Chayefsky's words, were "far and away superior to anything on the current Broadway stage or anything issued by the movie industry." Concurring with this assessment, Rod Serling declared that the anthology drama "consistently aimed high," it was "adult, never hackneyed, and almost always honest," and "rarely dull." Because of this, anthology writers achieved recognition for their scripts. "We became a household word," Horton Foote recalled, particularly as the networks merchandized their literary talents. One of the explanations for television's popularity was that people entrusted their democratic aspirations to it.[36]

The late 1940s witnessed deliberate efforts on the part of both government officials and network executives to make television a receptive environment for all manner of conviction on behalf of the "public interest." Aligning himself with those advocating "peaceful coexistence" with the Soviets, NBC chairman David Sarnoff declared that "we should be willing to carry on discussions and negotiations, however fruitless or frustrating they may appear at the time." By trusting in the deliberative process of disclosing Soviet aims, Sarnoff backed the government's moderate containment policy before 1950. Sarnoff and NBC president Niles Trammell had both been members of the Committee for the Marshall Plan, serving with renowned Cold War liberals who voiced scorn for anti-communist witch-hunters, among them Hubert Humphrey and Reinhold Niebuhr.

In what has been termed "the single most important programming policy document" in its history, the Federal Communications Commission in March 1946 issued the "Blue Book" of standards and practices — a document that implored broadcasters to take into account the "public interest" in programming matters. By defining the kind of programming that met the "public interest," the "Blue Book" spelled out exactly what it meant: to provide a balance to advertising — support material, to showcase the "unsponsorable"; to "serve minority tastes and interests"; and to "allow experimentation with new types of programs." The commission would look favorably on renewal applications "from stations that had met their public service responsibilities," with the latter including a "discussion of public issues, and no excessive advertising." Subsequently, FCC chairman Wayne Coy announced the commissioners' analysis of Section 315 of the Communications Act of 1934 and asserted that stations "may not censor political broadcasts because of allegedly libelous or slanderous material contained in them"—meaning the commission would insist that licensed broadcasters air political programs on the part of radicals and supposed "subversives." Television would be sustained in such a way as to allow the presentation of all kinds of perspectives—including those of the most incendiary nature.

During the "freeze" on station licensing imposed by the FCC between September 1948 and April 1952—an action arising from signal interference and other technological problems and one that also allowed the commission to regulate television's expansion—industry insiders devised significant standards and precedents. Stations would be under the gaze of a progressive FCC that demanded that they fulfill their "public service responsibility" to secure renewal of their broadcast licenses. And, by disproving allegations from the FBI in the matter of supposed communist ties of some broadcasting license applicants in California, the FCC deflected the efforts of zealous anticommunists who sought to transform television into a political weapon.

Taking its signal from the FCC, the National Association of Broadcasters (NAB) promulgated its own guidelines for the television industry—though, in this instance, such rules were meant to exercise strict control over broadcasting content. By bluntly declaring that "controversial issues" shouldn't be dramatized, the NAB especially hoped to eradicate profanity, foster the institution of marriage, and disallow "material tending to break down juvenile respect for parents, the home or moral conduct." "In short," Andrew J. Falk has written, "given the Cold War environment, the NAB urged networks to downplay, if not" completely eschew such controversial subjects.[37]

Executives at NBC, appreciating that they must exercise management of their programming before someone else did, set forth their own code of broadcasting conduct under the designation *Responsibility*. Issued for the purpose of altering policies initially set forth in 1934, *Responsibility* adopted much of what the NAB desired, yet claimed the duty of regulating what it aired, much the same way as other media had already done. Prior to its broadcast, everything heard and spoken had to receive clearance from NBC's bureaucracy. "Continuity acceptance," NBC's designation for its job as censor, was the network's responsibility, and in the late 1940s and early 1950, that area was the domain of those who (temporarily at most) were receptive to controversial subject matter.[38]

"The common values shared by a cadre of writers, directors, producers, and network executives," in Falk's words, "allowed for the proliferation of multilaterist themes in anthology dramas."[39] This favorable climate, however, would soon be dashed by the worsening of Cold War tensions after 1950 as broadcasters began to place their own interests and careers at the expense of those stained by the accusation of having communist sympathies. Cultural outlets, including television, were enlisted in America's war against Soviet ambitions, and blacklisting became a mechanism to stifle dissident voices in television.[40] Indicative of this new mood, the FCC, after 1950, redefined the "public interest" so as to confer legitimacy upon existing social institutions and to glorify the merits of capitalism — a new line that was advanced by several appointments President Eisenhower named to the commission.[41] "The guardians of television were few in number ... and they guarded the gate fiercely against apostasy of every sort. Anything appearing on screen was to be vetted for the aberrant, impure, or un–American. Inside that screen, fortress America fought back, defending itself against the ambushes of the forces of evil."[42]

Compromise became the order of the day for television writers. Television, Rod Serling lamented, had moved from "a medium best suited to illuminate and dramatize the issues of the times" to a "product pressed into a mold, painted lily-white," and one that had had "its dramatic teeth yanked one by one." Still it was enough for a few writers when they had the opportunity to merely voice certain issues. Such a course enabled television drama to survive — even though it was now gelded. As Reginald Rose put it, "I was surprised I got away with the stuff I did. Television was so sensitive to criticism, and the criticism almost always came from the right. The network people were really petrified for their jobs. Yet, they were also afraid of being that way, so sometimes things got through."[43]

Among the issues anthology drama delved into was nuclear anxiety and atomic testing. Where the government urged preparation to meet the possibility of atomic disaster, television conveyed unease. Atomic testing, in the government's view, could be shown as ordinary, scientifically significant, and a search for knowledge that would be employed to calm, instead of magnifying, anxieties. In the wake of a May 1951 atomic test at Eniwetok, General James Cooney declared, "The immediate radiation hazard from [an] air burst disappeared after the first two minutes. Rescue ... work can begin immediately in any area where there is life." And, just two months later, the AEC informed the American Institute of Architects that "special efforts would be made to gain information useful to architects trying to design atom-resistant buildings." Westinghouse president Gwilym Price declared, "I believe that we are within five years of the beginning of commercial atomic power." Westinghouse foresaw a time not far off when its TV spokeswoman Betty Furness would present a Westinghouse atomic toaster in what *Time* called her "electrified Utopia."[44]

Rod Serling took a dissenting view: Bomb testing was destabilizing instead of enlightening. "Nightmare at Ground Zero," a Serling script airing on a 1953 installment of the CBS program *Suspense,* was set in Nevada's Yucca Flat, and focused on George, who manufacturers "dummies" used in atomic tests, and his wife, Helen, who, put-off by her husband's engrossment in testing, prevails upon him to take her to the next atomic exercise. This, he does by placing her, sedated, as one of his "dummies" in the test house prior to the atomic detonation — leaving the viewer to wonder if she'll be rescued in time. In the story's opening shot, the audience is greeted by the site of a gate with a sign ("Restricted Area — Keep Out"), while, on the inside, armed guards are on duty. "In effect," Serling "is saying that the bomb is off limits and can never be contained or used by citizens in the beneficial ways the government and business had promised. Rather, Americans are reduced to the unthinking 'dummies' the military has carefully placed inside a home."[45] In Serling's story, as in real life, military planners went so far as to ensure that the tests were realistic by attiring "dummies" of both sexes with appropriate apparel. A painter tells his colleague, "Even dummies yet. And not just any place. Father here. Mother there. An' for what? At four A.M. they drop an a-bomb on it — an' there ain't nothin' left anyhow." To which the second painter says, "Kinda creepy, ain't it? Looks like a house. Furnished like a house. But it ain't a house. At four in the morning — *it's Ground Zero!*" In this way, Serling explains that people like George who support atomic testing are so involved with individual tests that they "don't care that I'm frightened to death!" Despite their realistic appearance, the mannequins aren't truly human — thus, how can authentic results be gleaned from tests that kill objects that merely "bleed plaster-of-Paris?"

Another issue that comes up in Serling's story is radioactivity. Addressing a mannequin "father," a military officer says, "Well, old man, this is it! By morning you'll be just so much dust. Dangerous dust I'll wager, too. Radioactive, you know." After leaving his wife in the doomed structure, a conscience-stricken George reassures himself that she "won't feel a thing. They tell me it's so quick." The viewing audience knows otherwise. George ultimately saves Helen from destruction.[46]

"Mr. Finchley versus the Bomb," Serling's 1954 script for NBC's *Kaiser Aluminum Hour,* is the account of an old man who momentarily brings an atomic test to a standstill. By now, the nuclear ante had risen to even greater heights. In January 1954, Secretary of State John Foster Dulles told the Council on Foreign Relations, "Local defense must be reinforced by the further deterrent of massive retaliatory power.... The way to deter aggression is for the free community to be willing and able to respond vigorously at places and with means of its own choosing." By citing "more security at less cost"—a phrase altered to "more bang for the buck"—Dulles serenely clarified the dependence on weapons of mass destruction. Emphasizing this even more was the subsequent launching, just days later, of the first nuclear submarine, the *Nautilus*. Thus, Serling's tale aired simultaneously with the enunciation of the massive retaliation doctrine. Continued government testing persuaded Serling of the need for another atomic yarn—one that, in Falk's words, confirms "the political nature of his cultural product." Subsequently, Serling became actively involved with the Hollywood branch of the Committee for a Sane Nuclear Policy (SANE), which "pushed the Eisenhower administration toward adopting a testing moratorium and a comprehensive nuclear test ban treaty."[47]

The same year of Serling's "Mr. Finchley versus the Bomb," *The Motorola TV Hour* presented "Atomic Attack," an adaptation of Judith Merril's novel *Shadow on the Hearth*. Published in 1950, Merril's work focused on a suburban New York housewife, Gladys Mitchell, who, upon learning that Manhattan has been bombed, worries about the welfare of her husband and children. Despite the destruction unleashed on the nation's cities by atomic bombs, Merril's work concludes on an upbeat note: Gladys and her loved ones will be reunited. H. Bruce Franklin believed the experience of dealing with the consequences of an atomic attack on New York contributed to Mrs. Mitchell's maturation: "The situation gradually forces her to unleash repressed strengths, and her selfless nurturing, now coupled to an awakening consciousness, helps save her family."[48]

Produced by Herbert Brodkin, written by David Davidson, and directed by Ralph Nelson, "Atomic Attack" starred Phyllis Thaxter, Robert Keith, and Walter Matthau, and begins with the words of an offscreen announcer intoning:

> The play you are about to see deals with an imaginary H-bomb attack on New York City, and with the measures that civil defense would take in such an event for the rescue and protection of the population in and around the city. The happenings that will now follow on your screen might be taking place in suburban communities some fifty miles from New York—but are entirely fictitious of course. It is the prayer of us that such happenings shall forever remain fictitious.

The broadcast now focuses on "a Westchester suburb of New York City" as a typical fifties family dines on breakfast before the children head off to school and the husband-father to work. The day begins normally—with no inkling that disaster is about to befall them and their neighbors. Once everyone has left, Mrs. Mitchell (Thaxter) attends to her routine household duties.

Later, as she tries to get her malfunctioning clothes washer working again, a sudden flash of light fills the sky and the house is rocked by an explosion; the air resounds with the wailing of an air raid siren.

Rushing upstairs and looking through her kitchen window, Mrs. Mitchell sees smoke rising from New York. The telephone doesn't work. A civil defense radio broadcast announces that a hydrogen bomb, carried by a submarine-launched guided missile, has been dropped on New York. Unable to reach her husband and children, Mrs. Mitchell is effectively cut off and confined to her home. Later reports confirm that the attack was one of several aimed at numerous other American cities.

Mrs. Mitchell's anxieties are partially alleviated when her two daughters return home safe and alive. The younger daughter, Ginny, to her older sister's Barbara's consternation, treats the emergency as if it were a game: "Oh, Mommy, there was a great big flash. I was looking out the classroom window and, all of a sudden, a big bang.... Some of the kids — they said there wasn't any New York anymore." Barbara's chief concern is their father's welfare. Their mother recalls that he was supposed to go to New Jersey to inspect a bridge his firm was building.

Word comes that radioactive fallout has spread as far as 70 miles from New York; for their safety, everyone should remain indoors. Barbara's high school science teacher, Dr. Lee (Keith), shows up at the Mitchell's front door, telling her mother that Barbara may have been exposed to radiation when the bomb fell and should be checked with a Geiger counter. Shortly thereafter, when the block civil defense warden arrives, Mrs. Mitchell asks him about having Barbara tested, and is directed to Dr. Spinelli (Matthau) who gives both daughters a clean bill of health.

Night comes. Gunshots ring out as the auxiliary police take aim at looters. Ginny briefly steps outside to bring in a stuffed animal, risking exposure to fallout. The block warden returns, asking that Mrs. Mitchell provide shelter in her home for evacuees from New York, which she agrees to do. As the days pass, the United States delivers a devastating retaliatory blow to the enemy homeland. Meanwhile, Mr. Mitchell's fate remains undetermined. And there are dangers other than fallout to contend with: When hoodlums try to break into the Mitchell residence, Dr. Lee, who once worked on the bomb program and has since turned pacifist and whom Barbara has hidden in the cellar, uses Mr. Mitchell's bird gun to drive off the intruders — an act that disgusts him, nonetheless.

The day finally comes when Mrs. Mitchell receives a phone call from her husband's secretary: Mr. Mitchell was in New York when the bomb fell and was killed in the attack. Dr. Lee provides an anchor of support to the widow during this time.

More trouble is in the offing: Ginny comes down with radiation sickness. Dr. Lee takes a blood count on her, followed by Dr. Spinelli, who, when he learns Lee has previously tested her, discovers he's Garson Lee, upon whom the medical authorities want to set up a research project on and who is now ill himself. At the hospital, Ginny's diagnosis requires long-term treatment. Mrs. Mitchell requests that she be allowed to treat Ginny at home, a request that is granted. The source of Ginny's illness was Michael, the stuffed horse she brought inside the house; the toy had been doused with massive doses of radiation.

Despite the trauma they've endured, the Mitchells have grown stronger for the experience. Back home, Ginny asks her mother if America is winning.

"Not yet, darling," her mother replies. "But we're going to. I promise you that, Ginny dear. We are going to win."

The broadcast concludes with an acknowledgment to the New York State and federal civil defense authorities for "their kindness in providing technical information and advice throughout the presentation of tonight's show...."

Reviewing "Atomic Attack," *Broadcasting* applauded the broadcast for conveying

> clearly and emphatically, the basic elements of the proper behavior following an atomic attack. If these instructions are remembered and if any watcher is stimulated to join some branch of his local Civil Defense setup, the program will be good proof of the commercial broadcasters' educational theory of teaching through entertainment.[49]

One way "Atomic Attack" could have motivated a viewer to become active in civil defense was by becoming a block warden of the type featured in the broadcast. Historian Andrew D. Grossman has written "As public policy, the Truman administration established the warden system as a coherent and politically acceptable way to militarize the neighborhood."[50] Like the Ground Observer Corps, the warden system had its origins in World War II, being set up along the lines of the community warden system that operated in the United States during that war. At that time, the neighborhood warden was a familiar figure to the average citizen who was hardly acquainted with the operations of municipal government and civil defense. In reviving the World War II warden system, FCDA planners revamped it for the nuclear age with updated instruction manuals and civil defense narratives to mirror the "realities" of global nuclear war. The critical component of the warden system was organized instruction and uniformity as the essential method for controlling mass hysteria. The latter was set forth in *Before Disaster Strikes: What to Do Now* (1951), the first warden's manual:

> Besides helping to save lives, the training you give your residents will be instrumental in preventing panic and confusion in an emergency. Knowing what to

do under emergency conditions will bolster their confidence and morale and they are less apt to give way to panic and emotional reactions. When an emergency occurs they will realize that there is remedial action that can be taken and that they must take such action. If they are well trained their reactions will be automatic, and the greatest possible amount of order and effective civil defense action will result.[51]

The warden system functioned as a type of social control: The local warden acted as the boss of the neighborhood in an emergency situation. Civil defense wardens were people everyone knew and trusted, and they supervised practice civil defense exercises. "Block wardens," in the FCDA's eyes, functioned as the principal link between local communities and Washington, D.C. "Thus, like the civil defense plan during World War II," Grossman has written, "the organizational structure of the warden system was premised on the theory that your neighbor could control neighborhoods more efficiently than could, for example, a soldier." The employment of local citizens allowed the FCDA to wield an ample amount of social control over those people who treated civil defense lightly. The training of wardens at the community level and the civil defense exercises they carried out augmented the notion of civic and national responsibility in a wartime environment and furthered a process of fortification in both the community and the home.

The FCDA took note of the additional advantages a comprehensive warden system provided: "It should be noted that while civilian defense in this country in World War II was not called upon for action against enemy attack, it served many useful purposes. It should not be forgotten that when air raid wardens patrolled the streets during blackouts, there were fewer crimes." "Certainly this type of community-based empowerment," Grossman continues, "was an effective type of state expansion, for the state was not represented by a soldier but by the 'citizen soldier,' the neighborhood warden." The warden, one's friend and next-door neighbor, imparted and strengthened "the core ideas that the central state deemed vital for home-front preparedness during the early Cold War period."[52]

Crime control, which the FCDA emphasized was an added by-product of the warden system, was also the responsibility of the auxiliary police who curb looters in "Atomic Attack." Yet, as suggested by *Alert Today—Alive Tomorrow,* an FCDA film produced two years after "Atomic Attack" aired on network television, criminals might not be the only people from which the auxiliary police would be called upon to protect the community in the wake of a nuclear attack. The film's theme was the role of traditional American neighborliness in the nuclear age, focusing on the civil defense organization of Reading, Pennsylvania, and its various components. In addition to the auxiliary police, Readingites volunteer for rescue teams, hospital, nursing, ambulance units, and fire departments. Volunteers for the Reading auxiliary police corps receive instruction at the Reading Pistol Club's firing range. The reason for the corps' existence, the film's narrator explains, is to "check possible panic." Apparently, should nuclear war come, the Readingites themselves, their civil defense unit notwithstanding, may constitute a hazard to law and order in their own community and require protection — by force if need be. In such an emergency, the auxiliary police would exert, in the film's words, a "strong stabilizing effect on the jittery populace."[53]

The Soviet nuclear bombing in "Atomic Attack" symbolizes both their barbarity and their defilement of that sacred ideal of fifties America: the middle-class nuclear family. "In the postwar years," Elaine Tyler May has written, "Americans found that viable alternatives to the prevailing family norm were virtually unavailable. Because of the political, ideological, and institutional developments that converged at the time, young adults were indeed homeward bound, but they were also bound to the home."[54] Popular television programs of the time (I Love Lucy, Leave It to Beaver, Father Knows Best, The Donna Reed Show) reflected and celebrated the traditional family as the norm. "Television," in Lori Landay's words, "brought the world into the home and the home into the world. Because American culture was engrossed in the ideas and commodification of domesticity, postwar society was a fertile field in which television expanded."[55] Given this, it is no surprise that the Soviet attack, coming as it does in the midst of the Mitchells' daily lives, is such a shocking disruption of this norm. The day begins quite ordinarily with the family having breakfast before their daily routines begin, then is irrevocably lost in the ashes of the enemy surprise attack — a permanent alteration signified by Mr. Mitchell's death in the bombing.[56]

In the character of Dr. Garson, the bomb maker-turned-pacifist, "Atomic Attack" argues strongly in favor of nuclear stockpiling. The pacifist aspect of Garson's character denotes a movement that briefly flourished during the late 1940s, when many of the scientists who worked on the wartime atomic bomb program and supported the international regulation of nuclear weapons set out to persuade Americans that such management must be undertaken. Though the scientists, as one historian has noted, did indeed knowingly manipulate public anxieties in the nuclear realm, their machinations were motivated by their sincere belief that the atomic destruction they portrayed was a strong probability, if not nearly inevitable, that the time to forestall a disaster was quite brief, and that the solutions they advanced did hold the minute possibility of hope.

Presently, though, backing for the scientists' movement's cause was surpassed by anti-communist sentiment favoring an arms race as the best course of action. Emblematic of the latter was the man known as the father of the

H-bomb, Edward Teller, who, in Paul Boyer's characterization, yielded more and more to total distrust of the Soviet Union, advocated the H-bomb's development, which "challenged nearly all arms-control efforts as naïve and dangerous" and called for "a nuclear arms build-up almost without control or limit."[57] Thus, in "Atomic Attack," Garson has to cast aside his pacifist convictions to protect the Mitchells from harm. At the same time, he fears he'll be killed for collaborating with the enemy because of his stance against the arms race. Indeed, the authorities have been searching for him—to ask his help in ministering to victims of radiation sickness.[58]

Its grimness aside, "Atomic Attack" nevertheless argues in support of the Soviet-American arms race by presenting the idea that a nuclear war can be won. Such a concept was buttressed by bomb shelters, civil defense drills, and popular magazine articles such as "How to Survive an Atomic Bomb" and "Survival Secrets for Atomic Attacks." The magnitude of the Soviet attack on the United States in "Atomic Attack" in no way impairs America's capability to inflict retributive force on the enemy's homeland. Thus, by the tenth day of conflict, an announcement is heard on the radio: "The enemy's will and ability to fight back have virtually been broken," allowing Gladys Mitchell to tell Ginny, "We are going to win." Despite its premise that an erratic Soviet regime might unleash its nuclear arsenal without any motive, "Atomic Attack" delivers a heartening message: nuclear war can be won, and survived.[59]

This optimistic message wasn't shared by an episode of one of early television's medical dramas. *Medic,* starring Richard Boone as Dr. Konrad Styner, differed from shows of its genre in that it was filmed on location in Los Angeles hospitals and presented a fictional treatment of genuine medical issues and practices. The debut episode, airing in 1954, depicted the on-air birth of a baby.[60] "Flash of Darkness," an episode of *Medic* airing February 14, 1955, on NBC, presented a scenario of survival after a nuclear attack which was sharply at variance with the hopeful message of preparedness that official civil defense sounded.

A nuclear attack on more than a dozen American cities, followed by a biological attack employing "airborne bacteria," temporarily traps Dr. Styner and his civil defense team in a shelter. Unable to reach the clinic after leaving the shelter due to an intense firestorm, Dr. Styner and his team establish a clinic in a school. The team is "out of everything" and facing an overwhelming crush of survivors, precluding any possibility of helping the numerous patients destined to succumb to radiation exposure. Styner ascertains that one survivor—a young girl—will die, and directs a nurse to take her to "isolation" from patients waiting for transfer to distant hospitals. The nurse asks why the girl isn't given morphine for her discomfort, a query that elicits Dr. Styner's explanation that they "haven't got enough for the ones I can save. I can't spare it for the hopeless cases." The nurse protests, "But it's not right! It's not human! She's suffering, she's in agony!" "You can call it inhumane — all right, it is," Styner explains. "But these aren't our terms, they're the terms that were handed to us." When, in another case, Dr. Styner asks a boy how his face was cut, the patient, in what Robert A. Jacobs calls "a clear dig at the civil

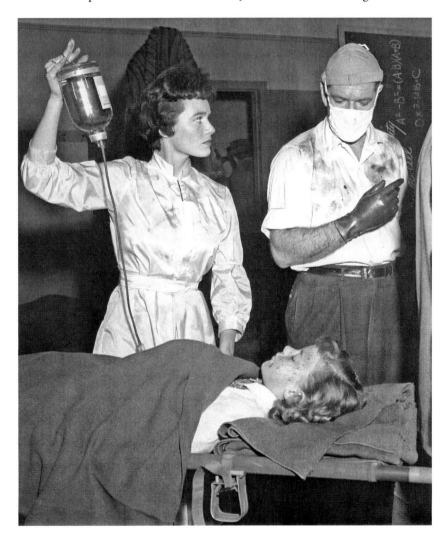

Grim reality: Dr. Konrad Styner (Richard Boone, right, wearing surgical mask) is forced to deny morphine to a survivor of a nuclear attack in a 1955 episode of the television series *Medic*, which presented a less optimistic view of post-apocalyptic life than the one official civil defense promoted. The nurse shown here is unidentified (NBC/Photofest).

defense program that emphasized the importance of 'Grandma's pantry' as a model of stocking a shelter with food," explains that his injuries resulted from glass shards from the jars of preserves in his basement sanctuary. Assured he'll be fine, the boy then asks about his brother: "He can't see," he says. His younger sibling suffered blindness when he ran upstairs to see the flash, and vomited several times thereafter. After the brothers are led away, Styner, asked if the younger boy will continue to be blind, answers, "That won't bother him for long. With the amount of radiation he's taken, he'll be dead." At the show's conclusion, Styner comforts the tearful boy when he tells him his brother has died.[61]

Such stories, in Jacobs's words,

> presented strong counternarratives to the official civil defense depiction of the impact and aftermath of a nuclear attack. Even as the show reinforced the value of civil defense preparedness and the valiant nature of those who worked hard to prepare for a nuclear attack, it framed that preparedness within the grim reality of a collapsing society and an overwhelmed response to the scale of destruction such an attack would bring.[62]

Live television dramas, of which "Atomic Attack" was a part, began fading from the small screen when mass audience programming began dominating the airwaves and television sets fell within in the price range of more people.[63] Other factors — the shift in the center of the television universe from New York to Hollywood, where the production of prerecorded programs became the TV norm, and commercial and financial considerations, contributed to live drama's demise. John Frankenheimer, one of the great directorial talents of the Golden Age, summed up how television had changed from an art form to a tool of commerce: "It exists to sell cigarettes, gas, lipstick.... I don't think any of us left television for financial reasons. What we all wanted to do was good things. They wouldn't let us. They told us, 'We don't want you guys. We want film situation comedies."

Two events in 1960 exemplified the changing face of television: the cancellation of the live drama production *Playhouse 90* and the debut, at the start of the fall season, of a show that embodied the new world of filmed, episodic television and the new decade: *Route 66*.[64] Where live dramas had been anthologies, presenting new productions, featuring new casts and characters each week, episodic series like *Route 66* featured actors playing continuing characters from week to week, in this case Martin Milner and George Maharis playing, respectively, Tod Stiles, a clean-cut collegian whose father's death wiped out his family fortune, and Buzz Murdock, a reformed juvenile delinquent from the wrong side of the tracks. Between the two of them, they buy a Corvette and set off on U.S. highway 66 "in search of America" and a new direction for themselves. Traveling cross country, they encounter various people in the midst of personal crises and set them back on course.[65] In contrast to other, standard television fare, *Route 66*, in *Newsweek*'s characterization, did have "an odd distinction: It had abandoned the cloister of the studio for the entire map of the U.S., taking its stars and cameras everywhere from the oil fields of Texas to the fish markets of New Orleans and the sheep ranches of Utah, simply to provide unorthodox backdrops for its fairly orthodox episodes.... The formula of sex, sock, and setting has given this Friday night series, according to the Nielsen ratings, better than a one-third share of the national TV audience in its one hour time slot."[66]

"A Fury Slinging Flame," the series' December 30, 1960, installment, written by Stirling Silliphant and directed by Elliot Silverstein, brought Tod and Buzz smack up against the era's fears of nuclear war in the form of a nuclear scientist who takes a drastic approach in response to the nuclear crisis. The scientist, Dr. Mark Christopher (Leslie Nielsen), convinced that a thermonuclear attack will strike the Western Hemisphere at 6 P.M., January 1, 1961, gives Tod his truck and trailer, then, accompanied by a group of fellow believers, seeks refuge from the impending holocaust by entering New Mexico's Carlsbad Caverns, despite it being a national park. Christopher's group intends to wait out the attack in the caverns, then rebuild the human race once it's over. Toward that end, they've brought animals with them. Despite the best efforts of the park rangers and an old colleague of Christopher's, the latter refuses to budge from his "sanctuary."

Back on the surface, Tod receives a visit from Fay Spain (Paula Shay), a newspaper correspondent sent to cover this unusual story. Examining the interior of Christopher's trailer, Spain finds a container of EDTA, an anti-radiation serum, as well as a calendar with December blacked out and January 1 marked, accompanied by a Latin phrase, translated as "Death from above."

The old year gives way to January 1, 1961— the day Christopher predicts doomsday will come. Revelers in New York's Times Square welcome the new year with their traditional frivolity, giving no indication they're worried about what the future holds. The news media has converged on White City, a community near Carlsbad Caverns, to seek what one newscaster calls "the answer to the $64 question: Does his retreat signal the imminent end of the world, a return to the caves for all who may survive whatever it is Dr. Christopher fears, or are we facing, not Armageddon, but a bright new year in the soaring sixties, filled with promise?" When a contingent of reporters descend into the caverns to interview Dr. Christopher, he refuses to answer their questions, telling them to take the matter up with Washington.

Fay Spain has an inspiration: She and Tod Stiles will pose as a husband and wife who want to join Christopher's group to survive the attack and then help repopulate the world once it's over. Believing that using people in such a way is wrong, Tod reluctantly consents to her scheme; he, Buzz, and Spain enter the caverns as part of a tour group. Breaking away from the tour, the trio make their way to Christopher's group.

"Dr. Christopher, do you really believe it?" asks Buzz.

"I'm here, aren't I?" Christopher rejoins.

Buzz presses his case: "Well, can't you give me a simple yes or no...? If you really think there's something to all this, why don't you warn people?"

"Because I'm told that in these times there are certain things that are better left unsaid."

"You mean like getting hit by H-bombs? It isn't cricket to tell people when to duck? We had a quarterback who takes a different point of view than you do, Dr. Christopher — Paul Revere. He gave a lot of important signals."

"I tried to call the signal," Christopher explains, "but what convinces me does not convince the others. It does not convince the authorities."

"Forget about the authorities," says Tod. "Let the people decide."

"Don't you understand?" Christopher asks. "I'm under orders. I can't say anything, I can't make a statement. This is not what I wanted. I wanted to shout it from coast to coast. Even Nikolai, if it meant his getting shot, I'm sure that's what he wanted me to do."

Spain asks Christopher who Nikolai is, but, at this point, Christopher's ex-wife appears, armed with a federal writ ordering him to return their son who is among those in the cave with Christopher to the surface, and a federal marshal to implement the writ. When Spain implores Christopher to tell them why a nuclear attack is imminent, the doctor finally relents: Two years earlier, he met Nikolai, a fellow scientist, at a conference in Geneva (Mrs. Christopher dubs him "as big a fool" as her former husband); during the conference they played chess, deciding to continue their match via air mail correspondence. Recently, Nikolai changed his strategy, repeatedly using the letters "KT" (the abbreviation for the chess term knight), convincing Christopher that Nikolai is referring to the word "kiloton," not knight. Nikolai then sent Christopher a Christmas gift: A pair of Chinese boots — misspelling the last word, leading Christopher to conclude that the misspelled word meant the name of a constellation, one the Earth moves in orbit with every year, being pummeled by a shower of meteors on January 1. All of this, combined with a series of false military alarms, has convinced Christopher that a nuclear attack will strike the United States at 6 P.M., on January 1, 1961.

Fed up with her husband's wild-eyed notions, Mrs. Christopher, determined to have custody of her son, directs the marshal to order Christopher to give up the boy. (Buzz correctly deduces that Fay Spain arranged the confrontation between the estranged couple to force Christopher to divulge the reason that he and the others entered the caverns so she'd have her story, regardless of the consequences to the Christophers' son). Forcibly taking the latter from his father, Mrs. Christopher hustles him out of the cavern into the daylight — with Christopher and the others in pursuit. Exiting the caverns, they discover that it's just after six o'clock, the time Christopher predicted that the nuclear attack would come — only the world is still intact.

"Will everything be OK now, Dad?" the boy asks his father.

"I — I don't know," is all the scientist can say in response.

"Well, if you don't mind me saying so," opines Buzz, "you got a lot of people stirred up for nothing if you don't know."

Dumbfounded by the failure of his prediction Christopher can only wonder when doomsday will come.

"Well, in the meantime...," Tod observes, "there's six other days in the week."

Looking at his son, Dr. Christopher says, "We're going to use them — for all they're worth. You use them."

While the fictional Dr. Christopher was going underground to flee the nuclear danger, his real-life counterparts were directly confronting the issue — and incurring the displeasure of the powers that be for their stands. Highly learned, these men virtually comprised the cloistered elite that frequently worked in the government's nuclear program. The first to speak out in protest was J. Robert Oppenheimer. The head of the wartime Manhattan Project that developed the atomic bomb, Oppenheimer lost his security clearance merely because he challenged the morality of developing the hydrogen bomb; he wasn't sufficiently "enthusiastic" about it. According to historians Douglas T. Miller and Marion Nowak, "Ralph Lapp, while also not a pacifist nor a proponent of nuclear disarmament, intelligently criticized official abuses of atomic energy."[67]

Lapp's efforts in this regard played a major role in compelling the AEC to provide further information about fallout in the mid-fifties. A nuclear physicist who had worked at Los Alamos, Lapp knew what he was talking about when it came to effects of the H-bomb. His articles that appeared in the *Bulletin of Atomic Scientists* in 1954 and 1955 charged the AEC with promoting nuclearism by encouraging an "official drought" of information that could quell freedom of expression and seriously harm democracy. Lapp furnished detailed appraisals of fallout and indicted the AEC for "sanitizing" public reports on the hazards of radioactivity. He demonstrated that a 15-megaton H-bomb detonated close to the ground could release sufficiently ample amounts of radiation to kill everyone in the open within 250 square miles. Within three hours of the explosion, Lapp forecast amounts of virulent and extremely dangerous radiation exceeding 1,200 square miles. Accurate awareness of the consequences of fallout would "kill civil defense [programs] in the country." Angry at Lapp's efforts to reveal the AEC's endeavor to minimize the fallout menace, AEC head Lewis Strauss did everything in his power to disparage Lapp to the media. One historian has observed that Strauss secretly perused Lapp's private correspondence — something that could only have happened with a helping hand from the FBI.[68]

The most eminent voice in the anti-nuclear effort was that of Linus Pauling, who unswervingly advocated the cause of nuclear disarmament. His 1956 book *No More War!* spelled out the hazards of Strontium-90. Pauling condemned AEC proclamations concerning a presumed threshold level of radiation exposure. It was the belief of scientists during most of the 1950s that humans could safely receive small amounts of such hazardous products as radiation. When it came to the threshold of safety in exposure to radiation, Pauling stressed there was no evidence supporting such a notion. Of great concern to him was the possibility of genetic damage: "*Any radiation is genetically undesirable.*"

Pauling's concern about the threshold notion raised other issues for him. If even small amounts of radiation presented a threat to people, then bomb testing wasn't that innocuous after all. Pauling denounced the notion promulgated by Dr. Edward Teller and Dr. Albert Latter, that fallout could be multiplied by a million before harmless consequences were evident. He reckoned in 1956 that birth defects worldwide had already risen significantly because of test fallout. "We may say that each year of bomb testing at the present rate is carried out with the sacrifice of 15,000 children, who would be born healthy and who would lead normal lives if the bomb tests had not been carried out that year," he declared. "Perhaps the testing of one large superbomb required the sacrifice of only 1,500 children. Perhaps it requires the sacrifice of 15,000 children or more.... The only debatable point is whether the victims of bomb-testing should be counted in the thousands, hundreds of thousands, or millions."[69]

Pauling's anti-nuclear testing campaign drew public and private condemnation from such prominent government officials as Lewis Strauss and J. Edgar Hoover. Pauling's critics characterized him as the pawn of a communist conspiracy, and possibly even a communist sympathizer himself. After 1958, he would receive no federal financing for research for the next two decades. The FBI kept its eye on him for quite some time, though the bureau never uncovered any proof of communist ties on his part.[70]

In June 1957, Pauling led about 11,000 scientists around the world, among them approximately 3,000 Americans, in putting their names to a petition advocating "immediate action ... to effect an international agreement to stop the testing of all nuclear weapons," a move that prompted an inquiry into Pauling's loyalty by the Senate Internal Security Subcommittee.[71] That same summer witnessed the birth of the Provisional Committee to Stop Nuclear Tests, which subsequently was rechristened the National Committee for a Sane Nuclear Policy, or SANE. Under the headline "We are Facing a Danger Unlike Any Danger That Has Ever Existed," a SANE advertisement in the *New York Times* that November urged the immediate termination of nuclear testing. The astonishing response the ad generated prompted SANE to expand its status of a temporary and select group to a permanent, nationally organized membership body — with the result that, by the following January, SANE groups had been established in 15 cities; each one of them being organized locally without any assistance from the national SANE office. The organization's initial national convention met that spring, and by the summer of 1958, SANE had swelled to 130 chapters comprising an estimated 25,000 members.[72] Among those on SANE's roster were such luminaries as Norman Cousins, Norman Thomas, Oscar Hammerstein II, Walter Reuther, John Hersey, and Erich Fromm. Other SANE members came from the ranks of the old left and the rising new left, as well as Quakers, and other organizations that had already been active in the peace movement.[73]

In May 1957, just before the convening of the gathering that would sire what ultimately became known as SANE, radical pacifists had created an organization of their own — Non–Violent Action Against Nuclear Weapons (NVAANW). Shortly thereafter, members of NVAANW gathered at the Camp Mercury test site, located approximately 70 miles northwest of Las Vegas, for the first-of-its-kind demonstration against a nuclear test. Incredibly, the AEC had slated August 6, 1957, the 12th anniversary of the atomic bomb attack on Hiroshima, as the date to hold one of the tests (inclement weather conditions forced a day's postponement of the test). On Hiroshima Day, 11 pacifists entered a restricted area at the test site and were arrested. While the majority of newspaper accounts of the incident appeared on the inside pages, the protest organizers still felt that they had scored a significant victory in the demonstration generally eschewed being branded as communist inspired; the protest, in the *New York Times*'s words, marked "the unusual employment in this country of the 'civil disobedience' tactics made famous by M. K. Ghandi, the late Indian independence leader."[74] Given suspended sentences for trespassing, the 11 protestors who had been arrested returned to the Camp Mercury gate, where they held an all-night vigil in anticipation of the bomb's detonation which occurred at 5 A.M., August 7, 1957. "It was," in the words of one demonstrator, "a nightmare come true."[75]

One of those arrested during the Camp Mercury protest, Albert Bigelow, came from a background one would hardly associate with that of a pacifist. Bearer of a Harvard degree, he had commanded Navy destroyers in the North Atlantic and South Pacific. His grandfather had a been a renowned Boston banker, and his father had been the Republican head of the Massachusetts state legislature's Ways and Means Committee for a number of years. But there was more to Bigelow than just the distinguished pedigree. During his childhood, his mother had taken him to Boston Common, where he visited a memorial to a Boston patrician, Robert Gould Shaw, who died a martyr while in charge of a company of Massachusetts free blacks during the Civil War. His political convictions remained those of an individual of his social station and education all during his military career, yet the crusading spirit of Yankee abolitionism came alive within Bigelow. Joining the Society of Friends in the mid–1950s, Bigelow's involvement with the Quakers brought him acquaintances that led him to the pacifist movement. In 1955, he and his family hosted two Japanese girls who survived the Hiroshima bombing and who had come to America with the "Hiroshima maidens" for plastic surgery on their scars resulting from radiation. A strong believer that nuclear weapons were morally wrong, Bigelow decided to take dramatic measures against the further development of such armaments. What followed was the "Pacific Project"— the voyage of the *Golden Rule*.

Bigelow and the other members of the *Golden Rule's* crew intended to sail their craft into the area where the United States planned to conduct nuclear tests near Eniwetok atoll in the Marshall Islands during the spring of 1958 — plans they disclosed in a message they issued to President Eisenhower in adherence to their Gandhian beliefs. Casting off from San Pedro, California, on February 10, 1958, the *Golden Rule's* initial attempt at executing its voyage was aborted seven days later on account of rough seas and a crew member's seasickness. Departing a second time on March 25, the crew reached Honolulu, where the ship laid anchor for refitting. In a move lacking sure legality and directed squarely at the seafaring anti-nuclear protestors, the AEC declared 390,000 square miles of open sea surrounding the test area "off-limits"; those encroaching upon this forbidden region would face up to two years incarceration and a $5,000 fine.

Appealing a restraining order preventing them from setting sail, the crew of the *Golden Rule* consented to postpone any further effort to cast off until after a hearing on their appeal scheduled for May 1, 1958 — an agreement members of NVAANW's executive committee considered an inexcusable compromise with unlawful authority. On May 1, an hour after a federal judge upheld the restraining order, the *Golden Rule* set sail once more, only to be halted two miles out by a Coast Guard cutter and compelled to turn back. Arrested for their defiance, the crew was confined after declining to post bond. Tried on May 7, the crew, despite challenging the legality of the AEC's action and asserting that they answered to a law far greater than that of the government, was convicted, with each member receiving suspended 60-day prison sentences.

The next act in the drama came when the crew took their case to the Circuit Court in San Francisco. The fears of NVAANW leaders that the legal wrangling surrounding the case would diminish public and media interest notwithstanding, just the opposite occurred. The crew's straightforward dignity in championing their cause touched a chord with many Americans, who, as a country, merged an ingrained commitment to "law and order" with an ingrained distrust of government. The combination of the crew's clearly genuine religious convictions and the war record of "Captain Bigelow" (as journalists called him) helped undermine the government's efforts to portray them as sinister subversives. A large number of people turned out to show their support for the *Golden Rule* sailors in nationwide demonstrations organized by NVAANW and other pacifist groups. In San Francisco, over 400 people appealed to the U.S. attorney to prosecute them along with the crew as backers or contributors to their expedition. The frenzy affected even those people who couldn't have cared less about the seafaring protestors, yet were caught up in the crusade in their behalf.

On June 1, 1958 — seven days after losing their appeal in San Francisco Circuit Court — the crew of the *Golden Rule* announced that they planned to make another voyage. Three days later, federal marshals arrested Bigelow on a "criminal conspiracy" charge. By a stroke of luck, Bill Huntington, the sole member of the crew next to Bigelow competent enough to command the vessel, returned to Honolulu from a trip to the United States to enlist members of a backup crew; he had also wanted time to ponder his future course, as he was less certain than anyone else that another voyage aboard the *Golden Rule* was worth the effort. Now, owing to Bigelow's incarceration, Huntington changed his mind. "What are we waiting for?" he asked his shipmates and took charge of the latest attempt to set sail. On this latest endeavor the ship traveled nearly six miles out before two Coast Guard cutters intervened. Both Huntington and Bigelow were confined in Honolulu city jail to serve their original 60-day terms; their shipmates would presently join them.

One final chapter of the story remained. While they waited out their appeal to the circuit court, the *Golden Rule* sailors had become acquainted with a pair of fellow sailors, Earle and Barbara Reynolds, who were moored near the *Golden Rule*. An anthropologist, Earle Reynolds had spent four years in Hiroshima working for the AEC's Atomic Bomb Casualty Commission; in this capacity, he had scrutinized how the bomb had impacted the lives and health of those children who survived the attack. Following the second interception of the *Golden Rule* by the authorities, the Reynoldses, accompanied by their two adolescent children and a young Japanese acquaintance, set out in their own boat, the *Phoenix of Hiroshima,* to complete the aborted voyage of the *Golden Rule.* Following a two-and-a-half week voyage, the Reynoldses' ship successfully penetrated the test area for several miles before the Coast Guard intercepted it and forced it to return to port. Convicted of entering the test-zone, Reynolds was vindicated when the San Francisco Court of Appeals threw out the verdict on the grounds that the AEC ban against entering the forbidden zone was fallacious—a decision that was a victory for the *Golden Rule*'s crew as well. In pursuing a course that was then viewed as a radical defiance of the United States government, both the *Golden Rule* and the *Phoenix* "had done so in a way that made the government look like the real threat to" America's "liberties and well-being."[76]

Other peace rallies and demonstrations would follow. While the actions of the peace movement failed to do much else, they nonetheless contributed to public debate on nuclear issues, even if most Americans weren't paying any attention to what the crusaders were saying, as well as disclosing the presence of views contrary to popular Cold War thinking and laying the groundwork for the subsequent anti-war movement of the Vietnam era.[77] And while Dr. Christopher had eschewed direct action to meet the nuclear threat head-on, he was, nonetheless, a prophet of sorts: He had "dropped out," literally, from society to avoid a nuclear attack long before that phrase entered the national lexicon.

4

The Kennedy Years: "Shelter Morality" and Survivalism

On the evening of July 25, 1961, slightly over six months after taking office as President of the United States, John F. Kennedy went on national television to deliver what has been described as "one of the most alarming speeches by an American President in the whole, nerve-wracking course of the Cold War."[1] Kennedy's remarks had been prompted by Soviet Premier Nikita Khrushchev's threat to sign a peace treaty with East Germany — an act that would terminate the West's access rights to West Berlin. That city, Kennedy told his audience,

> has now become — as never before — the great testing place of Western courage and will.... It is as secure ... as the rest of us — for we cannot separate its safety from our own. I hear it said that West Berlin is militarily untenable. And so was Bastogne. And so, in fact, was Stalingrad. Any dangerous spot is tenable if ... brave men will make it so. We do not want to fight — but we have fought before.... We cannot and will not permit the Communists to drive us out of Berlin, either gradually or by force. For the fulfillment of our pledge to that city is essential to the morale and security of western Germany, to the unity of western Europe, and to the faith of the entire world.... We will at all times be ready to talk, if talk will help. But we must also be ready to resist with force, if force is used upon us.... We seek peace, but we shall not surrender.

Kennedy announced that he was requesting an added sum of three-and-a-quarter billion dollars from Congress, with a large portion of this request to be allocated to improved conventional weapons. The total strength of the army would be raised by 15 percent, with draft calls sharply increased and certain reserve and national guard units mobilized. Ships and aircraft slated for mothballing were to be retained for active service.[2]

Kennedy then addressed "another sober responsibility":

To recognize the possibilities of nuclear war in the missile age, without our citizens knowing what they should do and where they should go if bombs begin to fall, would be failure of responsibility.... Tomorrow, I am requesting of the Congress new funds for the following immediate objectives: to identify and mark space in existing structures — public and private — that could be used for fallout shelters in case of attack; to stock those shelters with food, water, first-aid kits and other minimum essentials for survival.... In the event of an attack, the lives of those families which are not hit in a nuclear blast and fire can still be saved — if they can be warned to take shelter and if that shelter is available. We owe that kind of insurance to our families — and to our country.... In the coming months, I hope to let every citizen know what steps he can take without delay to protect his family in case of attack. I know that you will want to do no less.[3]

Kennedy's words marked the first time a president had spoken with such candor about the likelihood of nuclear attack.[4] They served as a catalyst for a nationwide shelter boom as Americans sought to learn how they could protect themselves should a nuclear war erupt.[5] Yet the Kennedy-inspired shelter craze would also ignite a debate over just how far shelter owners could go to protect their sanctuaries and families from others who sought to crowd into their neighbors' nuclear hideaways. In this, American's greatest civil defense crisis to date, popular culture would play a key role in how the American people ultimately decided whether or not to accept fallout shelters as the best means of surviving a nuclear war.

Berlin and the Shelter Craze

The Soviet-American confrontation over Berlin in the summer of 1961 wasn't the sole reason for the Kennedy civil defense initiative. Domestic political considerations early in his term also came into play. In December 1960, before Kennedy took office, the OCDM had recommended a program that, in addition to furnishing shelter spaces, would provide training, equipping shelters with supplies, radiometers, and postwar recovery planning to those potential victims of fallout. Initially suspicious of a program of such magnitude, Kennedy requested a study of the matter by his national security adviser, McGeorge Bundy.

Pressure on Kennedy to adopt a civil defense program began mounting in May 1961 when the Conference of Governors convened in Washington. Heading the Conference's Committee on Civil Defense was New York Governor Nelson Rockefeller, a strong fallout shelter advocate, who had convinced President Eisenhower to convene the Gaither Committee. In his own state, Rockefeller had begun a vast shelter program that included tax incentives and matching grants. Popular money also held that Rockefeller might face off against Kennedy as the GOP standard-bearer in 1964.

Meeting with Kennedy and Bundy on May 9, Rockefeller argued that a strong program was necessary to strengthen public readiness to back American employment of nuclear weapons if need be. Kennedy was skeptical about such an initiative. His advisers had informed him that the price tag for a nationwide fallout-shelter program might be $20 billion. Over time, what good would any kind of shelter program be given that the size of nuclear weapons would be expanding?[6]

Still smarting from his recent misstep with the Bay of Pigs, Kennedy asked two of his White House assistants, Marc Raskin and Carl Kaysen, to conduct a more thorough study of the civil defense issue. Kaysen decided that Kennedy had only two choices: Either stop squandering money on civil defense or treat it as a serious issue and hand responsibility for it over to the Defense Department. For his part, Raskin, though he authored the civil defense section of Kennedy's address to Congress, right from the start, cast skeptical eyes on any effort to create a civil defense program that amounted to anything worthwhile. In his words:

> We have also to decide whether we are building a world which is safe for democracy — or one only finitely safe even for a garrison state. I have great fear for this civil defense program. I do not think that it will decrease the probabilities of war. At best it won't change the odds, although it will utilize resources that can better be spent elsewhere. At its worst it will change our society and reinforce misperception and distort awareness of reality more than out senses are distorted already.

Raskin stressed that he had often cautioned Bundy that civil defense endeavors "could kid many people into thinking we could do many things (wrong ones I suspect) that some would be constrained psychologically to do" otherwise. Moreover, Raskin worried that both construction of blast and fall-out shelters and the acceptance of NUTS (nuclear utilization target selection) as policy would bring about a "dangerous and tragic turn in events for the United States and for the world."

All of this notwithstanding, Kennedy, on May 25, 1961, requested that Congress establish a national civil defense system. It is true that historically the public had regarded civil defense with indifference or chariness, but such attitudes had mainly been because earlier programs had been so "far reaching or unrealistic." Kennedy's program was meant solely to provide protection from fallout. It wouldn't provide safety from attack, but it would be useful in the event war erupted either accidentally or because of an irrational attack. Under Kennedy's plan, middle-class Americans could purchase or construct their own sanctuaries, while his proposed program would determine communities' fallout shelter space in existing buildings and furnish matching grants and additional incentives for building shelters in state and local government buildings. Though such an undertaking would be costly, it was deemed necessary and prudent. Kennedy transferred the program to the Defense Department as the Office of Civil Defense.[7]

In the aftermath of the U-2 incident and the dashing of hopes for improved Soviet-American relations, Soviet Premier Nikita Khrushchev apparently believed that Kennedy's election would signal a new opportunity to ameliorate relations between the two great powers, and the two heads of state agreed to meet in Vienna. By the time the Vienna summit convened, Khrushchev had revised his appraisal of the new president: The Soviets had orbited the first man in space and Kennedy had been humiliated by the failed attempt to oust Castro at the Bay of Pigs. Thinking Kennedy weak and inexperienced, Khrushchev felt he could bully the new president. Berlin would be the issue.[8]

The German capital had long been a Cold War hot spot. At the close of World War II, both Germany and Berlin had been partitioned into zones — a division that not only ultimately produced two nations (East and West Germany) but also divided Berlin itself into two halves — East and West Berlin.[9] In 1948, Stalin had imposed a blockade on West Berlin, which the Western allies had frustrated with their airlift. Khrushchev had taken advantage of the prestige the Soviets' success with *Sputnik* had provided to insist that Berlin become a demilitarized "free city," issuing the West a six-month deadline to accept his proposal. He deferred his ultimatum when Eisenhower stipulated that such a deferral would be necessary before Khrushchev could visit the United States. Conceding that the Berlin situation was "abnormal," Eisenhower offered to discuss the size of the Western garrison there and how much the city could be used as a station for West German propaganda and espionage operations.[10]

In seeking an end to the "temporary" accords that had governed Berlin since 1945 in favor of a permanent solution of the German matter, Khrushchev wanted a new Big Four summit conference, refusing to budge from his warning that if he didn't get his way by the end of 1961, he would initial a separate accord with East Germany, one that would nullify those agreements allowing Western access to Berlin that were already in effect. The motives behind Khrushchev's hard line were numerous: His various blunders — the U-2 incident, the widening breach with China, his unsuccessful efforts to enhance consumer items that were possibly debilitating the Soviet Union in the arms race with the United States — weren't passing unnoticed by his Kremlin opposition. Getting the West to return to the conference table to reach a solution to the German issue would greatly restore Khrushchev's standing, as well as mollify East German head of state Walter Ulbricht, whose people were fleeing the economic hardships of East Germany in favor of the flourishing West German economy. During the first six months of 1961, a total of 150,000 East Germans had fled. The key escape route into West Germany was Berlin.[11]

On the first day of their Vienna parley in June 1961, Kennedy and Khrushchev were unable to find agreement on virtually any point of discussion. In the words of one Russian historian, Khrushchev at that time had "the complete confidence of a man riding on the crest of history." The Soviet leader's truculence shocked Kennedy. Questioned by his aides as to what he thought of the American president, Khrushchev made a dismissive gesture with his hand, declaring Kennedy no match for Eisenhower.

When the talks got around to Berlin the next day, Khrushchev insisted upon a peace treaty and East German recognition. Berlin would become "strictly neutral"; the West would have to obtain East German consent to retain the right of access to the city. Any violation of East German territory would be viewed as an aggressive act against the Soviet Union. The United States would have to withdraw by the end of 1961. In response, Kennedy said that the West's presence in Berlin was a right resulting from its victory over Germany in World War II. America's national security was directly tied to Berlin's.

"I want peace, but if you want war that is your problem," Khrushchev bellowed as he pounded the table with his fist. The encounter ended on an unsettling note: Khrushchev threatened Kennedy with war, and declared that his decision to sign a peace accord with East Germany in six months was irreversible. Kennedy rejoined, "If that's true, it's going to be a cold winter."

Viewing Kennedy as he departed the meeting, a journalist remarked that he appeared "shaken and angry." Back in Washington, the president directed his foremost national security, diplomatic, military, and intelligence personnel to study the Berlin matter and devise courses of action to deal with it. Hardliners in the American government maintained that yielding on Berlin would signal defeat in the Cold War, while who those favored a moderate course wanted further negotiations with Moscow. With refugees still streaming into West Berlin, Kennedy spent the weekend of July 22–23 at his family residence in Hyannis Port, Massachusetts, formulating his decisions, then prepared his July 25 address.[12]

In the immediate aftermath of Kennedy's speech, The New York Times assured its readers that they were "calm" and "confident," and displayed "no shock and no sense of panic." Yet Times columnist James Reston accurately noted that Kennedy had frightened "the daylights out of people," particularly, in the words of a Chicago homemaker, when "he started talking about civil defense and bomb shelters." On July 26, Kennedy requested $10,000,000 for the National Emergency Alarm Repeater (NEAR), an alarm system that could be plugged into a wall socket in one's home; once installed, NEAR would be activated by the Air Defense Command should Soviet missiles be launched, providing those people equipped with the NEAR mechanism approximately a half-hour's advance warning of an enemy attack — provided that people, in Kennedy's words, built a home shelter "without delay." On July 29, the Federal Housing Authority announced that, those constructing home shelters would be eligible for insured home-improvement loans.

Kennedy's July 25 address set off a national frenzy for civil defense information. Telephone calls poured into civil defense offices, as did mail that soon reached "tidal wave proportions." Volumes of civil defense literature went out. The demand for civil defense officials as public speakers soared. The national state of mind that anxious summer was expressed in the words of a West Coast woman: "I don't want a war. I don't want to build a bomb shelter, but I don't see what else we can do about it." Events as the summer wore on further darkened the apprehensive mood. On August 13, the Communists erected a barrier of barbed wire around East Berlin — followed by the construction of the Berlin Wall.[13] (The Wall, Kennedy privately informed his aides, was Khrushchev's "way out of his predicament," and that while it wasn't "a very nice solution," a wall was far preferable to a war. During another private moment, Kennedy remarked that the East Germans had had 15 years "to get out of their jail").[14] The tension level rose again when, shortly thereafter, an American military convoy from West Germany crossed the Autobahn to West Berlin. Khrushchev frayed nerves even further when he announced, on August 31, immediate Soviet resumption of testing of nuclear weapons, suspending a three-year halt of such tests.[15,16] During the next month the Soviets exploded 30 major nuclear devices — nearly all of them atmospheric tests. By the time their last bomb had been detonated, the Russians had tainted the air with more radioactive poison than the Americans, British, and French combined.[17] On October 30, 1961, the Soviet Union detonated the Tsar Bomba — at 50 megatons the biggest nuclear device ever built — above the Arctic island of Navaya Zemlya. Despite its awesome megatonnage, the Tsar Bomba was highly impractical. The Tu-95 Bear bomber, a slow Soviet plane, was the only aircraft capable of transporting such a weapon; as such it was an easy target for American air defenses. Moreover, so immense was the bomb's yield that had it been dropped on Central Europe, it would have contaminated those living in Eastern Europe. The Tsar Bomba blast had been nothing more than a political stunt.[18]

With the public's interest in fallout shelters at a frenzied level, shelter advocates initiated an equally passionate crusade to convince people of the necessity for home shelter construction — what one publication termed "the greatest campaign of persuasion in the history of American public relations." Shelter partisans went so far as to endow their cause with an heroic patina. Building shelters, in the words of Assistant Secretary of Defense for Civil Defense Stuart Pittman, afforded Americans the occasion "to demonstrate their will to face up to thermonuclear war." The shelter builder was cast as a contemporary equivalent of the American who "plowed with a musket in his hand." Shelter proponents also maintained that home shelters were inexpensive and easy to build. "Survival stores" selling shelter supplies soon opened for business, as did shelter-manufacturing outfits, the majority of which were suburban and small-town contractors ready to make a fast buck by installing backyard shelters instead of swimming pools, while others offered completely prefabricated steel or concrete sanctuaries costing an average of approximately $2,000. What one magazine called "survival merchants" got in on the act with press advertisements, door-to-door selling, and erecting sales models of shelters in shopping-center parking lots. Such mock-up shelters could be found at nearly every state fair in America that fall. At the Dallas Fair, the Federal Bomb & Fallout Shelter company's shelter, priced at $1,350 and hyped as "the only precast monolithic concrete shelter approved by the Office of Civil Defense!" reportedly eclipsed prize-winning cattle and midway rides as the center of attention.[19]

In the midst of this frenetic activity there arose a debate over the issue of "shelter morality," specifically what obligation did a shelter owner have for his shelterless neighbors. The issue hadn't sprung up solely in connection with the Kennedy shelter initiative. In 1959 Los Angeles's civil defense director noted that one of the problems in knowing the precise total of fallout shelters there, was because there were many people who built shelters without specifying them as such through building permits. The reason for this was that some people wanted to keep their neighbors ignorant of the fact that they had a shelter. Similarly, in 1960, Leo Hoegh, Eisenhower's civil defense director, observed that numerous shelter owners had informed his office of their desire not to publicize their sanctuaries "and, therefore, have everyone in the neighborhood rush in and take over."[20]

What made the "shelter morality" issue more imperative in 1961 was the possibility that nuclear war would erupt between the United States and the Soviet Union over the Berlin confrontation — and an ugly every-man-for-himself mentality began manifesting itself. In its August 18, 1961, issue, *Time* magazine quoted a Chicago suburbanite who minced no words:

> When I get my shelter finished, I'm going to mount a machine gun at the hatch to keep the neighbors out if the bomb falls. I'm deadly serious about this. If the stupid American public will not do what they have to to save themselves, I'm not going to run the risk of not being able to use the shelter I've taken the trouble to provide to save my own family.

Mirroring the same sentiment, Charles Davis, an Austin, Texas, hardware dealer, fortified his shelter with four rifles, a .357 Magnum pistol, and a four-inch-thick wooden door; the latter's purpose, he explained, was to keep, not radiation, but people out of his shelter. Should shelterless neighbors enter his hideaway ahead of him, Davis was ready for that contingency as well: "I've got a .38 tear-gas gun, and if I fire six or seven tear-gas bullets into the shelter, they'll either come out or the gas will get them."[21]

Davis's stance elicited mixed reactions. A Los Angelino nominated him Neighbor of the Year, and a fellow Austin, Texas, resident seconded Davis's sentiments. A Detroit woman, however, characterized Davis as a "monster": "I have often pondered the advisability of a bomb shelter, wondering whether survival may not be the most horrible choice. If survival depends upon living with such monsters, Mr. Davis need not worry. I, for one, would not knock on his door." A Connecticut man agreed: "I was planning to get my parents to build a bomb shelter with a removable top that could double as a swimming pool [but] "after reading about the Davis family, I decided that it would be much better to die from the bomb's fallout than live in a world ridden with people who would gun down their neighbors." Still, owing to her family's experience with friends and neighbors after constructing a shelter, one California woman championed Davis's position: "For the most part we have met with smirks or polite indifference. Since we have spent our time and money to prepare for something we sincerely hope will never come, we would not hesitate to defend ourselves with guns if necessary against these same people who would be threatening our lives because of their ignorance."[22]

Davis and like-minded others received the blessing of Father L. C. McHugh in "Ethics at the Shelter Doorway," an article he wrote that appeared in the September 30, 1961, issue of the Jesuit magazine *America*. Taking exception to the words of one cleric *Time* had quoted ("If someone wanted to use the shelter, then you yourself should get out and let him use it. That's not what would happen, but that's the strict Christian application"), Father McHugh declared that he couldn't accept that statement "as it stands. It argues that we must love our neighbor, not as ourselves, but more than ourselves. It implies that the Christian law runs counter to the instinct of self-preservation that is written in the human frame." If he, Father McHugh was correct, not only did humans require "blueprints for shelter construction. They also need a little instruction in the grim guidelines of essential morality at the shelter doorway."

"This aspect of nuclear warfare," Father McHugh explained, "has received no attention, but its relevant principles were the common property of Catholic moralists long before Hiroshima. They are generally treated under the discussion of what kind of activity is permissible when one's life is under attack."

Observing that the "right to life and its equivalent goods is a curtain of invisibility drawn around the human personality," Father McHugh then stated that should this curtain be "torn aside by the unwarranted interference with one's freedom, nature still provides a second line of defense against injustice ... the right to use violence as a last resort or emergency measure for securing the just needs of the human person. This right to employ violence," termed "co-activity" by the moralists, was "a *limited* grant of power, just like the rights for whose protection it is given." Operating from this foundation, "Catholic moralists teach that the use of violence to defend life and its equivalent goods is justifiable, when certain conditions are met, even if the violent defense entails the death of the aggressor." Father McHugh then enumerated these criteria:

1. The situation is such that violence is the last available recourse of the aggrieved party. Either you take desperate action now or, in your best judgment, you are going to be done in.

2. The violence used is employed at the time of assault.... The violence is leveled against an attack which, in the prudent estimation of the victim, has been actually initiated....

3. The violence is employed against an attack that is unjust. In other words, the violence is used to ward off an unwarranted invasion of one's undoubted rights.

4. Finally, when one uses violence to defend his essential rights, he may employ no more violence than is needed to protect himself.

Father McHugh further declared: "Nowhere in traditional Catholic morality does one read that Christ, in counseling nonresistance to evil, rescinded the right of self-defense which is granted by nature and recognized in the legal system of all nations." Addressing the immediate issue, whether a shelter owner could morally employ violent force to protect his family and shelter from outsiders clamoring to get inside, Father McHugh noted that

the father of a family is tied to his wife and children by bonds of both love and justice. His every moral instinct prompts him to nourish and protect his dependents. He cannot carelessly squander their essential welfare for the needy stranger and call this irresponsibility an act of charity. He may not idly stand by while his brood is robbed of what is necessary for life and then explain that his cowardice is actually a wholehearted obedience to the Biblical injunction to overcome evil by good.

If a man builds a shelter for his family, then it is the family that has the first right to use it. The right becomes empty if a misguided charity prompts a pitying householder to crowd his haven to the hatch in the hour of peril; for this conduct makes sure that no one will survive. And I consider it the height of nonsense to say that the Christian ethic demands or even permits a man to thrust his family into the rain of fallout when unsheltered neighbors plead for entrance. On the other hand, I doubt that any Catholic moralist would

condemn the man who used available violence to repel panicky aggressors ply-
ing crowbars at the shelter door, or who took strong measures to evict tres-
passers who locked themselves into the family shelter before his own family had
a chance to find sanctuary therein.... If you are already secured in your shelter
and others try to break in, they may be treated as unjust aggressors and repelled
with whatever means will effectively deter their assault. If others steal your family shelter space before you get there, you may also use whatever means will
recover your sanctuary intact.[23]

McHugh's article didn't directly say that people should install "protective
devices" in their shelters, but simply declared the absence of any actual hin-
drance toward such measures. In a subsequent television interview, however,
McHugh amplified his position:

Let's say you got your family in your shelter, the attack is on, a question might
come up of admitting anyone over and above the number for whom the shelter
is designed. I'd say that we should rely on the best prudential judgment that the
father or the one responsible for the shelter can make in the circumstances. But
I say let him think twice before he admits the needy stranger if admitting the
needy stranger is going to cut down the chances of survival of the group that's
already there. And then that final point: Can a man have protective devices in
order to protect his family once they are in the shelter from, let's say, strangers
that try to use a crowbar to get in? I'd say, from what I have been talking about,
the matter of self-defense, it would be wise for a man to at least weigh the possibility of putting some protective devices in his shelter along with other elements of his survival kit.[24]

Against this backdrop of war fears and shelter mania, American popular
culture would enter the fray over "shelter morality" with an episode of one
of the most acclaimed programs of early television, providing an example of
the medium's ability to address social issues in the guise of entertainment.

Rod Serling's Shelter Morality Tale

On the evening of October 2, 1959, CBS unveiled a television anthology
series that carried its viewers to "a fifth dimension beyond that which is known
to man.... This is the dimension of the imagination. It is an area we call *The
Twilight Zone*.[25] Its creator, Rod Serling, had surprised many with his
announcement that he intended to develop a weekly fantasy and science-
fiction television series. "To go from writing an occasional drama for *Playhouse
90*, a distinguished and certainly important series, to creating and writing a
weekly, 30-minute television film," Serling said, "was like Stan Musial leaving
St. Louis to coach third base in an American Legion little league."
What others viewed as a step down from the realm of highbrow drama

to the "less important" sci-fi arena, Serling viewed as an appropriate course. Serling's decision was motivated primarily by his displeasure at the powers of censorship wielded by network sponsors. Complaining about such treatment given one of his stories, Serling lamented, "By the time 'A Town Has Turned to Dust' went before the cameras, my script had turned to dust. They chopped it up like a roomful of butchers at work on a steer." Science fiction afforded Serling greater flexibility in presenting controversial themes. Where the censors wouldn't allow two senators to discuss current political issues, they wouldn't object if two Martians treated the same subject allegorically. "There won't be anything controversial in the new series," Serling explained, albeit insincerely. "I don't want to fight anymore. I don't want to battle sponsors and agencies. I don't want to fight for something I want and have to settle for second best ... which is in essence what the television writer does if he wants to take on controversial themes." When it came to *The Twilight Zone*, Serling's wife, Carol, explained, "The TV censors left him alone, either because they didn't understand what he was doing or believed that he was truly in outer space."

The disappearance of live television productions in favor of series television was another contributing factor to Serling's decision to enter *The Twilight Zone*. The series gave Serling a new outlet for both his ideas and ideals and boundless imagination. "Rod felt that drama should be an assertion of social conscience," Carol Serling observed. "He found that in *The Twilight Zone*, through parable and suggestion, he could make the same point that he wanted to make with straight drama."[26]

The Twilight Zone was especially popular with young people, who eagerly awaited each week's episode. "Did you see it?" they asked each other the following Monday morning. "As a cultural icon," Serling's biographer Joel Engel has written, *The Twilight Zone* "became part of the same historical wave that swept John Kennedy to win the presidency and the Beatles to alter music history." Engel also felt that the show made an important contribution "to the youthful idealism of the 1960s. Unlike science fiction, which often takes imaginative joyrides just for the pleasure of going, 'The Twilight Zone' traveled to worlds in which honesty and ethics and principles" were as important as gravity. Essentially, most *Twilight Zone* stories were morality tales. Each week, audiences received a dose of Serling's social vision, one where malefactors received their just desserts, and "peace and love were noble." By the time the series concluded its network television run in 1964, most of the "entire emerging generation had received regular doses of subtle moralizing." And with America's growing involvement in Vietnam, a "cause that lacked immediate identification, many of this same generation" that had grown up watching *The Twilight Zone* would presently be demanding reasons for why we were fighting this war, explanations "that fit, coincidentally or not, Serling's ethos."[27]

Before then, *The Twilight Zone* had already found its way into the national landscape, with the show's title a part of the national lexicon. "Man, I was in the Twilight Zone!" was how boxer Archie Moore described what it was like to be KO'd in a 1961 bout. That same year, Secretary of Defense Robert McNamara cautioned the communist world about initiating "twilight zone" wars. "Man," Serling declared upon hearing this. "Now we really have arrived!" And in his "vast wasteland" speech decrying the content of television programming, especially that in the dramatic and children's genres, FCC chairman Newton Minow cited *The Twilight Zone* among those shows that stood out from the usual TV fare.[28]

Nuclear war was a recurring theme on *The Twilight Zone*. Long before the series debut, Serling, in 1955, had joined Citizens for a Sane Nuclear Policy, and was one of the most energetic members of the group's Hollywood branch. During its first season, on November 11, 1959, *Zone* had presented "Time Enough at Last," whose bank-teller protagonist, Henry Bemis (Burgess Meredith), secludes himself in the bank vault to pursue his love of reading, and thereby becomes the sole survivor of a nuclear attack. Discovering the remains of a library, he is about to pursue his passion, uninterrupted, for years to come when he shatters his glasses![29] "One More Pallbearer," a third season installment, directed by Lamont Johnson, featured Joseph Wiseman as a man seeking vengeance against those he felt wronged him by fabricating a bogus nuclear attack.[30]

And it was also during that same third season, which began in the midst of the national fallout shelter craze Kennedy's Berlin speech had ignited, that Rod Serling and *The Twilight Zone* entered the fray with an episode, titled simply "The Shelter," that examined just how far one's neighbors would go to save themselves from annihilation by attempting to force their way into one man's nuclear sanctuary.

The genesis of the episode had begun months before the storm clouds erupted over Berlin, when Serling took part in an NBC program on shelters that aired early in 1961. Meeting with Frank R. Dunbar, survey director of the Los Angeles Shelter Survey, Office of Civil Defense, Serling requested background information on how to build a shelter and what would be required to survive a foreign-based attack. Dunbar didn't immediately respond to Serling's request; when he finally did so, Serling explained that "this show has already been filmed and will be shown sometime next fall. What mistakes are in it, I'm afraid, will remain."

In a letter to Serling after he read the script for "The Shelter," Walter Hiller, Jr., of Ashley-Steiner was very direct and emphatic in his reaction to Serling's tale: "WOW!" Hiller recommended the casting of Lloyd Nolan as the story's shelter-owning protagonist, Dr. William Stockton, arguing that the character of Stockton would "come to life" if Nolan filled the part. Instead, Larry Gates won the role of Stockton. Calling Serling's script "first-rate," Gates subsequently told author Mark Phillips:

> My character of Dr. Stockton believed he was doing the most reasonable thing with his shelter, but it turned out he had hopelessly misjudged the results of his actions. We had a wonderful cast and an excellent director, a happy company and crew and a fascinating script. When I saw the episode years later, I didn't like my performance. I thought I had overacted. But the script, direction and cast made it work.

Before filming of the episode commenced, Serling submitted the script to the scrutiny of the De Forest Research Group, whose principle concern was the Conelrad announcement heard at the beginning of the story. Such proclamations as, "A state of martial law is hereby declared..." were viewed as erroneous as neither the yellow nor red alert announcements mentioned such a condition. De Forest recommended the deletion of one line — "No commercial traffic of any kind will be permitted on streets and highways" — as a yellow alert didn't prohibit vehicles but provided exact guidance for local dispersal of traffic by means of automobiles. Serling's suggestion in the script that "off in the distance we can see search lights" also came up for elimination because the high speed and high altitude of modern aircraft and missiles rendered searchlights antiquated and useless as a component of anti-aircraft defense. Another aspect of Serling's script — "...the angry screaming cries of the people ring in their ears..." — was also considered an error as the heavy doors of shelters would dampen sounds outside the sanctuary.

Neither the U.S. Air Force and Civil Defense had any say — official or otherwise — in the preparation of the script.[31] Following two days of rehearsal, "The Shelter" went before the cameras for filming between May 19 and 23, 1961.[32] Originally scheduled to air in November, the episode was moved up to an earlier date owing to the acceleration of developments on the civil defense front, and on September 29, 1961, viewers of *The Twilight Zone* got their first look at "The Shelter."[33]

Dr. William Stockton, the honoree at a birthday party thrown by his neighbors, has built a home fallout shelter. He is acclaimed as "a very beloved fellow" whose patients hold him in high regard. The festivities end quickly, however, when Stockton's son tells him that the television broadcast has been interrupted by an announcement to turn to the Conelrad station. The president has announced that radar had detected unidentified flying objects which are flying due southeast. As they haven't been identified, a yellow alert has been declared and everyone is directed to take refuge in a shelter or basement. The party breaks up as everyone scurries to take cover. As the Stocktons have already prepared a shelter, they're ready for doomsday. Considering the wasteland that would result from a nuclear attack, Stockton's wife wonders, aloud, "Why it is so necessary to survive? What's the good of it?" Indicating their son, Stockton replies, "That's the reason.... He may only inherit rumble now. But he's twelve years old. He's only twelve years old."

As Stockton goes upstairs to get the rest of the water, one of his neighbors, Jerry, knocks on his kitchen door, pleading with him to let him and his family share Stockton's shelter. Stockton refuses: "I kept telling you ... all of you — get ready. Build a shelter. Forget the card parties and the barbecues for maybe a few hours a week ... make the admission to yourself that the worst was possible. But you didn't want to listen. To build a shelter was to admit to the kind of age we lived in. And none of you had the guts to face that. So now you've got to face something far worse, Jerry. Oh, God, please God, protect you, Jerry. Its out of my hands. It's simply out of my hands. It's got to be done...."

With that, Stockton shuts the door to his shelter behind him. When another neighbor, Marty, wants in and Stockton again declines, Marty, pounding the shelter door, screams, "You probably will survive, but you'll have blood on your hands. You're a doctor. You're supposed to help people!"

Soon a dog-eat-dog, everyone-for-himself mentality seizes Stockton's neighbors as each one of them, in Robert A. Jacobs's words, betrays "a hidden hatred of the others."[34] One of Marty's neighbors says, "That's the way it is when the foreigners come over here. Pushy, grabby, semi–Americans." When someone else suggests getting a battering ram to break down the shelter door, the question arises that another neighborhood will know about Stockton's shelter, bringing "a whole mob to contend with" over " a whole bunch of strangers."

"Sure," says the wife of one of Stockton's neighbors, "what right have they got to come over here? This isn't their street! This isn't their shelter!"

"Oh, this is *our* shelter," replies Jerry. "And on the next street — that's another country.... You fools. You're insane — all of you.... I wanna see the morning sun come up, too. But you're acting like a mob. And a mob doesn't have any brains! You're proving it by what you're doing!"[35]

By now, reason and common sense have fallen by the wayside. Stockton's neighbors have turned into rampaging, single-minded fanatics, determined to save themselves at whatever cost — the latter symbolized by a scene in which, having secured their battering ram, they rush into the Stockton residence, knocking over the furniture, letting nothing stand in their way, severing the

Opposite: Mob fury: In "The Shelter," an episode of *The Twilight Zone,* a friendly dinner party devolves into chaos after an announcement of incoming bombs is heard. Neighbors determined to save themselves at any cost batter their way into a basement fallout shelter. The episode aired during the shelter craze and "shelter morality" debate that followed President Kennedy's civil defense initiative during the 1961 Berlin crisis (CBS/Photofest).

bonds of neighborliness and friendship they've had for years. (Considering the national debate over the right of shelter owners to repel intruders with force, it is ironic that Stockton himself takes no action to protect his shelter from being overrun — apparently not having equipped it with firearms or any other sort of self-defense mechanisms). Just as the mob breaks down the shelter door, Conelrad comes to life with a new announcement:

"The President of the United States has just announced that the previously unidentified objects have now been definitely ascertained as being satellites ... there are no enemy missiles approaching.... They are harmless, and we are in no danger. The state of emergency has officially been called off.... Repeat, there is no enemy attack."

With that, the neighbors come to their senses. The experience, however, has left Stockton shattered and disillusioned. When Jerry says everyone will pay for the damages to Stockton's home, it elicits a bitter commentary from Stockton:

> Damages? I wonder. I wonder if anyone of us has any idea what those damages really are. Maybe one of them is finding out what we're really like when we're normal: The kind of people we are just underneath the skin. I mean all of us: A lot of naked, wild animals who put such a price on staying alive that they'll claw their neighbors to death just for the privilege. We were spared a bomb tonight. But I wonder. I wonder if we weren't destroyed even without it.

Serling then simply concluded the episode: "No moral, no message, no prophetic tract. Just a simple statement of fact: For civilization to survive, the human race has to remain civilized. Tonight's very small exercise in logic from The Twilight Zone."

Asked if that was the ending he wanted to take, or if he wanted "to leave it a little bit stronger than that," Serling announced, "I was up in the air about it, morally and ethically. I didn't know how to end that thing. I didn't know what position, philosophically, I could take." Serling's remarks were part of an interview he gave to radio dee jay (and future *Hogan's Heroes* star) Bob Crane over Los Angeles radio station KNX shortly after "The Shelter" episode's broadcast. Commenting on its impact, Serling noted, "We had 1,300 letters and cards inside of two days. I think we hit some kind of a nerve." In the same interview, Serling revealed that he and his wife had discussed "the possibility of building a shelter.... We were struck with the moral and ethical problem of what would happen if ... there were an alert sounding, we get into our shelter, happily, because we built one. And neighbors with children came to the door and said, 'Please, let us in....'" That was the problem. I can't answer it. I don't know what is the ethical rightness and justice of this. I haven't figured it out yet." When asked by Crane if he was building a shelter, Serling replied, "No, we're not now."

CRANE: Were you?

SERLING: For awhile we thought very seriously of it ... and now we've decided that no, we're not going to build it.

CRANE: Why?

SERLING: ... For a very realistic ... stringently realistic reasons, and it's my feeling now that, if we survive, what do we survive for? What kind of a world do we go into...? If its rubble and poisoned water and unedible [sic] food and my kids have to live like wild beasts, I'm not particularly sure I want to survive in that kind of a world.[36]

Writing to Serling the very day "The Shelter" aired, one *Twilight Zone* fan expressed his opinion of the broadcast very directly: "I dug your 'The Shelter.'" Another viewer wrote in *The Kansas City Star:* "I have no intention of buying a shotgun to keep neighbors out of my basement and the thought of 'one out of ten' who have already done is sickening! It makes a great deal more sense to get together with our neighbors and build together a refuge for each neighborhood. Let's remember the old slogan: United we stand; divided we fall!" Kenneth H. Campbell, chairman of Civil Defense in Frazier Park, California, wrote: "We thought the film very good, most provocative and thought producing. Due to our distance from Los Angeles, we have met with some apathy here, people believe there would be little danger. However Civil Defense has stressed the need for shelters and the high danger from fallout. We think your film would make people think." Conveying how much he enjoyed "The Shelter," another civil defense official, Jack B. Schmetterer, assistant director of the Northbrook, Illinois, Civil Defense Corps, inquired about the availability of a copy of the episode. Urging viewers to tune in to the broadcast the day of its airing, *The Albuquerque Journal* called it "a show that should not be missed."[37]

Shelter Backlash

Rod Serling's treatment of the "shelter morality" issue and his plea for the maintenance of civilized values in so dire a situation as a nuclear attack was soon followed by a public outcry against the "nuclear ethics" Father McHugh championed — with Father McHugh's fellow clerics leading the charge. On October 13, 1961, the Reverend Angus Dun, Episcopal bishop of Washington, D. C., branded the use of a gun to turn back shelterless neighbors "utterly immoral." Bishop Dun was shocked "at this business of preparing people to push their neighbor's children out of a shelter.... I do not see how any Christian conscience can condone a policy which puts supreme emphasis on saving your our skin, without regard to the plight of your neighbor."

Bishop Dun was joined in his sentiment by Protestant, Catholic, evangelical, and Jewish clerics — among them Protestant theologian Reinhold Niebuhr and evangelist Billy Graham. Consequently, shelter builders fell into disrepute. In Bishop Dun's words: "The kind of man who would be most needed in a post-attack world is least likely to dig himself a private mole-hole that has no room for his neighbor."

The clergy's condemnation emboldened other shelter critics, who had kept their misgivings private, to raise their voices. Speaking to journalists five days after Bishop Dun voiced his objections, former President Dwight D. Eisenhower announced he wouldn't build a shelter: "If I were in a very fine shelter and they [Eisenhower's wife and children] were not there, I would just walk out. I would not want to face that kind of world."[38] Another former president would soon add his voice to the anti-shelter ranks: Speaking in Nebraska in December, Herbert Hoover condemned public and private shelters. Rather than burrowing underground, "We should keep our heads up looking for honorable solutions."[39] Scientists and technical authorities also did much to discredit the cause of shelter advocates. The latter had long maintained that radioactive fallout posed the greatest threat to life in a thermonuclear clash. That argument was challenged by scientists at the Rockefeller Institute. Should the Russians detonate a bomb high above ground — as had been the case at Hiroshima — little or no radioactive fallout would result. The real danger from such a blast would be a firestorm able to wipe out everything miles beyond ground zero. A 50-megaton bomb, explained the publisher of *Scientific American*, Gerard Piel, would yield a firestorm 100 miles in diameter — with the result that every home fallout shelter within that expanse would become a "fire-trap"— which is what suburban and exurban shelters would be transformed into should the Russians explode their large bombs high above American cities. Piel branded fallout shelters "a hoax on public opinion."[40] Piel further sided with those who argued that civil defense, instead of deterring an enemy attack, merely stoked the arms race:

> The civil defense program of our Federal Government, however else intended, must be regarded as a step in the escalation process. It gives the sanction of action to the delusion that a thermonuclear war can be fought and survived. It encourages statesmen to take larger risks predicated on First-Strike Credibility and Post-Attack Recuperative Capacity.[41]

An open letter to President Kennedy, bearing the signatures of hundreds of Midwestern professors, branded fallout shelters a "quack cure for cancer."[42] In "Are Shelters the Answer?" an article appearing in the November 26, 1961, edition of the *New York Times Magazine*, anthropologist Margaret Mead made reference to Serling's "Shelter" episode to advance her argument that "the armed, individual shelter is the logical end" to the moral direction America had traveled since World War II. Mead declared that Western Europeans were appalled at the American crusade to construct private bomb shelters and utilize force to safeguard them against their "less provident neighbors." Europeans viewed this as "one more example of Americans' inexplicable affinity for violence," and "set beside such terms as 'overkill' and 'megadeath,' the picture of members of the richest and most technically advanced country in the world regressing to a level lower than that of any savages, to the level of trapped animals, made Europeans shudder." Mead continued: "Perhaps the world did not have to wait for a nuclear war to bring about the physical dissolution of civilization: perhaps it was dissolving morally now." This moral disintegration stemmed from American culture during the Berlin crisis:

> A clergyman sanctioned the right of a man to kill his neighbor in order to protect his own family — a right accorded to no member of a society which calls itself a society. A nation-wide television program, depicting the fictional response to an alert, showed a frantic group of neighbors battering down in violent rage a family's shelter which, once destroyed, could protect no one.

The American government, in Mead's view, was responsible for a good part of such shelter selfishness: Its advocacy of individual shelters had nullified its communal defense pledge and destroyed any recognition of community obligation. Moreover, Mead contended that the kind of American moral breakdown seen in the shelter mania was "symptomatic" of the overall and continuing changes in American attitude that had taken place since World War II. Mead declared that "the fantastic, unrealistic, morally dangerous behavior in which citizenry and government have indulged in thinking about the shelter program was an expression of a much wider ethical conflict — one in which Americans have been involved ever since we dropped the first nuclear bomb on Hiroshima." The latter had terminated two eras: first, America's isolation from the world and, second, the easy dependence on war to resolve and protect national honor, as war entailed risking "suicide" and "murder against all bystanders." Because of Hiroshima, "We were no longer protected by fixed boundaries," hence "we extended our defenses around the world." The augmentation of post-war American interests produced discord in American society and culture and, in a shrinkage of the spirit that found ultimate assertion in the venal immorality of the day's shelter ethics — an attitude that could be seen in the prejudices Stockton's neighbors exhibited toward another neighborhood knowing about his shelter in Serling's teleplay:

> Countering this centrifugal movement was the centripetal pull of fear and dread — dread of the danger of mass destruction with which mankind now must live, perhaps forever; dread of the strain of living always related to distant and still alien peoples and having somehow to assimilate their experiences, good and

bad, to our own; dread of the vast population spurt that is already being likened
to an atomic explosion; and closer to home, dread of the surging masses of
young people, uneducated and unprepared for urban living, turning to drugs
and crime; dread of our crumbling, dangerous cities. As American feeling was
stretched to the utmost, moving even further outward, those who were ill-pre-
pared to take these unexpected, giant steps turned inward. Drawn back in space
and in time, hiding from the future and the rest of the world, they turned to the
green suburbs, protected by zoning laws against members of other classes or
races or religions, and concentrated on the single, tight little family. They idealized the life of each such family living alone in self-sufficient togetherness, protecting its members against the contamination of different ways or others'
needs.... The armed, individual shelter is the logical end of this retreat from
trust in and responsibility for others.[43]

Official efforts to persuade Americans to build home shelters aside, very
few actually were built. In Cook County, Illinois, where 260,000 copies of
the brochure "Family Fallout Shelter" had been disseminated, merely 19 people
out of a population exceeding three million had applied, as of November 19,
1961, for permission to construct a home shelter. A full year after the shelter
mania had taken off, the Federal Housing Administration announced that
only 3,500 people had requested a home-shelter loan. The final death knell
for the shelter boom came when the bubble burst for shelter merchants.
Declaring in May 1962 that the shelter market was dead, the president of
Chicago's Atomic Shelter Corporation calculated that approximately 600 shelter manufacturers had closed their doors. That same month an Oklahoma
City contractor announced that he had received only one shelter-related query
for all of the preceding month. One indigent Los Angeles manufacturer called
it "a real loused-up deal." In what political writer Walter Karp called the symbolic end of the shelter craze, on April 1, 1962, a destitute Oakland, California,
firm, the Living Circle Company, which had sold only one prefabricated shelter in fifteen months, disposed of its remaining inventory at a public auction,
selling nine shelters for roughly six hundred dollars each. One shelter pur-
chaser felt it would make "a dandy darkroom." Another planned to use his as
a storage facility for garden tools.[44]

Other events, domestic and international, contributed to the demise of
the shelter boom. Kennedy was aware that, should his potential Republican
rival Nelson Rockefeller fail in his crusade to secure public backing in New
York for shelters, then his own campaign for nuclear hideaways would be virtually meaningless. Early in 1960, the New York state legislature had vetoed
Rockefeller's plan to make fallout protection a requirement in all new and
existing buildings in the state. Rockefeller attributed this loss to the "absence
of a well-defined national civil defense policy." Owing to Rockefeller's behind-
the-scenes machinations, his civil defense program was rammed through a

special session of the New York legislature on November 9, 1961, with such speed the majority of the lawmakers didn't have time to study the legislation before voting on it. The legislature sanctioned $100 million to underwrite the construction of fallout shelters in all state buildings and to furnish assistance to educational institutions, among the latter private and public universities and colleges, up to $25 per shelter space.

Mark Lane, a 34-year-old, first-term member of the New York legislature, was responsible for driving the final stakes into Rockefeller's civil defense crusade. The first blow came when Lane disclosed that Joseph Carlino, majority leader of the Assembly and Albany Speaker of the House, had concealed his financial investment in a firm that built fallout shelters, a disclosure that prompted an investigation into the matter by the New York State Assembly's Committee on Ethics and Guidance. In exonerating Carlino of any misconduct, the committee observed that "much distrust and suspicion was unduly generated" in the press, and proposed additional study of a tougher legislative code of ethics for future lawmakers. Lane's next move came in early February 1962, when he orchestrated an anti-civil defense march on the New York state capital, Albany, in what the *New York Times* called the largest protest demonstration Albany had witnessed since "the rent and discrimination protest of the late nineteen-forties." Most of the demonstrators were middle-class housewives and students.

Rockefeller, refusing to face the reality that there was opposition to his civil defense drive, told the Office of Emergency Planning in New York City on April 2, 1962, that he was convinced that people were prepared for civil defense and would presently achieve it with faith in democracy and God. Shortly thereafter, his speech-writing aides cautioned that the next time he addressed the civil defense issue, he should be aware that they knew "for a considerable time" of the existence of

> considerable public opinion ranged against both the Federal and New York State fallout shelter programs. It is also quite evident that the critics of shelters are not merely crackpots, or unilateral disarmers, or any other fringe group. They include men who have thought deeply on the issues involved, and they also include persons of considerable stature.... Some of the most vehement opposition to the shelter program comes from (a) certain scientists, many of whom are highly regarded in the scientific world; (b) liberal writers (the *Nation, New Republic*); and c) certain conservatives, including most notably Hanson Baldwin and Arthur Krock.

Baldwin and Krock were, respectively, the military editor of the *New York Times* and one of that paper's most esteemed journalists. Now appreciating that his cause was lost, Rockefeller immediately refocused the direction of argument in favor of shelters to their usefulness during dangerous weather —

an argument future presidents would also use to justify civil defense measures.[45]

Months earlier, Kennedy himself had been forced to face realities. As anti-civil defense sentiment accelerated, presidential staff members such as McGeorge Bundy, originally a civil defense proponent, were compelled to retreat. Writing to Bundy in October 1961, presidential science adviser Jerome Wiesner explained that the minimum cost of a fallout shelter for everyone would be $10–20 billion — and would merely cover the small number of people not in, or close to, target areas. Another administration staffer, Ted Sorensen, subsequently reminded the president that one of the most perilous canards was *Life* magazine's assertion "that 97 percent of the population or anything like it could survive a major nuclear attack if we had a massive shelter program." "Civil Defense," Sorensen wrote his boss, "is rapidly blossoming into our number one political headache, alienating those who believe we are doing too much or too little, or with too much confusion. What is needed most of all is an all-out effort to get it back into perspective." In November, Wiesner arranged a personal meeting between Kennedy and civil defense advocate Edward Teller about the need for shelters. Wiesner was certain that once Teller began talking about the necessity of countering the Russians' development of larger and improved bombs by burrowing ever deeper underground, Kennedy would further appreciate how essentially foolish was the notion of building fallout shelters.

Meeting several important advisers at Hyannis Port during the Thanksgiving holiday weekend in 1961, Kennedy decided to diminish public discourse regarding civil defense and redirect the focus of the federal shelter system to community or group shelters — a move intended to placate those critics who objected that the prior focus on home sanctuaries left out those who were impoverished and who weren't homeowners. All future efforts in the civil defense realm were to be limited to finishing the shelter survey that had been funded in 1961. This study would designate and mark structures furnishing 46 million shelter spaces and provision approximately one-fifth of them. Implored by Defense Secretary Robert McNamara, Carl Kaysen, and OCD head Steuart Pittman, Kennedy agreed to request an additional $700 million from Congress for a Shelter Incentive Program that would provide federal funds to nonprofit health, educational, and welfare institutions that would build fallout shelters capable of accommodating at least 50 people of up to $25 per shelter space. The purpose of this new program was to foster construction of 100 million spaces at a cost to the taxpayers of just $2.2 billion.

When Kennedy submitted his funding request for the Shelter Incentive Program to the House Appropriations Committee, the Democratic chairman, Clarence Cannon of Missouri, long a critic of civil defense, turned the matter over to fellow Democrat and congressional civil defense adversary, Albert Thomas of Texas — an action seen as an attempt to crush the civil defense program, and one by which the Kennedy administration made clear that it wasn't really disturbed. After pro-civil defense witnesses had had their say before Thomas's subcommittee, Thomas did something extraordinary for that day: He permitted the testimony of nongovernmental, anti-civil defense witnesses — the latter including members of SANE, the Quakers and other religious groups, and numerous academic and scientific organizations. When all was said and done, Thomas' subcommittee sanctioned a mere $75 million of the sum for which Kennedy had asked, sustaining only the most fundamental civil defense functions. When the House voted 368–12 to approve the attenuated civil defense allocation in August 1962, the White House again lodged no serious protest. "The final congressional allocation," minus funding for the Shelter Incentive Program "was $128 million for the OCD in fiscal year 1963."[46]

By then the Berlin crisis, the main catalyst for Kennedy's fallout shelter drive, had long since cooled. Episodes of East German harassment along the access route to West Berlin occurred during the fall of 1961; late October witnessed a tense moment when Soviet and American tanks confronted each other at the border between East and West Berlin, producing a 16-hour standoff, with both sides' military forces facing each other less than one hundred yards apart. Allied troops stationed in West Berlin went on alert. The crisis passed, and "both sides on the whole seemed more conciliatory and cordial."

Speaking before the United Nations, Kennedy hewed to a tough line regarding the Soviet Union and Berlin, yet advocated more dialogue and less provocation: "I pledge you that we shall neither commit nor provoke aggression, that we shall neither flee nor invoke the threat of force, that we shall never negotiate out of fear, [but that] we shall never fear to negotiate." Additionally, Kennedy strongly advocated global disarmament and challenged the Soviets to a "peace race" instead of an arms race. Formal diplomatic discussions concerning the Berlin issue began. Khrushchev started a personal correspondence with Kennedy that continued until JFK's death. Both men accepted a proposal from Kennedy's press secretary, Pierre Salinger, for a series of international televised debates — an agreement that fell through owing to Kennedy's decision to resume atmospheric nuclear testing. Khrushchev gave interviews to American journalists and invited Salinger and Kennedy's brother Robert to Moscow. JFK, for his part, gave an interview to Aleksei Adzhubei, Khrushchev's son-in-law, and the editor of the Soviet government newspaper *Izvestia*. The latter's Moscow edition featured the interview in its entirety. The Russians relinquished their call for a three-man secretary-generalship of the United Nations. According to historian Thomas C. Reeves: "Khrushchev did not sign a treaty with East Germany, and the access route to West Berlin remained open."[47]

In addition to the criticisms lodged by the clergy, scientists, and technical authorities, as well as the calming of the Berlin crisis, one final consideration must be added to those that defused Kennedy's civil defense crusade: The criticism of fallout shelters presented by pop-culture instruments such as *The Twilight Zone.* In this regard, Kenneth D. Rose has written that shelter advocates failed both to win the moral high ground and the hearts and minds of the American people to their cause in good part "because they lost the metaphor war":

> They were incapable of summoning images as brilliant as those commanded by their adversaries. In this cultural struggle, critics of shelters were aided greatly by a general unease in regard to fallout shelters. To many Americans, there was something inherently shameful about burying themselves under the earth to save their lives, despite the excellent utility of a nuclear attack. Compounding the shame was the barbarism of threatening to kill one's neighbor to protect one's shelter, what Walter Lippmann called the "evil" of "each family for itself, and the devil take the hindmost." In Arthur Washow's words, the shelter issue "strained the web of community." By "excluding neighbors, or people from the next block, or strangers from the next county, or casual visitors to town.... Suburbia has been pitted against city, one state against another." The "mole," the "caveman," and the "barbarian" thus became metaphors for the shelter owner, while the "Maginot Line" and the "garrison state" were used to describe a national shelter system. Perhaps more than any other factor, the images that these metaphors called forth — of a militarized nation and a fearful people huddled beneath the ground in dark shelters — would spell doom for a national shelter system.[48]

Not even the Cuban missile crisis could galvanize Americans to push for civil defense. Dwindling of media interest, public drills, and the building of private shelters clearly signaled an acute decline in interest in the subject. "However," Alice L. George has written, "as in so many issues that relate to Americans and civil defense, there is a disconnect between what people said and what they did." A 1964 University of Pittsburgh survey revealed that 35 percent of Americans said the missile crisis heightened their interest in civil defense. "Still, it seems apparent that most Americans walked away from the crisis accepting what their leaders had been afraid to say: A minimal program was pointless and that a more effective program would be very expensive and still would offer no guarantees for many Americans." American leaders' deduction that the electorate wouldn't support another gigantic and exorbitant federal bureaucracy that intervened in everyday life had been correct. A second 1964 survey, this one conducted by the Hudson Institute on behalf of the

Office of Emergency Planning, "supports the belief that war is a not-inconceivable possibility, supports the idea of shelter or other civil defense programs as a form of protection, but is little inclined to do anything about it.... It seems plain that most of the public would accept a cost-less, effortless civil defense program if it were given to them." Indeed, in the wake of the missile crisis, the majority of Americans evidently "accepted that defenselessness was a part of the nuclear age" or "simply prolonged their state of denial about nuclear war and its dangers."[49] As civil defense dwindled as an issue, Americans adapted the kind of foreign policy that sought to avoid nuclear confrontation. Kennedy's 1963 remarks at American University catalyzed a new foundation for peaceful coexistence with communism, and there is little doubt that Barry Goldwater's bid for the White House the following year was harmed by the voters' conviction that he might push the nuclear button to defeat the Communists. (During the Vietnam War, no broader voter backing for using nuclear weapons in that war existed.) JFK's evident hard line in the Cuban missile confrontation may have provided him new flexibility by blunting censure from the Right, but the true legacy of the crisis was that it led to far more cautious employment of nuclear saber rattling by both East and West.[50]

Other indications of the public's rejection of civil defense could be found in the termination of such programs by communities around the nation. Portland, Oregon's disenchantment with civil defense stemmed from a severe windstorm that virtually immobilized the city on Columbus Day 1962. When the foremost civil defense official, who was hunting deer in the eastern part of the state, couldn't be contacted, civil defense workers were unable to sound the alarm to Portlanders or render assistance in the storm's aftermath. On election day the following month, Portlanders overwhelmingly vetoed a special five-year levy of $75,000 for the local civil defense office. This was followed, on May 23, 1963, by the Portland city council's decision, by a vote of 4–1, to shut down its Kelly Butte civil defense communications center, terminate its entire civil defense staff and the federally funded shelter program, and abandon more than $1 million worth of civil defense equipment that had already been purchased and inventoried. Moreover, the city council, by relinquishing future disaster operations in the hands of Portland's police and fire departments, claimed it had saved nearly $100,000 a year. Shortly thereafter, led by progressive Senator Wayne Morse, Oregon's legislature scuttled its civil defense program by slashing the annual budget from $410,000 to $56,000, leaving Governor Mark Hatfield incapable of vetoing the legislature's action. Simultaneously, Lincoln County, Oregon, voted to terminate its local civil defense offices. What happened in Oregon was just the beginning. That summer, Baltimore and Los Angeles officials sharply reduced their civil defense budgets — a move resulting in part because of civil defense protests on the part of organized mothers that presently became a common occurrence in cities nationwide.

Even earlier, the Wichita, Kansas, superintendent of schools terminated civil defense drills in classrooms, citing as his reason the futility of civil defense as a shield against thermonuclear war. After Operation Alert for 1962 was canceled, anti–civil defense activists in New York City continued their fight as the Citizen's Committee to Abolish School Drills. Students had begun protesting such exercises. Dozens had been suspended for their actions, and a junior high school teacher, James Council, was fired from his job for declining to participate because of his conscience. The year of Council's firing, 1963, Jackie Goldberg, who subsequently became an important figure in the free speech movement, formed Campus Women for Peace and mounted a successful campaign to shut down the fallout shelters on the University of California's Berkeley campus.

That fall, the OCD's request for $346.9 million for fiscal year 1964 came up for House scrutiny, and faced those old foes Albert Thomas and Clarence Cannon. "We haven't changed our minds," Thomas declared. "We're not building any fallout shelters, period." To this, Cannon said, "[Fallout shelters] will never be needed because there will never be another world war. With modern weapons, an international war amounts to international suicide. Most of the people would die and all cities would disintegrate within three days after hostilities started." Once more, with nary a word of objection on the administration's part, the congressional appropriation for fiscal 1964 was trimmed to $111 million, which provided maintenance of only the most fundamental CD functions. By then, Kennedy had been assassinated. The death knell for funding the Shelter Incentive Plan was sounded in early 1964 by the refusal of Senator Henry Jackson, Democrat, of Washington State and chairman of the Senate Armed Services Subcommittee, to continue hearings on the new civil defense bill. Disgruntled, Steuart Pittman resigned as OCD head in March. Shortly thereafter, the OCD was demoted and federal civil defense operations transferred from the office of the secretary of defense to the office of the secretary of the army.[51]

One final question remains: What would have happened if a shelter owner had actually shot someone trying to crowd into the shelter defender's sanctuary? An answer of sorts was provided by a 1991 episode of the television series *Quantum Leap*, which starred Scott Bakula as the time-traveling Dr. Sam Beckett, who travels to various periods of history, correcting wrongs from the past. One of Beckett's travels takes him to Florida during the Cuban missile crisis, where Mac, a fallout shelter salesman, is enjoying a profitable business. In the person of Mac's brother, who is working his way through college selling shelters, Beckett takes a potential customer on a tour of a super deluxe shelter "designed to give you the most modern space-age conveniences to protect you and yours well into the '60s."

According to official records, Burt Rosencranz, the man to whom Beckett is showing the shelter, was shot by Mac when the former tried to get into the shelter. Mac did time for the shooting. Beckett's mission is to prevent the shooting from occurring. Toward that end, he empties the bullets from the shotgun in Mac's shelter, burying them in the backyard.

That evening, a power blackout (occurring just as President Kennedy is about to make a statement) sends Mac's family into the shelter, thinking an actual attack is imminent. When Burt tries to enter the shelter, Beckett gets into a struggle with Mac, trying to get the gun away from him. Unnoticed during the excitement, Stevie, Mac's young son, lays his hands on a pistol in the shelter, exits the shelter entrance, and shoots at Burt, thinking the latter is a Russian. Beckett averts the tragedy by telling Stevie a bomb is falling, and to "duck and cover." Feeling a sense of guilt over the affair, Mac took the rap for Stevie's action. With the missile crisis over and orders for his shelters being canceled, Mac decides to go into the swimming pool business.

Panic in Year Zero!

The survival-at-any-cost tone of the "shelter morality" debate reflected how harshly attitudes toward surviving a nuclear war had changed from the optimistic quality of the early Cold War era. Civil defense literature during the early Cold War period presented the idea that people would live through an atomic attack mostly in the same manner that they survived natural disasters: Survival depended on good citizenship and survivors would contribute to society's restoration. Such literature was usually devoid of politics in that they never mentioned which nation was responsible for launching the attack. Frequently the literature cited the metaphoric link between the individual and the nation, emphasizing the notion that personal survival and national victory were one and the same.

Survival narratives, along with other elements of nuclear-era pop culture, underwent a noticeable change in tone once the Cold War entered the thermonuclear age in the mid–1950s. Now such narratives were more likely to be more fatalistic, presenting uncompromising self-interest as essential to survival and nuclear war as inexorable with no survivors. Survival itself became the paramount issue, sanctifying whatever means were necessary to guarantee that one remained alive before and after the war.

"In popular culture narratives of survival," Robert A. Jacobs has written, the individual is removed from society, isolated, while the grotesque surgery of nuclear warfare is performed. These narratives assume that, to make it through this period of intense self-reliance and isolation, it might well become necessary for people to revert to a primitive level of behavior and to commit acts that in peacetime would be considered abhorrent. All such acts were justified by the extremity of the situation and by the imperative to survive, and all must be considered acts of self-defense.[52]

Jacobs also notes that the revolution in warfare thermonuclear weapons wrought, where missiles, not bombers, would rain mass destruction on a global scale within mere minutes, also changed how the survivor was presented: "The conscientious citizen-survivor of the early atmospheric testing era gave way to the rugged survivalist of the H-bomb era."[53]

This harder-edged survivalist concept was depicted in the feature film *Panic in Year Zero!* Released in 1962,[54] *Panic* was to movie audiences what Rod Serling's *Twilight Zone* "Shelter" episode was to television viewers. Directed by Ray Milland (who also starred in the film), written by Jay Simms and John Morton, and filmed for American International Pictures (the company behind numerous Roger Corman epics[55]), *Panic* took Father McHugh's survivalist message to an even greater extreme, showing what lengths to which a man would go to protect his family from the chaos resulting from a nuclear attack.

The breakdown of civilized behavior is a recurring theme in apocalypse stories. Long before *The Twilight Zone* and *Panic in Year Zero!* presented this motif within the context of nuclear war, George Pal's 1953 science fiction classic *The War of the Worlds* showed looters running amuck in downtown Los Angeles as the Martian invaders advance on the city. Comparing *Panic in Year Zero!* with *On the Beach*, film historian Kim Newman has observed that, whereas the survivors in *On the Beach* are resigned to their fate, *Panic*, despite the savagery of the post-apocalyptic world it presents, still offers the conviction "that there will be plenty of things worth fighting for" to make life worth living.[56]

As the film begins, a family of four — Harry Baldwin (Ray Milland), his wife Ann (Jean Hagen), son Rick (Frankie Avalon), and daughter Karen (Mary Mitchel)[57] — sets out with their camper/trailer in tow for a fishing trip. While they listen to the car radio, the sky suddenly lights up, prompting Harry to pull over and check the trailer's windows. A second burst of light appears. When Ann suggests that the light my have originated from an atomic test site in the vicinity of Las Vegas, Harry points out that the light came from the direction of Los Angeles. Checking their car radio, the Baldwins pick up an early morning weather report; otherwise, none of the Los Angeles stations are on the air, including CONELRAD. Driving farther down the road, they stop at a roadside pay phone; trying to call L.A., Harry discovers that all phone lines to Los Angeles are temporarily out of commission. The cause of the disruption then becomes apparent: The sky above Los Angeles is filled with an enormous mushroom cloud — evidence that the bomb has been dropped on the city. The fact that the Baldwins left before the attack occurred spared their lives.

Driving back home, the Baldwins are nearly run off the road by cars fleeing Los Angeles. Finally coming to life with news, the car radio picks up a message from the Emergency Broadcasting Network that the Los Angeles area has apparently been the target of a nuclear attack. Pulling into a roadside gas station, Harry discovers a refugee from the attack, who says he heard L.A. "being torn apart and watched it being tossed into the air." The man had pulled in to have his car refueled; when he tells the station attendant he has no money with him and the attendant insists on payment, the motorist

Post-apocalyptic survival: Harry Baldwin (Ray Milland, second from right, in hat) became a ruthless survivalist determined to protect his family, in 1962's *Panic in Year Zero!* Also pictured: Harry's son, Rick (Frankie Avalon, far left); daughter Karen (Mary Mitchel, center); and wife Ann (Jean Hagen, far right) (American International Pictures/Photofest).

punches him. Observing the incident, Harry tells the dazed gas station oper-ator, "I hope I'm wrong but there may be a lot of business transacted like this from now on." His words prove prophetic.

Encountering more panicked motorists along the way, concerned that looting and chaos now reigns in Los Angeles, Harry decides not to return there and resume his family's vacation as planned. Survival is now his primary concern. "What do you want to do?" his wife, Ann, asks. "Write off the rest of the world?"

"When civilization gets civilized again," Harry replies, "I'll rejoin."

Harry presently demonstrates his new moral ethic: Stocking up on food and other supplies in a town off the beaten path, he tries to purchase a handgun but the store owner refuses to sell it to him, citing a state law. Harry loads the weapon, aims it at the proprietor, telling him to write a receipt for his purchases, and promises that he will pay for everything. Handing Harry the receipt, the owner punches him, precipitating a brawl that ends when Harry's son Rick breaks up the altercation by pointing the gun at the owner. Stocking up on additional firepower, Harry and his family high-tail it out of town. Shocked at her husband's behavior, Ann says, "I can't get over it. After all these years, I thought I knew you, but you turn out to be a stranger. Robbing and mauling people like some kind of a cheap hoodlum."

"We're fighting for our lives, Ann," Harry retorts. "My family must sur-vive."

Siding with his father, Rick says, "We're on our own.... No rules, no reg-ulations, and no laws."

"Don't write off the law," Harry tells him. "The law'll come back. I just want us to be around when it does."[58]

Harry's descent into barbarism is exhibited once more when, pulling into another gas station for refueling, he punches out the station owner when he discovers the latter has taken advantage of the crisis by hefting the price of gas per gallon, then orders Rick to ride shotgun for him in the trailer with his mother and sister. "If I stop the car, grab a shotgun. Don't get trigger-happy. But don't be gun-shy, either. If you have to use it, use it."

Encountering a roadblock along the way, Harry plows his car and trailer right on through it. (The roadblock was intended to keep Los Angelinos out of town. In reality, such an idea wasn't limited to the screenwriters' imaginations. The idea of Los Angelinos stampeding into Las Vegas in the aftermath of a nuclear conflict occurred to Las Vegas's civil defense chief J. Carlton Adair. "A million or more persons might stream into this area from Southern California," he declared, "and pick the valley clean of food, medical supplies, and other goods." Adair's solution to this dire possibility was the establishment of a militia, numbering 5,000 members, to protect Las Vegas.

Adair wasn't the only civil defense official who feared an invasion of Los Angelinos. Keith Dwyer, civil defense coordinator of Riverside County, California, recommended that county residents arm themselves as well. Waving a pistol above his head while speaking to police reservists in Beaumont, California, Dwyer cautioned, "Get one of these and learn how to use it." Bakersfield police chief Horace V. Grayson — who did double duty as Kern County's civil defense coordinator — asserted that "the greatest danger to Bakersfield would not be from an atomic bomb or its fallout, but from hundreds of thousands of displaced residents from the Los Angeles area." Grayson anticipated that up to one million such people would inundate Bakersfield from the south following the nuking of Los Angeles. "They must not come here," Grayson said. "They must be stopped south of town and shown a route to some kind of refuge on the desert." The task of halting this influx would be the responsibility of local law enforcement officers, who undoubtedly drew scant encouragement from Grayson's words: "We have plenty of them, and they are expendable."[59]

After running the roadblock, the next challenge the Baldwins face comes in the form of thugs who try to kill Harry and molest Ann and Karen. A shotgun blast from Rick scares the would-be molesters off. When Harry then learns that Ann pushed the gun aside just as Rick fired it, he goes ballistic: "Would you rather see one of us lying dead at your feet? Make up your mind!" Harry then tells his son that both he and his mother want to save civilization: "And don't you forget it." The next obstacle the Baldwins overcome is the crowded main highway: Pouring gasoline on it, Harry sets it ablaze, allowing Rick to drive their car and trailer to the other side of the road. This memorable scene reminds film historian Jack G. Shaheen of Moses parting the Red Sea; however, "Unlike Moses, Harry was not waiting for a miracle; his is the religion of survival" — his and his family's.[60]

Finally reaching a campsite, the Baldwins take refuge in a natural bomb shelter — a cave, setting up house there. They soon discover they're not alone: Johnson, the hardware store owner with whom Harry had fought, appears, telling him there are others in the area, keeping to themselves — "Everyone's trigger-happy." When Johnson asks if he and his wife can visit, Harry refuses him. Ann's desire for civilized people changes her husband's mind; he tells her he'll visit the Johnsons in a few days and bring them back to the cave with him. However, when Harry makes good on his promise, he and Rick discover both Johnson and his wife dead at their own encampment.

Harry and Rick make their gruesome find while they investigate the source of some gunshots they heard. Continuing their investigation, they check out a nearby farmhouse, which they find occupied by the three hoodlums they encountered earlier. When two of them rape Harry's daughter,

Karen, her father and brother exact revenge by killing them. They also find and rescue a girl, Marilyn, whose parents were murdered by the gang. In exacting vengeance for his daughter's rape by killing her violators, Harry experiences guilt at his action, but his wife, who up till now had been repelled by her husband's violent actions in defense of his family, now confirms that his course was the appropriate one. Unless decent people like themselves survive (compared to the lowlifes they've crossed paths with since the nuclear holocaust), civilization would be doomed.[61]

When a radio bulletin announces that a relocation center has been established in the area in which the Baldwins are holed up, Harry refuses to leave, arguing that there's some measure of control where they are. Shortly thereafter, Carl, the last surviving member of the trio of hoodlums, shows up, pulling a gun on Marilyn. When Rick throws a stick at him, Carl shoots Rick, seriously wounding him, while Marilyn downs Carl with a rifle. Driving into town, Harry finds a doctor who temporarily patches up Rick. (In commenting on Harry's reaction to the doctor saving his son's life, Jack G. Shaheen writes: "Civilization and the hope of mankind return. The film, for the first and only time, suggests technology may be used for humanistic ends; technology is not evil at all; it is neutral." It is merely an extension of whatever use humanity puts it to. It is evil if man fashions weapons from it, good if he fashions lifesaving instruments from it.)[62]

Rick still needs a blood transfusion to save his life. En route to a hospital for the procedure, the Baldwins encounter an Army patrol that directs Harry to a medical facility ten miles away. As Harry drives off into the night, the screen flashes the words: THERE MUST BE NO END — ONLY A NEW BEGINNING.

Boxoffice thought *Panic in Year Zero!* "well produced on a modest budget" and believed that "Avalon [turned] in his best screen performance to date." Writing in the Los Angeles *Herald-Examiner*, David Bongard cautioned that the film "will scare the daylights out of you." Milland, in Bongard's opinion, "directs economically and pointedly.... This very unhappy and demoralizing picture is told with all the stops pulled out. It wasn't too expensive to make, but the story is a blockbuster." Considering the film a "good, sound melodrama," the *Hollywood Reporter's* James Powers felt that Milland directed it with "some dignity and intelligence." The script, in Powers's judgment, was "generally superior to its class, with some of the dialogue very sharp. The story itself tends to run down in the closing minutes of the film ... but the approach to a ticklish subject is generally good."[63]

In equating *Panic in Year Zero!* with other post-nuclear films, Toni A. Perrine notes: "The nuclear family is set against the needs of the larger society, because it is the fabric of the society and must survive intact. It also assumes that a disaster of the magnitude of nuclear war will bring out the worst in people and implies that it may even get rid of some of the scum of the earth and leave decent, law-abiding citizens to start again."[64]

Panic is also indicative of the gender roles of its era. In taking charge of his family's survival in the post-attack word, Harry Baldwin reflects the social ethos of the time: Men are the leaders; women follow them. "This," Shaheen writes, "is an accurate reflection of the way in which early-sixties women's magazines, such as *Family Circle* and *Ladies' Home Journal*, stressed the importance of the family unit. Togetherness was the prevalent theme with dad as leader."[65] Shaheen continues that Ann Baldwin's primary purpose in *Panic* "is to occasionally counterpoint the moral disintegration of the men. Dubiously, she represents love, goodness, Christian morality, and civilization; and in retrospect, a typical treatment of women in disaster films." However, when she tries to kill the two hoodlums who raped Karen, she demonstrates that she can discard her saintly posture when the situation warrants, and, in this instance, she is justified in doing so. "This is a realistic gesture, unlike the violent reactions of the men, who are constantly in search of potential victims."[66]

Once it is clear that civilization will prevail — as symbolized by the elimination of Carl, the remaining hoodlum — it becomes clear that it is time for Harry to resume civilized behavior, a point manifested by the appearance of soldiers at the film's conclusion. Now that they're present, order will be restored and everything will be fine. Compared to the likes of Carl, the Army epitomizes acceptable violence that maintains the status quo. The character of Carl represents the antithesis of the values Harry Baldwin symbolizes. The post-nuclear world is Carl and company's world, "but," in Bill Warren's words, "they are also burned away by the nuclear fire-represented by Harry." Indeed, *Panic in Year Zero!* makes a strong case that nuclear war is a purifying, cleansing force that leaves a new and better world in its aftermath — if one ignores the unpleasant aftershocks in the postwar world (radiation sickness, the degeneration of civilized behavior and attendant complications, such as lawlessness). The war was merely "a hitch in civilization's gitalong, nothing really to concern ourselves with."[67]

Violence was the dominant theme of the pop culture representations of nuclear war in the Kennedy years — violence that threatened the social fabric. Dr. Stockton's neighbors sought to batter their way into his shelter in *The Twilight Zone*, and Harry Baldwin drops out of civilization at the first sign of its disintegration, deciding for himself what's right and wrong in *Panic in Year Zero!* Not only were the Kennedy years the closest that mankind came to nuclear Armageddon, civilized values came close to an armageddon of their own during that time — in real life (the shelter owners who threatened to shoot those seeking to crowd into their private havens) and in the pop culture depictions of those tensions.

The Kennedy years marked both the apex and the climax of the "Golden Age of civil defense." Paradoxically the chaos of the sixties and the disappointments of the seventies would soon make those anxious Cold War times look quite attractive to Americans.

5

Nuclear Nostalgia
in the Seventies

In the aftermath of the Cuban missile crisis, nuclear fears began calming. A factor in this was the 1963 Limited Test Ban Treaty which relegated nuclear testing out of sight — underground — and out of the public consciousness. Civil defense, only recently a serious national concern, also faded from view as mounting evidence indicated that "duck and cover" and bomb shelters were insufficient protection against nuclear weapons. "The fear of possible nuclear war and actual radioactive fallout that had been building since the mid-fifties suddenly dissipated in the absence of the constant reminders that had typified the preceding decade."[1]

Throughout the missile crisis, civil defense went unmentioned by American leaders, including President Kennedy; nor did they urge Americans to take sanctuary in shelters. Implicit in this silence was the realization on the part of the government what the ordinary citizen knew from the beginning: Civil defense was a fallacious, impractical, and dangerous notion — one that neither awed nor frightened the Soviets. Kennedy's Secretary of Defense Robert McNamara eventually appreciated that all the Soviets needed do to counter the most exorbitant American civil defense concept was to boost both the numbers and mega tonnage of their retaliatory strike force.[2]

Other issues began to command the attention of scientists and the government. The scientists became engrossed in weapons development, nuclear power generation, and arms limitation; government officials became focused on Vietnam and the domestic anti-war movement which the Southeast Asian conflict produced. Civil defense was relegated as a ridiculous relic of the past.

Nonetheless, American presidents and their principal aides did advocate civil defense on those occasions when it benefited their larger strategic goals. Lyndon B. Johnson called "an effective civil defense program an important element of our total defense effort." Gerald Ford maintained that "our civil defense program continues to be an essential element of the nation's deterrent posture." Such proclamations aside, neither president was committed to the sort of sweeping program that had been previously advanced.

The OCD continued surveying, designating, and supplying shelter spaces. Civil defense officials, though they campaigned for a wider effort, appreciated that hardly more could be done as legislative interest in the subject ebbed. When, in fiscal year 1967, Congress turned down $10 million that had been requested to finance an experimental program of shelter subsidies, Defense Secretary Robert McNamara decided to stick with the ongoing limited program. By the end of the 1960s, authorities had designated more than two hundred million shelter spaces and distributed more than 165,000 tons of supplies.

This program remained in place as the seventies began, as civil defense began incorporating both wartime and peacetime calamities. Convinced that appropriate planning would enable the United States to survive any crisis, Richard Nixon's Secretary of Defense Melvin Laird maintained that the Defense Department "can and should contribute to total civil disaster preparedness — civil defense and natural disaster." A pair of agencies — the Federal Preparedness Agency in the General Services Administration and a Federal Disaster Assistance Administration in the Department of Housing and Urban Development — continued activities akin to those conducted by the Defense Civil Preparedness Agency in the Defense Department until President Jimmy Carter sanctioned a stronger civil-defense effort, and Congress amalgamated all civil defense operations into the Federal Emergency Management Agency (FEMA).[3]

Civil defense wasn't the only '50s relic to fall by the wayside during the post–Kennedy era. The same years witnessed a decline in '50s rectitude, which emphasized stringent boundaries on sexual behavior and extolled the nuclear family. The late–1970s witnessed the apex of this disintegration with the popularity of disco music as possibly the greatest manifestation of this break with the past. In addition to the catchy dance music that had been part of the New York City club scene for quite some time, disco represented a more uninhibited lifestyle when it came to matters of drugs, free sex, gender bending, and sequined attire. The public's growing acceptance of sexually explicit books and motion pictures were further evidence of America's changing sexual probity. "The sexual liberation movement of the mid–1970s," one historian has noted, "was particularly aimed at young women who were embracing the laxness of sexual morality as a manifestation of the expanding movement for women's rights." The sexual revolution was finding converts, not only among young people, but their elders as well. "Swingers" would have sex with each other's partners or participate in "more free-form orgies." Finally, there was the rise of the homosexual and lesbian community into mainstream culture and politics.[4]

Not everything about the 1950s was scorned. Beginning in the early Seventies, a nostalgia craze for all things fifties swept the nation, finding expression in various pop culture outlets: motion pictures (*American Graffiti*, *The Last Picture Show*, *Let the Good Times Roll*, *The Way We Were*), television (*Happy Days*, *Laverne and Shirley*, *M*A*S*H*), Broadway (*Grease*), popular music (the return of Elvis Presley and other fifties artists to live performances, the issuing of golden-oldies LPs featuring popular fifties songs, the appearance of fifties-themed pop groups such as Sha-Na-Na, Flash Cadillac and the Continental Kids, and Vince Vance and the Valiants), and clothing styles (the popularity of leather motorcycle jackets, pedal pushers, pleated skirts, and strapless evening dresses). Compared to the traumas of the recent past (political assassinations, Vietnam, racial discord, Watergate, the energy crisis, and rising inflation), the fifties seemed like a tranquil, more innocent and simpler era. A Cleveland DJ explained that "my audience wants to forget its problems and return to — or at least recall — those happy high-school times — the prom, no wars, no riots, no protests, the convertibles and the drive-in." Another DJ felt the fifties music revival afforded young people an opportunity to span the generational divide between them and their elders: "I get the feeling that through this music some of the kids are finding a back-door way of getting together with their parents."[5] Fifties nostalgia also reflected the yearning of some older Americans for the time of their youth before they got caught up with adult responsibilities and sixties turmoil. As was frequently the case in the wake of strife-torn times, people tried to forget the present by recalling an earlier, less complicated period they never experienced themselves or, for the older Americans, wishing for a now irretrievably past era.[6]

Fifties nostalgia, however, overlooked some harsh truths about the decade. "There's no Joe McCarthy revival, and nobody is longing for the days of the H-bomb tests," observed Jeff Greenfield. "People listen to '50s songs and go to '50s movies because it's fun."[7] Still, not all fifties nostalgia ignored the dark side of the era — as was the case with a popular fifties-themed television sitcom of the '70s and the sequel to one of the '70s' most popular fifties-themed motion pictures — both of which touched upon Cold War–era nuclear fears and one of its most familiar manifestations: the bomb shelter. Both would also suggest that bomb shelters could serve purposes other than that for which they were originally intended.

Happy Days and *Grease 2*

One of the television series to ride the wave of fifties nostalgia had initially aired as a February 1973 segment of ABC's *Love, American Style*. When *American Graffiti* scored in movie theaters that same year, *Happy Days* debuted as a mid-season replacement on ABC during the 1973–1974 season. Far removed from the socially relevant Norman Lear sitcoms then airing on CBS, *Happy Days* totally immersed itself in the world of fifties teen life, focusing on the Cunningham family of Milwaukee, Wisconsin, and the adventures of the Cunninghams' son, Richie (played by Ron Howard, already a familiar face to television viewers from his earlier appearances on *The Andy Griffith Show*), and his friend, Potsie Weber (Anson Williams), as they came of age during the fifties. Though it embraced the popular revisionist view of the 1950s,[8] *Happy Days* didn't completely sugarcoat its presentation of the era. Such was the case with its May 7, 1974, installment, "Be the First on Your Block," which focused on how the Cold War tensions of the time affected the Cunningham family—specifically, Richie's father, Howard (Tom Bosley), who resolves to take proactive measures to protect his family.

After viewing an Edward R. Murrow documentary on the Cold War, Howard Cunningham informs his brood that Ernie (Ronnie Schell), a bomb shelter salesman, will be dropping by that evening. When Howard's wife, Marion (Marion Ross), objects to such an idea, saying it will frighten their children, Howard says, "Now listen.... The Russians now have the bomb and they could decide to drop it on us. The Cold War is a fact of life, and everyone, including our children, has got to live with it. Now look, I'm not trying to scare anyone. I'm merely trying to protect my family." Howard Cunningham's argument here mirrors the Eisenhower administration's position that the civil defense frontier extended to the American family, making them the primary agency responsible for domestic safety in the Cold War. Howard proposes to pay for the shelter with the money the family has saved in its vacation fund for a trip to Carlsbad Caverns—an idea that doesn't go over well with the rest of the Cunninghams, who decide to veto the proposed shelter.

When Ernie, the shelter salesman, arrives at the Cunninghams' residence, he immediately plunges into his pitch, only to be informed that they've decided against the shelter.

"You're not going to try harder to sell us?" Richie asks.

"Richie, what I'm trying to sell you is something for your own good.... this is something that I honestly believe in.... You just don't hard sell safety."

When Howard inquires of Ernie if he has a bomb shelter of his own, Ernie doesn't hesitate to answer: "Of course I do.... I like to think of my little bomb shelter as sort of a personal little secret message to Nikita Khrushchev that the good old U.S. of A. is not going to be pushed around.... I mean that it's very possible that, in case of nuclear attack, there are going to be very few survivors left around here to repopulate this beautiful town."

The implied sexual connotations the latter statement holds make Marion Cunningham uncomfortable that her children are hearing it; they, on the other hand, are intrigued. "I'd like to try repopulating," says Richie. When his father expresses shock at these words, Richie remonstrates, "Dad, I just want to do my part as a good American." What emerges here is a theme that would reappear in similar end of the world scenarios: Nuclear war as an excuse for sex, ostensibly to ensure the continuation of the human race.

This theme continues when, asked by Potsie if he's really going to build a shelter, Richie answers affirmatively. "Boy," says Potsie, "have you got it M-A-D-E. It'll be a great place to take the chicks."

"Oh, wait. I don't think that's exactly what my dad has in mind."

"Yeah, but what your dad don't know won't hurt him." When Potsie then asks Richie if he has a place in the shelter reserved for him ("I mean, you wouldn't forget your best friend?"), Richie answers affirmatively but tells him not to spread word of the shelter's existence. Yet, in order to get a date with a girl, Richie has to tell her himself about the shelter. Smooching with him later, she asks for more information about the shelter.

"Well, did you ever think that ours is the first generation to grow up with the bomb?" Richie asks.

"No, I never thought that."

"Well," Richie continues, "it's made our generation different — more serious. Not that I don't like having fun. But ... we're responsible for future generations."

"Future generations?"

"Well, yeah. Just suppose that you and I were in the bomb shelter, and it happened...? Then, afterwards, you and I would have the responsibility of rebuilding, of repopulating this entire town."

"Richie, if I were going with someone and things were ... serious ... could I bring a date to the shelter?"

Presently, word that Richie's father is building a bomb shelter gets out among Richie's friends — all of whom, including Fonzie (Henry Winkler) who rides in on his motorcycle — converge on the Cunningham residence when Howard holds a practice civil defense drill for his family. Aghast at the presence of so many uninvited participants in his shelter space, Howard orders everyone out. The experience alienates Richie's friends from him. Richie confronts his father over the issue:

"Dad, the way I figure it is if they drop the bomb, then I won't have any friends. And if they don't drop the bomb, I won't have any friends. So what good is this bomb shelter?"

Richie's father adamantly holds to his position: "I'll tell you what good it is. If you sit in it, you have peace of mind."

"While all your friends are pounding on the door?" rejoins Richie.

Fed up with his family's resistance to the idea, Howard Cunningham decides to take matters into his own hands, exercising his prerogative as head of the household to build the shelter: "Being the head of the house is a lonely job."

When we next see Howard, he is truly alone: Standing in his shelter space, all by himself, during another civil defense exercise. Richie tells him the rest of the family had had a meeting of their own:

RICHIE: We voted not to survive.... Dad, I don't understand what's happening. You're a nice guy who's talking about trying to lock his friends out.
HOWARD: In the words of Leo Durocher, "Nice guys finish last."
RICHIE: In an atomic war, does anybody finish first?
HOWARD: Are you telling me that living through a bomb isn't worth losing a few friends?
RICHIE: Dad, we figured that, if things come down to somebody dropping the bomb, then we'd better live now than survive later. Understand?

Richie's words finally hit home. Both he and his father break down the rope and stakes demarcating the boundaries of their shelter area.

HOWARD: Richard, what do you think of a man who gets so carried away by his owns fears that he forgets about other people?
RICHIE: I'd say he's human.

With the shelter issue now resolved, Howard Cunningham decides to take his family to see Carlsbad Caverns after all.

The serious message in this sitcom, the utter futility of civil defense measures such as bomb shelters as protection against nuclear war, had already been realized in real life years earlier. By 1955, President Eisenhower and the National Security Council (NSA) realized that the federal government could provide little or no protection to American citizens from the hazards of nuclear war; this realization, however did not stop them from advancing civil defense as a way of "managing nuclear terror" and quashing public resistance to the Cold War effort. Toward that end, the government undertook a massive crusade extolling the benefits of civil defense involving the production of literature, exhibits, motion pictures, and filmstrips. Civil defense advertisements adorned billboards and milk cartons, and were displayed in hotel rooms. Nearly every item of promotional material beamed at the public urged people to make a purchase in behalf of the civil defense effort.

Ultimately, though, the civil defense advertising crusade failed in its objective of persuading the public to make preparations for war. A study commissioned by the Defense Department found that a tiny portion of American families (2.2 percent) ever owned a private shelter, while a 1961 Gallup poll revealed that only 5 percent of those taking part in the survey had "made any changes in [their homes] to protect [themselves] in the event of an enemy nuclear attack."[9]

The antagonistic relationship between Congress and the various federal civil defense agencies meant that the latter consistently lacked funding. To counter this situation, the civil defense agencies were able to generate inexpensive, first-rate advertising material by characterizing civil defense as a public service. In this effort, they were assisted by advertising agencies, newspapers, radio and television outlets, and celebrity endorsements.

The main thrust of the federal civil defense campaign was consumer-oriented. Americans were asked to buy their own civil defense provisions. Such a pitch extolled the virtues of free-enterprise capitalism and individual initiative as opposed to the compulsory, state-run Soviet civil defense system. Consumer purchases on behalf of civil defense could also ensure the continued health of the American economy.[10] Thus, people like Howard Cunningham who purchased shelters for their homes not only were looking out for their family's welfare, they were staving off recession. Those in charge of the civil defense promotional effort appreciated that if they were to convince a nation of consumers of the rightness of their cause, they had to *sell* civil defense as a commercial product. An instance of this was FCDA administrator Val Peterson's defense of utilizing professional advertising methods in an appearance before a House subcommittee in 1954, on the grounds that his agency "is simply using the best American technique to sell something, and we are selling in the most difficult market in the history of the world." On numerous occasions, Peterson likened the FCDA's public information program to the marketing efforts of Coca-Cola, Pabst, Planters Peanuts, General Motors, and the Ford Motor Company.[11]

Nearly all the advertisements created under the eye of the federal civil defense agencies implored Americans to buy items to support civil defense — with the fallout shelter the most costly and most recognized form of civil defense merchandize on the list. After 1958, when private shelters officially became the primary focus of the federal civil defense effort, Washington supervised the production of numerous materials — brochures and motion pictures — promoting shelters. The brochure receiving the broadest dissemination, "The Family Fallout Shelter," a 1959 OCDM booklet, featured plans for five different shelters — with the first and least expensive set stressing a do-it-yourself approach to survival; the price tag for the necessary building materials was merely $150–$200. The remaining blueprints necessitated the services of a contractor and could cost as much as $1,500. The cost of a "deluxe shelter" in the OCDM motion picture *The Invisible Enemy* was $25,000.

In their efforts to sell civil defense to the public, federal officials portrayed shelters as a new kind of insurance the atomic age now required. Possibly cognizant that the insurance angle was too depressing to encourage shelter sales, civil defense publicists also stressed that shelters could be used for purposes other than nuclear war — although the notion of shelters as a playground for sexual shenanigans probably never entered their minds. The Federal Housing Administration (FHA) declared in 1961 that "shelters could be part of the overall rehabilitation of a home or could qualify as a basic improvement. They could serve in a dual role as laundry rooms, dark rooms, studies, etc." Even earlier, the OCDM proclaimed the development of a new above-ground shelter "usable as a spare bedroom." This new design, in the words of OCDM chief Leo Hoegh, was "a better improvement from the property-value standpoint as well as from the standpoint of protecting your family." An article targeting women in a 1959 OCDM newsletter declared that shelters "may be used as a playroom, darkroom, or storage area." In *Walt Builds a Family Fallout Shelter: A How-to-Do-It Project*, a 1961 film co-produced by the National Concrete Masonry Association (NCMA) with assistance from the OCDM, Walt's friend declares that he might build a shelter, especially as he is already considering installing a dark room in his home. Referring to his own hideaway, Walt says, "And when those grandchildren come, it'd be a great place to put them." Similarly, his wife's friend notes that it would also be a great "extra bedroom for company."[12] Civil defense ads, moreover, linked shelters and modernity. At the conclusion of *Walt Builds a Family Fallout Shelter*, Hoegh contends that "no home in America is modern without a family fallout shelter. This is the nuclear age." "The implicit argument in many of these statements," John Gregory Stocke has written, "was that a fallout shelter was as necessary as the most modern appliance."[13]

Private industry also climbed aboard the civil defense bandwagon. Local building contractors were more than willing to lend support to the government civil defense campaign, possibly because, as one contractor phrased it, a fallout shelter was "just a swimming pool upside down."[14] Most likely the business community's recognition of the potential earnings that could be made from civil defense dated to 1951 when the *New York Times* reported an epidemic of "bombshelteritis" in California. The boom quickly subsided, but revived during the tense Cold War period characterizing the end of the Eisenhower Presidency and the beginning of Kennedy's administration, only to fade again after the shelter mania of the early sixties, and then die out completely after the 1963 nuclear test ban treaty and the redirecting of the Cold War toward conflicts in the Third World.[15] Other factors may have contributed to the collapse of the survival industry.

Essentially, a good many Americans simply believed that the sheer destructiveness of nuclear weapons negated the effectiveness of fallout shelters or other civil defense measures. Other people subscribed to the belief that the survivors of such a war might envy the dead — and thus weren't eager to invest in shelters. On the other hand, those people who were willing to invest in a shelter were likely discouraged from doing so because of civil defense's ability to attract con artists. Many shelters failed to comply with federal standards, and some were indeed death traps, lacking appropriate ventilation and liable to flood easily. Numerous shelter salesmen also played the fear card to get people to purchase shelters. Despite the government's efforts to rein in fraud, the damage swindlers inflicted on the shelter industry proved irreparable. Moreover, the kind of fear necessary to sell shelters, directly confronting people with the genuine possibility of nuclear war, was something they chose not to dwell on — as Val Peterson acknowledged in a 1955 report to a Senate subcommittee when he noted that "all of this can probably be summed up in the fact that continuous readiness for possible nuclear attack requires that people live in constant apprehension. This, in large measure, they simply refuse to do." Civil defense was a reminder of just how ephemeral the affluence of the time was, that it was recently removed from the Great Depression, and that, historically, Western civilization had only a short time earlier found the way to remedy such essential economic problems as starvation and plague. An atomic war could easily wipe out such gains — and reduce everything to a primitive level. Civil defense also entailed sacrifice, something that Americans, after the long years of depression, war, and consumer shortages, no longer wanted to think about. In the words of U.S. Army General Benjamin W. Childlaw, "Simply put, it is possible to have convenience if you want to tolerate insecurity, but if you want security, you must be prepared for inconvenience." American consumers opted for convenience.[16]

The harsh realities of the 1950s, such as nuclear war and bomb shelters, may have seemed less unpleasant to subsequent generations because they hadn't experienced such unpleasantries firsthand and because the passage of time had softened the sharp edges of the '50s. Thus, civil defense could be viewed in a nostalgic, almost comedic light. *Happy Days* was one such example. Another was provided by the 1982 feature film *Grease 2*. A sequel to the 1978 film adaptation of the Broadway play *Grease*, the film chronicles the efforts of an Australian student, Michael Carrington (Maxwell Caufield), to win the hand of Stephanie Zinone (Michelle Pfeiffer), a member of the Pink Ladies, Rydell High School's girl gang. Learning that Stephanie's ideal man is the biker type, Michael earns money to buy himself a motorcycle by writing essays for other students, composing these literary works in his uncle's fallout shelter (the film is set in 1961, making shelters a timely topic). Upon seeing the nuclear hideaway when he comes to pick up his essay, one of Michael's clients, DiMucci (Peter Frechette), observes that it is "a neat joint ... it's private. Good for homework and other activities involving student bodies." Later deciding to put his observation to the test, DiMucci brings his girlfriend, Sharon, (Maureen Teefy) to the shelter. When Sharon expresses doubts about coming there, DiMucci, tries to calm her: "You trust President Kennedy, right?.... Kennedy says we got to be prepared for a *nucleid* war." To make certain everything goes according to plan, DiMucci has arranged for some friends to secretly wait outside the shelter and, at the right minute, turn on an air raid siren to make his girl think an actual attack is imminent. DiMucci tries to convince Sharon that for patriotic reasons she should have sex with him before they're blown to bits. Finally convinced that sacrificing her virginity is in America's best interest, Sharon decides it would be better if they performed their patriotic duty at *her* house. Scurrying over to the shelter door, she opens it to discover DiMucci's friends waiting outside where they've been trying to eavesdrop on the proceedings inside. Enraged, she hurries out.

As can be seen from all this, both *Grease 2* and *Happy Days* suggested that shelters weren't such grim places after all; they could even be fun when put to uses other than their original intent. Such an idea wasn't limited solely to film and television. Noting the sizable number of science-fiction stories involving shelters that were published in 1961 and 1962, when shelters were a hot national topic, Paul Brians, in his survey of nuclear writings, surmised that nuclear fiction, like the culture, spurned shelters:

> Fall-out shelters have been used in a number of ways in fiction: as a high-pressure environment for the blossoming of love affairs, as a refuge for religious cultists, as emotional pressure cookers provoking violent conflict, and even as time-travel machines. Indeed they have usually served every purpose except that for which real bomb shelters are ostensibly designed: the protection of their inhabitants from blast and radiation. Whatever their perspective, all but a handful of authors writing about shelters view them as metaphors for racial suicide, a symbol of the self-destructing nature of nuclear weapons, which make us our own prisoners of war.[17]

Like the Baldwins' running the roadblock meant to keep "invaders" from overrunning surrounding communities in *Panic in Year Zero!*, the notion of the fallout shelter as a make-out place in *Grease 2* was an instance of art imitating life. For some adolescents and young adults, the possibility of nuclear destruction during the Cuban missile crisis was an occasion, not of fear, but a chance that offered "good fortune." Literary agent David Obst recalled how he sought to forfeit his virginity by asking his girlfriend "whether she wanted to live without ever having made love."[18] Obst had hooked up with Jill, a popular girl in school, who seemingly was way out of his league: Girls League vice president, pom-pom girl, and endowed with a great personality and an astonishing figure. "She had become that most extraordinary of suburban American creatures: well rounded." On the day they were to meet for a study date, President Kennedy appeared on television to announce the presence of Soviet missiles in Cuba. For Obst, this both constituted the manifestation of his "worst fears of nuclear annihilation" and placed his date with Jill in jeopardy. In the midst of Kennedy's address, Jill telephoned to say she thought it would be better to stay home and be with family that evening, a sentiment Obst understood.

Hanging up the phone and returning to the TV, Obst suddenly realized he was going to die a virgin!

The day after Kennedy's speech, Jill began clinging to Obst, seeking comfort. "The world might be coming to an end," Obst would recall of that moment, "but I'd never been happier in my life."

As Soviet vessels neared the American blockade line around Cuba, Obst told Jill that, in the event Khrushchev tried to penetrate the blockade, war might result. "This could be out last sunset ... would you like to watch it with me on the beach?" Jill consented. For the occasion, Obst borrowed his mother's car. "We sat, looking out at the Pacific ocean, listening to the radio. I had one arm around Jill and she had her head on my shoulder. I kind of wanted to change the station to find some make-out music, but there was nothing on but news."

Suddenly there was an announcement that 20 Russian vessels had come to a dead stop. When the Soviet fleet began reversing course, Secretary of State Dean Rusk said, "We're eyeball to eyeball and I think the other fellow just blinked."

"In my car," Obst wrote, "Jill gave me the biggest and deepest kiss I'd ever had. I too blinked."

The following day, Jill accepted Obst's invitation to come to his house after school. No one else was there as they watched Kennedy's UN ambassador Adlai Stevenson challenge the Soviet representative to deny the presence of Soviet missiles in Cuba. During the course of this televised encounter, Obst kissed Jill and asked if she would go out Saturday night. When Stevenson produced photographic evidence of the missiles' presence in Cuba, Jill kissed Obst: "Yes, I'd love to go out Saturday night."

On Friday, the Cubans feverishly continued work on the missile sites. "Their first missiles would be ready for firing sometime" that day. Obst desired "the world to survive until Saturday. At school, people said good-bye for the weekend as if they might not ever see each other again. It was very emotional."

The place Obst had chosen to consummate his relationship with Jill was a fallout shelter his friend Jeff's father had built: "It was a large, comfortable room with garish green concrete walls, matching pre–Astro Turf plastic carpeting, and a ton of storage space for such useful items as bottled water, canned food, a Sterno stove, a portable radio, and a Geiger counter." The facility was also equipped with "a couple of shovels ... so the family could dig out after the war. It was a great place to hang out and, most importantly"—for what Obst had in mind—"it had two large beds."

Luckily for Obst, Jeff's parents were in the East, visiting his ill grandmother. Obst managed to persuade Jeff to give him the key to the shelter. The missile crisis reached its height on Saturday, October 27, 1962. In the midst of the seeming drift to nuclear Armageddon, Obst's primary issue was finding a rubber. Obst and Jill were going on a double-date with Jeff and his girlfriend JoAnne. After going out to dinner, everyone was to return to Jeff's residence. Obst's plan

> was to take Jill into the fall-out shelter and talk about the future—or, rather, about the very likely possibility that we had no future. Okay, my strategy was pretty simple. "Jill," I'd say, "there's a pretty good chance that this is going to be our last night on earth. Do you really want to have lived without ever having made love?" Or something like that.

That evening, Obst and Jill sat in the backseat of Jeff's car, holding each other as they listened to the grim news. Obst casually told Jill about Jeff's father's fallout shelter "and that it might be a good place to spend the evening." Jill looked confused. While cruising Sunset Strip, Obst and Jeff almost got into an altercation with three people wearing Nazi regalia that was broken up by the police. Held at West Hollywood police headquarters for disturbing the peace, Obst and his friends were bailed out by his parents. Returning to her home, Jill whispered to Obst that she'd like to see him at the shelter the following morning.

Rising early on what he believed would be the most important day of his life, Obst hurriedly drove to Jill's residence where he was warmly greeted by her parents, then by Jill herself. The reason for their joy was word that the Soviet government had ordered the dismantling of the missiles and their return to the Soviet Union.

Declining Jill's and her parents' invitation to attend church with them, Obst drove back home, suddenly realizing that he and Fidel Castro "were probably the two most disappointed men in the Western Hemisphere."[19]

Jill may not have understood Obst's intentions, but other young girls at the time received clear warnings about remaining chaste during the missile crisis. Such was the case with a female sophomore at West Chester University, who recalled being summoned to an assembly where officials counseled young women not to surrender their chastity to doomsday warnings.[20]

Fifties nostalgia made nuclear war seem less frightening. But, in the 1980s, nuclear anxieties would again become real, attaining their greatest level since the Kennedy era–setting the stage for the most controversial pop culture treatment of such fears.

6

Reagan, the Nuclear Freeze Movement, and *The Day After*

At the same time America was waxing nostalgic for all things 1950s, the country was turning right politically. Elected governor of California in 1966, former film star Ronald Reagan unsuccessfully sought the Republican presidential nomination in 1976. Though Watergate harmed the GOP and Richard Nixon's successor, Gerald Ford, Jimmy Carter's ill-starred presidency came to symbolize the woes bedeviling America during the '70s. Economic miseries and an unremitting oil crisis prevented the Democratic administration from realizing the promises of the liberal Democratic Party. America's economic problems, along with a rise in Middle Eastern terrorism, and a prevailing sense that the nation's morals were disintegrating, produced a mounting aura of malaise that would come to characterize the late '70s.

The frustrations of this period spurred the rise of the religious right as a national and cultural force. The origins of this movement, which sought to amalgamate fundamentalist religious tenets and politics, lay in the 1964 Goldwater presidential campaign, which merged McCarthyite anti-communism with anxieties about "secular humanism." By exploiting concerns about women's and homosexual rights, the religious right made headway during the '70s. As the decade ended, the movement gave life to the New Right which pledged, in one historian's words, to "restore a world of simple virtues, an old America based on family, church and the work ethic."[1]

The Ford-Carter years were also an unhappy time for American anti-communists, who saw their warnings about the communist movement fall into disrepute. The most grievous transgressions of countersubversive anti-communism were dug up from secret FBI files, and presented to the public as anti-communism's true face. Meanwhile, those individuals against whom the anti-communists had sounded the alarm were recast as martyrs in a shameful crusade and the historical events that had prompted American hostility toward domestic communism and the Soviet Union were cast aside. Anti-communists were appalled as the Ford and Carter administrations substituted containment of international communism in favor of accord with the Soviet Union — a state that some believed was no worse than others with whom the United States had dealt. All of this was apparently giving the Soviets the impression that they could pursue the Brezhnev Doctrine, which laid the entire world open to Soviet designs, without any countermoves on the part of the United States. Hence, Cuban troops were utilized in Africa in support of Marxist governments fighting anti-communist uprisings, while Soviet-backed revolutions triumphed in Laos, Ethiopia, Mozambique, Afghanistan, and Cambodia.

A pair of events in late 1979 — the seizure of the American embassy in Teheran, Iran, by Iranian militants and the Soviet invasion of Afghanistan — seemingly validated the fears of those who believed that the diminution of American defenses had loosened a restraining hand on Soviet ambitions. In an about-face of his position regarding the Soviets arising from the Afghan invasion, President Carter withdrew the American ambassador from Moscow, terminated grain sales and technology exports to the Soviets, halted fishing privileges, withdrew the SALT II accord from Senate consideration, and, in April 1980, announced a boycott of that summer's Olympic games in Moscow. He also dispatched a greatly enhanced defense budget request to Congress and planned to reinstate draft registration. On April 24, 1980, Carter launched an ultimately abortive rescue mission to free the American hostages in Iran — a disaster that anti-communists viewed as "the lowest point of America's fortunes in this century."[2]

By then the anti-nuclear movement, which, like civil defense, had disappeared from the public spotlight, had been galvanized once more to activism. The 1963 test-ban treaty was one of several factors that contributed to the movement's decline. Exhausted by their years of struggle, many anti-nuclear protestors temporarily withdrew from the cause. The 1970s had witnessed a number of Soviet-American arms control accords. The 1972 Strategic Arms Limitation Treaty (SALT) I restricted the number of nuclear delivery weapons, while permitting the installation of multiple warheads on a single missile. The same year's Anti-Ballistic Missile (ABM) Treaty limited the United States and Russia to only two ABM sites, and curbed the number of missiles. Finally, and most importantly, the anti–Vietnam crusade became the primary focus of the protest effort after 1963.[3] Save for brief appearances in fiction and popular music, nuclear issues also faded from television and film after 1963.[4]

By the early 1980s, the nuclear issue was once more in the forefront of public and pop-culture consciousness, owing in part to one of the most controversial broadcasts in the history of American television — *The Day After*. Even before its network airing on November 20, 1983, the broadcast ignited a furor — likely pleasing the network that aired it, ABC, as it came during a ratings sweeps period. A letter to President Reagan from a nine-year-old Kansas City girl (advocating that the United States and Russia exchange workers to disassemble the other country's stockpiles of nuclear weapons) was transformed into a major story by the Associated Press. Another letter to Reagan, this one from the mayor of Lawrence, Kansas, where *The Day After* was filmed, extended an invitation on the mayor's part to host a summit between the American president and Yuri Andropov. "Nuclear freeze groups obtained advance copies of" the film "and organized" teach-ins nationwide. So great was the attention surrounding the film, an audience reckoned at one hundred million tuned their televisions to ABC the evening of its airing — making it the second-largest TV audience in history.[5]

The Reagan Doctrine and the Nuclear Freeze Movement

In 1980, Ronald Reagan finally won the presidency. In both the political and cultural realms, the Reagan years (1981–1989) signified conservatism. Politically, Reagan's program featured such traditional Republican themes as larger defense budgets, reduced taxes, and far fewer social welfare programs. Culturally, the Reagan era was characterized by a dramatic rise in the religious Right, featuring a new kind of politically adept and outspoken fundamentalist who would dominate American culture. Motivated by a literal interpretation of the Bible and committed to the notion that '50s America was a better, less complicated, and more devout place and time, the "moral majority" would work to reverse the cultural permissiveness and experimentation that characterized the past 20 years.[6]

During his campaign, Reagan promised to renew America both in its power and its determination to lead the free world in the anti-communist crusade. At his initial press conference after taking office, Reagan branded détente "a one-way street" that the Soviets had employed to advance their own objectives. Bringing his long-standing anti-communism with him into the presidency, Reagan declared that it was the Soviets' conviction that they could take any action to "further their cause, meaning they have the right to commit any crime, to lie, to cheat in order to attain that [end]." Reagan's worldview resembled the simple value system of an old Hollywood film: communists were the villains, the West at the helm of a "crusade for freedom" that would consign Communism to the "ash heap of history." Two years into his administration he characterized the rulers of the Soviet Union as "the focus of evil in the modern world" and their realm "an evil empire." Reagan totally accepted the rejection of détente and enhanced the defense spending Carter had initiated as the primary thrust of American foreign policy under his watch.

Reagan wasted no time in making good on his pledge of renewing American military might. Within two weeks of moving into the White House, he boosted the defense budget by $32.6 billion. Defense Secretary Caspar Weinberger declared his task was "to rearm America." During Reagan's first term, defense spending climbed by almost 50 percent — soaring to 7 percent of the gross domestic product. Among the armaments the Pentagon acquired was the B-1 bomber (which Jimmy Carter had junked), an expanded navy, and reinforcements of conventional armaments. New defense guidance directives advocated plans to fight a nuclear war "over a protracted period," urging "nuclear decapitation" of the Soviet political and military leadership should war begin and he emphasized that America must "prevail" in any nuclear war, and called attention to the necessity of "special forces" in clandestine operations. The bill for all this was footed by enormous budget deficits and cutbacks on domestic welfare programs. During the 1980s the national debt rose from $1 trillion to $4 trillion.[7]

American rearmament was one aspect of the Reagan Doctrine. It also included backing of anti-communist uprisings in the third world and anti-communist dissidents within the Soviet bloc itself—with the latter playing the crucial role of hastening the Soviet Union's eventual demise.[8] Of all the components of the Reagan Doctrine, the one that stirred the most controversy was the installation of intermediate-range missiles in Europe.[9]

The controversy originated with the Soviets' deployment in 1977 of the SS-20, a triple warhead mobile missile. This was intended to comply with the restrictions stipulated by the 1972 SALT I accords regarding missiles, the range of which exceeded 5,000 kilometers. Because the SS-20 imperiled all of Europe and Asia, President Carter, pressured by America's European allies, the Germans especially, consented to the installation of 108 Pershing IIs and 464 cruise missiles on European soil to counter the SS-20s. Simultaneously, he offered not to deploy the "Euromissiles" should the Soviets consent to new restrictions on the SS-20s. This was Carter's "dual-track strategy." The Euromissile issue would give rise to what became known as the "nuclear freeze movement."[10]

By the conclusion of the Vietnam conflict in 1975, the American anti-nuclear campaign had surfaced again to take on matters relating to disarmament and nuclear proliferation. During the seventies, the movement initially focused on nuclear power and was scattered over several hundred local bodies.

Reinforced by the new environmental activism, the anti-nuclear movement took on the hazards arising from nuclear power plants, the release of radioactivity, the production of fissionable material for utilization in nuclear weapons, and the discarding of nuclear waste. Inspired by the success of anti-nuclear activists in Wyhl, Germany, who successfully blocked construction of a nuclear reactor, American protestors across the country opposed the construction of nuclear reactors at Seabrook, New Hampshire, and California's Diablo Canyon. By the time of the 1979 Three Mile Island crisis, the anti-nuclear drive was burgeoning into an expanded crusade against nuclear weapons. The Mobilization for Survival, created in 1977, joined 280 groups, among them 40 national organizations, to urge governmental action banishing both nuclear power and nuclear weapons, and to bring the escalating arms race to a conclusion. The Mobilization for Survival was intended to amalgamate various activists — supporters of the anti-nuclear testing campaign of the late '50s and early '60s, the anti–Vietnam war and anti-nuclear power protest movements of the '60s and '70s. Swiftly growing, the Mobilization for Survival became a potent anti-nuclear conglomeration seeking to create affiliations with religious organizations, in the manner of the civil rights movement, and with women's and environmental crusades.

The anti-nuclear movement's resurgence during the late '70s prompted calls for disarmament on the part of the American Friends Service Committee, the Fellowship of Reconciliation, and the Catholic Conference of 350 bishops. Other groups — the Physicians for Social Responsibility, the National Organization for Women, the Women's International League for Peace and Freedom, and Women Strike for Peace — enlisted in the cause as well. During the 1980 Women's Pentagon Action, 2,000 women circled the Pentagon to the sound of drumbeats and moans, obstructing entrance to the building, and yelling such chants as "Take the toys from the boys." The arrest of 150 of the protestors drew interest from the media and served to inspire others to become part of the crusade against employment of nuclear weapons.[11]

Ronald Reagan, more than anyone else, was responsible for further energizing the anti-nuclear crusade and creating what Richard Perle dubbed "the nuclear allergy." The Reagan administration revealed that it would boost spending on nuclear weapons by 40 percent, and administration officials frequently talked about "winning" nuclear conflicts: One said, "We are living in a pre-war and not a postwar world"; another declared that the Soviets could either change their system or go to war.[12] With its new push to rearm America, the Reagan administration also breathed new life into civil defense. In a notorious interview with the *Los Angeles Times*'s Robert Schemer, Deputy Under Secretary of Defense T. K. Jones asserted that Americans could survive a nuclear attack: "Dig a hole, cover it with a couple of doors and then throw three feet of dirt on top," he said. "It's the dirt that does it.... If there are enough shovels to go around, everybody's going to make it."[13] With that in mind, and notwithstanding the sensible doubts on the part of the Joint Chiefs of Staff and the Office of Management and Budget, the administration chose to underwrite a major civil-defense program. Its request for civil defense appropriations in the 1983 fiscal year — $252 million — was twice the sum of the year before. FEMA, in the meantime, initiated a seven-year plan, the price of which was estimated at $4.2 billion.

Acting on the somewhat absurd notion that warnings of an attack would furnish a full week for preparation, the Reagan administration revived the evacuation idea, proposing that millions of people be relocated into host areas in the countryside. Acknowledging the enormous complications such a relocation would entail, FEMA's Louis O. Guiffrida nevertheless asserted, "But do we just throw up our hands and say, 'Forget it, the job's too big'? Do we give up?"[14] Shelters were another option to which the administration gave thought. Rejecting an extremely costly estimate of $70 billion for permanent sanctuaries for the entire American population, FEMA chose another course: temporary shelters in rural areas to be constructed with the assistance of evacuees. FEMA was delighted that private companies, like the American Telephone and Telegraph Company, had started fabricating their shelter facilities for high-ranking executives. Simultaneously, government officials began preparing directives for sustaining the American economic system in the postwar era. In the words of a Federal Reserve System brochure: "Victory in a nuclear war will belong to the country that recovers first." Federal Reserve banks would strive to honor all checks, "including those drawn on destroyed banks," explained a National Plan for Emergency Preparedness. Moreover, credit cards could still be used in the post-attack economy.

Critics found the new plans mind boggling. Columnist Ellen Goodman "couldn't decide whether to giggle or shiver" after perusing FEMA's publications. "The calm, chatty descriptions of how to survive nuclear war with just a touch of inconvenience had what Yale professor of psychiatry Robert J. Lifton calls 'the logic of madness,'" she wrote in one piece. FEMA's theme song, she wrote in another, was: "Pack up your troubles in your old family buggy and drive, drive, drive."[15] T. K. Jones's credulous words of advice were ridiculed by folksinger Fred Small in his 1983 album *The Heart of the Appaloosa*:

Just dig a hole in the ground
Climb right on down
Lay some boards on top of you
And sprinkle dirt around
You won't have to be dead

If you only plan ahead
You'll be glad you kept a shovel on hand.[16]

Less sardonically, Congressman Edward Markey declared that civil defense was still merely "a band-aid over the holocaust," and fellow critics repeated the same argument voiced in earlier times: civil defense was incapable of furnishing satisfactory protection from a nuclear war. "Yet," as Allan M. Winkler has noted, "the government persisted in its approach for several years, until it became preoccupied with still another kind of protective shield."[17]

Reagan's hard line toward the Soviets was intended to accomplish two things: To pave the way for enactment of his military preparedness program and forestall a Soviet challenge to the new American administration while the latter focused its primary attention on the nation's economic situation. But it also had a third and unintentional consequence: It prodded millions to protest in Europe and generated an unparalleled outpouring of anti-nuclear feeling in America.

Numerous people — peace activists such as Helen Caldicott and Randall Forsberg and an increasing number of church leaders — declared that the way to call a halt to the nuclear arms race was merely for the superpowers to "freeze" their stockpiles of nuclear armaments. Such a concept wasn't new. It had initially been proposed in the early seventies by Richard Nixon's arms negotiator, Gerard Smith, and offered a pair of simultaneous advantages: It provided a means to halt the arms race while maintaining nuclear deterrence. The concept received national notice in November 1980 when it won 59 percent of the vote in a nonbinding referendum in western Massachusetts. Support for the freeze gathered momentum and quickly led to the creation of a new national organization with chapters nationwide and a peace crusade involving an unprecedented number of participants — far surpassing those who had been involved in prior crusades in American history.

The example of America's Roman Catholic bishops proved inspirational for others to get involved. Defying pressures form prominent laymen with close connections to the Reagan administration, the bishops issued a pastoral letter declaring that it was immoral to employ nuclear weapons, except as a response to a nuclear attack, and that it was also immoral to amass such armaments, except in the interim, while disposing of them. Going beyond this, some bishops advocated an emphatic condemnation, unilateral disarmament, tax resistance, and refusal to take part in the fabrication of such arms. When they were criticized for lacking the expertise pertaining to the relevant issues, the bishops declared that the Bomb involved the paramount moral issue confronting humanity, hence the only apparent qualification people required to speak out about the nuclear issue was, in Richard J. Barnet's words, a matter of "moral sense and a searching mind."[18] Thus other people, who, as a rule, wouldn't get involved in social activism, chose to do so as the Freeze movement appeared to furnish an avenue for them to have a sense of control over their future. "It was as much a movement for democracy as for peace."[19] Nine states and more than 50 cities — among them Philadelphia, Chicago, Galveston, and Miami — approved referenda supporting the freeze. In June 1982 Central Park was the site for a peace demonstration including nearly one million participants. The finding of some opinion polls revealed that nearly eight out of ten Americans supported a bilateral, verifiable freeze, and members of both the House and Senate hastened to show their backing of it.

The initial response of Reagan and his chief advisers to the nuclear freeze movement was harsh. On October 4, 1982, the president charged that the movement was "inspired by not the sincere, honest people who want peace, but by some who want the weakening of America and so are manipulating honest ... and sincere people." He followed up this accusation, just weeks later, with another that foreign agents were dispatched to "help instigate" the freeze. Other administration officials such as Robert McFarlane presented a less sharp but equally dismissive line: Because freeze supporters were unfamiliar with the technical issues pertaining to arms control, they had no right to speak out about it. Reagan's argument that America was dangerously "behind" notwithstanding, most Americans apparently believed that the differences in the nuclear forces were of no substance. Polls revealed that backing for military spending and Reagan's stance on the nuclear issue were sharply dwindling.[20]

Anxieties arising from talk by members of the Reagan administration concerning a "winnable nuclear war" were reflected in a pair of popular films, both released during the early 1980s. The fifth biggest moneymaker of 1983, *WarGames* focused on what could happen in the event that an unauthorized individual — in this case a teenager — could access the superpower weapons system, as when the film's protagonist, using his own computer, unintentionally locks into the American nuclear defense system. Enjoying great popularity with college audiences, *The Atomic Café* (1982), an independently produced documentary film featuring clips from 1950s nuclear war and civil defense propaganda films, effectively showed how film was utilized for propaganda purposes during the early years of the Cold War; it also disparaged the idea that the majority of Americans could survive a nuclear attack.[21] Elsewhere on the pop culture front, for the first time in years, a mushroom cloud appeared on the cover of an issue of *Time* magazine. Taking exception to the administration's conception of organized crisis relocation, the CBS television series *Lou Grant* dramatized how even a *rumored* nuclear attack could, in all probability, generate turmoil in a teeming city. "In addition to film and television,

Paul S. Boyer estimates that here at least nine novels and some forty science fiction stories of the early 1980s explored themes related to nuclear war."[22]

And, arguably, the most memorable pop culture production to weigh in on the debate over Reagan's nuclear defense policies was the made-for-television film *The Day After*, a production that would sire as much controversy as the nuclear freeze movement itself.

"TV's Nuclear Nightmare"[23]

ABC Motion Pictures president Brandon Stoddard called it "the most important movie we or anyone else have ever made."[24] Unlike other nuclear apocalypse stories that dwell on those most closely involved in decisions that could ignite nuclear war (politicians, generals, diplomats, and soldiers), *The Day After* focused on those on the opposite end of the spectrum. "The film is simply about you and me," observed screenwriter Edward Hume. "It shows what would happen to ordinary Americans after a nuclear war." Network executives took great efforts to emphasize *The Day After*'s apolitical stance. In Brandon Stoddard's words, "I don't think audiences will be able to find a political statement. It does not say there would be less nuclear bombs or more nuclear bombs. We do not deal in great detail with the causes." Vice-President Stu Samuels declared, "We are not a news division. We do not have the franchise to editorialize. This is not a docudrama because, thank God, it didn't happen." The film's director, Nicholas Meyer, dissented: "ABC gave us millions of dollars to go on prime time TV and call Ronald Reagan a liar."[25] Janet Michaud, executive director of the Campaign Against Nuclear War, applauded *The Day After* for "bringing what is the most critical issue of our times right into America's living rooms." Conservatives didn't share that view: *National Review* publisher William A. Rusher took the film to task for contributing to "an ignorant public hysteria."[26]

"From the television industry's perspective," noted *Newsweek* at the time of *The Day After*'s airing, the fact that the production was ever broadcast in the first place "may be the most remarkable thing about it." From day one of prime-time television's existence, "The networks have operated under two sacrosanct dictums: never leave viewers politically aroused or emotionally depressed." Thus, it came as a surprise that ABC, given its history of airing escapist fare such as *The Love Boat* and *Fantasy Island*, would break those rules. Brandon Stoddard, the man who dreamed up *The Day After*, was already responsible for such productions as *Roots* and *Friendly Fire*; when he submitted the idea for a televised end-of-the-world story, his network colleagues at first were astonished by his proposal. "Most ABC officials felt that if you put on anything terrifying, no one would watch and no one would make any money," Stoddard explained; he then added, "Of course, that still may be true."

After three directors declined to helm *The Day After*, Stoddard found his man in Nicholas Meyer, who had written a best-seller (*The Seven Percent Solution*) and directed such box-office successes as *Time After Time* and *Star Trek II: The Wrath of Khan*.[27] A "bankable" director owing to *Star Trek II*'s success, Meyer understood why the others approached for the directorial assignment for *The Day After* had rejected it: "Who wanted to learn about this god-awful stuff...? Like most people, I preferred to avoid the entire terrifying topic. What sort of person willingly immerses himself in the prospect of nuclear annihilation? Everyone knows the bombs are out there, Damoclean swords dangling over our necks, and that knowledge — semiconsciously carried around inside our heads — is more than sufficient for most of us."[28] A session with his psychoanalyst changed Meyer's mind about directing the film: While he was discussing his feelings about the project, Meyer's analyst broke in with "one of the most dreadful (and useful)" words anyone ever told Meyer.

"I think this is where we find out who you really are," he said. It was a phrase that proved quite helpful to Meyer in bringing others aboard the project.[29]

One person who readily signed on was actor Jason Robards, who played a doctor in the film who loses his wife in the nuclear holocaust. Meyer had previously met Robards at a friend's house, and now chance brought them together again on a flight to New York. Asked by Robards what he was currently working on, Meyer explained that he would be filming a movie about nuclear war that summer in Lawrence, Kansas.

"Really."

With no television executives or agents around, Meyer decided on the spot to offer Robards a part in the film: "So, Jason, what are you doing this August?"

"Not a thing."

"Would you like to be in this movie?"

"Beats signing petitions," Robards replied unequivocally. Meyer, who had a copy of the script with him in his suitcase, promised to show it to him when they landed.

"Great." A handshake sealed the deal. Unfortunately, upon arriving in New York, Meyer discovered that TWA had lost his bag.

"It's a really great script," he told Robards as he searched the luggage carousel for his missing suitcase.

"Don't worry about it," Robards simply said. "Just have someone get it to me one of these days."[30]

Meyer believed *The Day After*, originally conceived as a four-hour, two-night "event" broadcast, could be shortened to a one-night presentation that would have a greater impact on the audience. Moreover, Meyer doubted that the film would actually air: "You don't really think you're going to get this thing on the air, do you? I mean, the American people watch *Charlie's Angels* — they're not prepared to be exposed to anything like this."

"Oh, it'll go on the air alright," he was assured.[31]

Before filming began, Meyer discovered that the script he had agreed to direct was going to be censored by the network's Standards and Practices department — an idea he found baffling: "If they were gonna censor this script, wouldn't it have been more appropriate to censor it *before* I was offered it to direct...? Seems to me if they had wanted to tone it down they should have done that *before* I agreed to direct it." The network objected to the use of a term racially objectionable to Japanese members of the viewing audience; a scene in which a character bought a diaphragm (here, the network wouldn't assume a stance viewed as pro-birth control); and the portrayal in the film of the electromagnetic pulse (EMP) — an effect that occurs in a nuclear blast that neutralizes electricity. ("They were scientific experts now. We found ourselves arguing over scientific data none of us was qualified to evaluate.")[32]

When filming commenced in Lawrence, Kansas, Meyer disregarded every deletion the network had demanded. After production had been underway for about ten days, Meyer received an outraged telephone call from Los Angeles.

"Nick, what do you think you're doing!?"

"Shooting the script you offered me to direct."

"But we agreed, *you* agreed —"

"'I agreed to nothing,' I pointed out, having been waiting for this moment, 'except to shoot the script you offered me. But rather than have this discussion,' I went on, by way of preempting his next expostulation, 'let me make this easy for you. Fire me.'"

"What?"

"Fire me. I didn't want to make this depressing movie anyway. Fire me, and I'll have a perfect out."

"You're kidding."

"Not me. Look, you're only ten days in, it shouldn't be too hard to reshoot. You get a new director and some new actors —"

"New actors?"

"'Well, if I walk, Jason's gonna walk, maybe JoBeth Williams, too, but that shouldn't be a problem,' I hastened to assure him, warming to my topic. 'You just replace Jason, replace JoBeth, replace Gayne Rescher (Meyer's cinematographer on *Star Trek II*), and before you know it, you'll be —'"

"Hang on." There was a pause, then the call resumed.

"Nick, we'll get back to you."

"Do that." Meyer's caller got back in touch with him the following day —
the tone of his voice this time characterized by "patronizing serenity."

"N-i-c-k, it's your movie, you shoot it the way you want, but, as an
officer of ABC Circle films, I must tell you that legally none of that stuff can
be in the picture."

"Fine, you've told me."

When all was said and done, not a single scene Meyer filmed — including
the ones pertaining to the diaphragm and the EMP — was excised.[33]

In the wake of this confrontation with ABC, filming on *The Day After*,
first in Lawrence, Kansas, and subsequently at an abandoned Los Angeles
hospital, proceeded quite satisfactorily.

Once filming was completed, Meyer faced the task of editing the footage
he shot into a completed film. He persuaded the network to let him edit the
production down from the original two-night "event" broadcast; if they didn't
like it the way he cut it, he would restore it to the way they wanted it. ABC's
decision to let him proceed in this manner was rooted in the network's problems in finding sponsors for the broadcast, and, if ABC couldn't acquire sponsors, "it made no sense to stretch out the movie beyond a single night."
Commodore computers and one of the smaller car rental companies were the
sole sponsors to remain with the program. At a running time of two hours
and twenty minutes, Meyer's one-night version of *The Day After* was screened
before a gathering of network brass. The latter's reaction, when the final scene
had played out, was astonishing: All of them were crying. "These were television executives," Meyer wrote, "but they were also human beings — they
had families, they had children, they had lives of their own, a stake in the
planet like everyone else — and they had been deeply and obviously affected
by what they had seen.

"Based on their response, I imagined I was home free."[34]

Nothing could have been further from the truth. A six-month tussle now
ensued over the production's final form. Meyer's editor, Bill Dornisch, refused
to edit the film according to ABC's directives — an act of defiance that cost him
his job. Meyer himself exited the project for a time while someone he referred
to in his memoirs as "X" — an aide to Brandon Stoddard — entered the editing
room, with an editor of his own, only to make a mess of the production. In the
version that emerged from X's labors, the Soviets were depicted as the instigators
of the conflict. The new version left Meyer devastated. Asked about the film
by *Chicago Sun-Times* columnist Marilyn Reed, Meyer suggested in his own
way that the film had been re-edited due to corporate pressure. The threat
worked: Meyer was called back to "repair X's carnage in the cutting room."[35]

Ultimately, *The Day After was* censored, "and," Meyer wrote, "many
things weren't the way I intended them." Moreover, it "was preceded and

succeeded by all manner of disclaimers"; just the same it had sufficient impact to unsettle the likes of William F. Buckley, Jr., and Phyllis Schlafly. The latter pair "ran around the country like Chicken Littles, warning anyone who'd listen that the sky was falling, while on its editorial page the *New York Times* demanded to know why Nicholas Meyer was doing Yuri Andropov's work for him."[36] To Meyer's astonishment, the sole interest the press had in *The Day After* wasn't its content but whether America or Russia instigated the nuclear war the film presented. Subsequently, Meyer realized that the press, like everyone else, couldn't face the issue of nuclear war and its aftermath directly — which, in the case of the press, signified commercial disaster, preferring instead to focus on the safer, more comfortable issue of who started the war in the first place.

Prior to its telecast, the Reagan White House viewed *The Day After* and called to present what Meyer called "editing 'notes'!" Looking back on the episode, Meyer wasn't surprised that this happened. "The President, an old Hollywood pro, doubtless had always longed for final cut. (So did the Army, when we asked for their cooperation before shooting. We didn't get their helicopters; they didn't get to rewrite our script)."[37]

Interviewed by CBS News for a *60 Minutes* segment on *The Day After*, Dr. Jerry Falwell, head of the Moral Majority, voiced his opinion that the film served, in correspondent Ed Bradley's words, as "outright propaganda for those favoring disarmament": "ABC," in Falwell's view, "has, in essence, shut down the debate ... they've said, 'This is the way it is. Deterrence has failed. The U.S. is going to cause World War III. The debate should be closed down and we should disarm.' I don't like it." On the other side of the argument, Congressman Ed Markey declared, "I think that people do a grave injustice to ABC and their motivations in criticizing them, condemning them for something that they ought to be praised for ... in making the public think about an issue without prescribing for them the way in which they ought to deal with it." The same broadcast featured Brandon Stoddard saying that the film didn't "discuss whether deterrence is good or bad. There's no discussion about that. We don't even deal with that." Yet, as Bradley said, "That's just the problem with *The Day After*, according to John Fisher." The president of the American Security Council, an organization promoting peace through strong deterrence, Fisher said:

> There isn't even a pass at saying, "Well, deterrence has served us up till now." It ends up as being a very strong political statement, regardless of what ABC intended. I'm not saying that ABC is wrong as far as their intentions are concerned. What I'm saying is the net effect is that an audience is going to be in great shape for the nuclear freezers.[38]

The Day After proved disturbing to Reagan's White House staff who received a preview of the film in advance of its scheduled public airing. After watching it himself at Camp David, Reagan noted his impressions in his diary:

Monday, October 10
    Columbus Day. In the morning at Camp D. I ran the tape of the movie ABC is running on the air Nov. 20. It's called "The Day After." It has Lawrence, Kansas wiped out in a nuclear war with Russia. It is powerfully done — all $7 mil. worth. It's very effective & left me greatly depressed. So far they haven't sold any of the 25 spot ads scheduled & I can see why. Whether it will be of help to the "anti nukes" or not, I can't say. My own reaction was one of having to do all we can to have a deterrent & to see there is never a nuclear war.
    Back to W. H.[39]

Seeking to formulate a response to the film, White House aides convened several meetings and considered the option of a televised presidential rebuttal of the film. Believing that a direct challenge to ABC would be unwise, presidential assistants contacted friendly reporters as well as having the Republican National Committee issue talking points to GOP officials in every state. Such fears proved unwarranted. Presidential aides who screened the film beforehand observed that television diminished its emotional impact — an effect attributable to the commercials aired during the broadcast; the ads had a reassuring effect on viewers.[40]

As *The Day After* opens, the SAC Airborne Command Post plane at Omaha, Nebraska, takes off for its patrol station in the event of a nuclear war. On the ground below, life proceeds normally in America's heartland. Against this backdrop, potentially unsettling news emanates from abroad: Soviet military forces are massing along the West German frontier — an action that has precipitated Western economic sanctions and which the Soviet ambassador characterizes as nothing more than Warsaw Pact training exercises.

The film depicts the impact of a nuclear attack on the town of Lawrence, Kansas, as seen through the eyes of various residents in the area. The Dahlbergs, a farm family, are preparing for their daughter Denise's wedding. The crew of a missile silo checks in for its tour of duty at the site. A local physician, Russ Oakes (Jason Robards), is dealing with the news that his daughter is moving to Boston. Another farm family, the Hendrys, carries out its routine right next to a missile silo needing maintenance.

The international situation then worsens: East Germany, responding to mutinies within its armed forces, closes off access to West Berlin. The president of the United States places all American servicemen on alert status. Oakes's wife likens the situation to the Cuban missile crisis: "Do you remember Kennedy on television? Telling Khrushchev to turn his boats around?"

"Full retaliatory response," Oakes replies. "He didn't bat an eye."

"We were in New York, in bed...."

"We got up," says Oakes, "went to the window, looked for the bomb." "Didn't happen," Mrs. Oakes says. "It's not going to happen now." "People are crazy, but not that crazy," Oakes replies.

His wife then says their neighbors left that day for Guadalajara, dovetailing "their vacation with the rising international tensions.... What if it does happen? What'll we do?"

The crisis mounts as NATO forces enter East Germany, bound for Berlin. The situation frightens Oakes, who is afraid to listen to further radio broadcasts. A fellow doctor tells him that rumor has it that Moscow is being evacuated and that some people have left Kansas City due to the proximity of the missile silos there.

"What's going on?" Oakes asks. "Do you understand what's going on in this world?"

"Yeah," his colleague answers. "Stupidity — has a habit of getting its way."

Owing to the escalating crisis, the Russians then invade West Germany; raising the possibility that NATO will employ tactical nuclear weapons to halt their advance. Steven Klein (Steve Guttenberg), a pre-med student at the University of Kansas in Lawrence, decides to hitchhike home to see his family. Then the word goes out to those in transit in the Kansas City metropolitan area to take shelter. Panic buying ensues in a supermarket. When word comes that three low-kiloton nuclear weapons were exploded over advancing Soviet troops, SAC bombers take to the skies. The command is given: The silos disgorge their missiles toward their Russian targets. The Dahlbergs take refuge in their basement. When the Russians retaliate with an ICBM attack of their own against the United States, pandemonium breaks loose in Kansas City: Air-raid sirens sound, people scurry through the street seeking cover, traffic jams ensue. At this instant, a bright light fills the sky above the city as an air burst occurs, shutting off electric power.

What follows next, in *Newsweek*'s description, was "four minutes of the most horrifically searing footage ever to pass a network censor: building implosions, group immolations, a carnage of mass vaporizations."[41] Trapped in his car by the power failure, Oakes takes cover in the front seat. The Dahlbergs' son Danny is flash-blinded when he looks directly at the explosion. Unable to reach his family, Klein takes refuge in a building.

In the aftermath of the attack, nuclear winter sets in. Dazed, Oakes reaches the campus hospital at the University of Kansas which is overrun with survivors. Klein makes his way to the Dahlbergs' farm. In a scene recalling the "Gun Thy Neighbor" controversy during the 1961 fallout shelter mania, Jim Dahlberg, the family patriarch, is reluctant to let Klein come in, thinking others will demand to be allowed admittance; he relents when Klein assures him he's the only one present—everyone else is dead. Breaking under the strain of living in the family farm's basement day after day, Denise Dahlberg runs upstairs and out into the daylight, exposing herself to the lingering radiation from the nuclear blast. Klein chases her back into the farmhouse.

Security at the campus hospital is strained to the limit; one hospital worker asks a doctor if there's any truth to a rumor that firing squads are maintaining law and order. The doctor dismisses such a notion as absurd. (A later sequence proves that the rumor is quite true.) Elsewhere, one of the missile silo crewmen who survived the attack comes to the aid of a straggler who is fighting to get a drink of water, giving him one of the Baby Ruth bars he collected earlier. The two then set out for the hospital in Lawrence, reaching a survivors encampment.

Eventually, the radiation level diminishes to safe levels, allowing the Dahlbergs and Klein to emerge into the daylight. When Denise begins bleeding from her womb, Klein takes her and Danny aboard a horse-drawn carriage to Lawrence for treatment. The radio brings word from the president of the United States that a cease-fire with the Soviet Union is in effect. The pressure finally becomes too great for Oakes: Haunted by memories of his family, he

Dr. Oakes (Jason Robards) surveys the ruins of his home at the conclusion of *The Day After* (ABC/Photofest).

collapses. Upon reaching Lawrence, Klein helps with the burial of bodies in a mass grave and witnesses a food riot when the Army tells a group of people lining up for food that there are no supplies left for them, that what's left is slated for another camp. Additional violence erupts when, returning to his farm from a farmers' meeting, Jim Dahlberg is shot dead by a group of squatters encamped on his property.

Wanting one last look at his home before he dies, Oakes sets out in an Army vehicle for Kansas City. Once there, he sees the extent of the devastation the attack has wrought. He also discovers that his home has been destroyed and, with it, his wife. Seeing a group of people encamped where his home once stood, Oakes becomes enraged: "Get out of my house."

One of the people there offers him some food. Turning away, Oakes collapses, heartbroken with grief at his loss; the man who offered him the food then comes over and comforts him as the film fades to black. The now blackened screen features, not "the There Must Be a New Beginning end" of other post-apocalyptic films, but rather a very simple message[42]:

> The catastrophic events you have just witnessed are, in all likelihood, less severe than the destruction that would actually occur in the event of a full nuclear strike against the United States.
>
> It is hoped that the images of this film will inspire the nations of this earth, their peoples and leaders, to find the means to avert the fateful day.

Polls taken before and after *The Day After*'s airing revealed that it had done nothing to change public opinion regarding U.S. defense policy. "The peace movement," in Steven F. Hayward's words, "had made its last throw, and lost."[43] Seeing the peace movement's impotence in halting the deployment of the Euromissiles, the Soviets proposed to diminish their intermediate range warheads to the combined totals of those in the British and French arsenals if the United States didn't deploy the Euromissiles. Paying no heed to the Soviet proposal, Reagan and the allies moved forward. A measure calling for a unilateral freeze on nuclear weapons went down to defeat in the Senate by a vote of 58 to 40. On October 31, 1983, Britain voted for deployment, followed by the West German vote to deploy on November 22. The missiles were flown in the following day, prompting the Soviets to walk out of the Strategic Arms Reduction Talks (START).[44] The final tally on the number of Euromissiles deployed in Western Europe reads as follows: 108 Pershing and 96 cruise missiles in West Germany, 160 cruise missiles in Britain, 112 in Italy, and 48 each in Belgium and the Netherlands. The episode had demonstrated both the steadfastness and determination of the NATO alliance despite substantial internal and external pressure. The *New Republic* acknowledged Reagan's leadership: "It is hard to think of a single Democratic candidate for President who would have toughed it out the way Mr. Reagan did."[45] Given the failure of the Western peace movement to halt the Euromissile deployment, the onus was now on the Soviets to resume negotiations and make concessions, as it was evident that given the absence of additional arms control accords, Reagan would speedily arm the Western alliance.[46]

Still the message of the nuclear freeze movement reached Reagan's ears — an example of his extraordinary ability to perceive changes in public opinion. Reagan now became, in his own words, the "leader of the peace movement."[47] In a move that caught top officials of his administration completely off guard, Reagan, in a March 23, 1983, television address, called on "the scientific community in this country, those who gave us nuclear weapons, to turn their great talents now to the cause of mankind and world peace, to give us the means of rendering these weapons impotent and obsolete." What Reagan had in mind was a missile defense shield that would discard America's longstanding deterrence policy of averting war through the threat of mutual destruction. "Wouldn't it be better to save lives than to avenge them?" he asked. Furthermore, Reagan pledged that, once the knowledge that emerged from this Strategic Defense Initiative (SDI, or, as skeptical journalists soon called it, Star Wars) was completed, it would be shared with both the Soviets and America's allies to guarantee global nuclear disarmament. Speaking to reporters shortly after announcing the Star Wars initiative, Reagan said, "To look down to an endless future with both of us sitting here with these horrible missiles aimed at each other and the only thing preventing a holocaust is just so long as no one pulls the trigger — this is unthinkable."

Reagan's aides knew full well that SDI technology didn't exist and that the majority of defense experts refuted its viability. Despite this, and despite Democratic jeers that it was a Darth Vader fraud, numerous Americans applauded Reagan's appreciation of the hazards and uselessness of nuclear weapons. Defense contractors were appreciative as well, and showed it with well-priced favors to politicians. The results were soon evident: By 1985, SDI became the biggest military research program in American history. Just over a decade later, SDI and related missile defense programs had devoured $51 billion, with further sums spent thereafter, though none of this effort yielded any concrete technical achievement.

Probably the best account of SDI's origins is the one provided by Pulitzer Prize-winner Frances Fitzgerald who concluded that the explanations for the background of the SDI speech contained contradictions and implausibilities. Moreover, there

are pieces of evidence scattered about, particularly in the work of the official [SDI] historian, Donald R. Baucom, and that of the Naval War College historian, Frederick H. Hartmann, that do not fit this story at all. Finally, except in interviews with Baucom, the participants fail to mention a phenomenon of great importance to them at the time. Once this element is introduced, the story begins to make sense — otherwise it is like the score of a piano concerto with the piano part missing. The phenomenon is, of course, the antinuclear movement: the freeze.

The truth of the matter was that SDI was Reagan's response to the grave political crisis confronting him in early 1983 over his military strategy, and a nuclear strategy in case of limited nuclear war. The anti-nuclear movement's remarkable domestic and foreign popularity, particularly the nuclear freeze movement's success, was the paramount conundrum for the administration. Reagan's SDI speech contributed greatly to softening his militant public image, with positive results soon evident: His approval rating rose, he won a landslide reelection victory, and the nuclear freeze movement dwindled. To a large extent, the latter occurred because the movement was co-opted by Reagan's new dovish persona and by the movement's ostensible allies in the Democratic party. To a smaller extent, the movement was also devitalized by the vast sums of money lavished upon it by large foundations, which then believed they had to exercise a mitigating hand over the movement. In 1983, freeze leaders threw their backing to a "quick freeze," which signified their decision to step back from their advocacy for halting nuclear weapons production, while sustaining their ambition that testing and deployment might be halted. That same year, the House approved a version of the freeze resolution advocating a negotiated, verifiable, and mutual freeze with the Soviets — yet was so attenuated that it was rendered inconsequential. "Still," as Dee Garrison has written, "Nuclear Freeze and the nonviolent anti-civil defense protests were at the center of the peace movement that permanently established the public right and need to challenge government 'experts' and other nuclear 'strategists' on all issues concerning nuclear war."

Another consequence of SDI was its impact on the nuclear debate. In promoting SDI, Reagan was doing the same thing peace crusaders had long been doing: He denounced deterrence strategy as lunatic and unprincipled and pledged to discover, then share with the world, a means of rendering nuclear arms archaic, permanently eradicating the nuclear threat. By denouncing SDI as being years from realization, anti-nuclear activists were left in the ironic position of justifying the very deterrence policy they themselves had condemned and which Reagan pledged to terminate with his SDI program. The latter flourished as both an idea and a budget line item. The annual research funds bestowed on SDI rapidly spawned a powerful bureaucratic and corporate constituency that hastened to Reagan's backing, guaranteeing that SDI would remain alive. The absence of any successful research discoveries notwithstanding, support for the development of a workable missile defense system would continue beyond Reagan's presidency.[48]

One final question might be asked: What part, if any, did *The Day After* play in moving Reagan toward a less hawkish stance? Bearing in mind that his SDI proposal was made eight months before the film's broadcast — and primarily in response to the nuclear freeze movement — Meyer has called *The Day After* "probably the most worthwhile thing I ever got to do with my life." Based on their statistics from a survey taken after the broadcast as to whether it had altered people's minds about nuclear war, however, the press told Meyer that no one's opinion had been changed. What was his response?

I answered truthfully that it was too soon to say what effect the film had had on viewers and whether any were prepared to admit — even to themselves — if it had.... But at least one person's mind *was* changed by the film. When President Reagan signed the intermediate range missile treaty in Iceland, I got a lovely card from someone that said, "Don't think your film didn't have something to do with this," which turned out to be intuitively prescient. Some years after I had a weird confirmation of this fact. I was speaking at Oxford, and a student asked if I'd ever read Reagan's autobiography. I said I hadn't, whereupon he handily produced a photocopied page for me in which the president described his reaction to the film essentially allowing as to how it had altered his perception of the nuclear subject. Remember, this was a president who saw life in terms of movies, and it had taken a movie to help him see that nuclear wars are unwinnable. Later, when I met Edmund Morris, author of Reagan's biography *Dutch*, he confirmed the paragraph in his book that stipulates the only time he ever saw Reagan depressed was after viewing *The Day After*. Reagan, who had come to power contemplating a winnable nuclear war ("if we have enough shovels..." etc.), had changed his mind.[49]

7

From the Nineties
to September 11

During the mid–1980s, Soviet Premier Mikhail Gorbachev repeatedly declared that "the nuclear era requires new thinking from everybody," and "the backbone of the new way of thinking is the recognition of the priority of human values, or, to be more precise, of humankind's survival." Starting during Reagan's presidency, Gorbachev began announcing backing for openness, freedom, and decentralization; he recommended vast reductions in Soviet arms, and advocated the superpowers' elimination of all nuclear weapons.

Both Reagan and his successor, George H. W. Bush, collaborated with Gorbachev to curb their nations' nuclear arsenals. The 1987 Intermediate-Range Nuclear Forces (INF) Treaty eradicated ground-launched ballistic and cruise missiles and permitted inspections on both sides to guarantee adherence to the treaty. By the summer of 1991, the Strategic Arms Reduction Treaty (START 1) was in effect, stipulating that both the United States and the Soviet Union reduce their strategic nuclear armaments to 6,000 warheads each. Gorbachev called the signing ceremony "a moment of glory for the new thinking and the foreign policy stemming from it." Bush declared, "For me this was more than ritual; it offered hope to young people all over the world that idealism was not dead."[1]

At the same time, the Soviet Union was unraveling. Facing grave economic problems and informed by Gorbachev that the Red Army wouldn't come to their rescue, Poland's Communist leader had no choice but to hold free elections, with the result that Lech Walesa's anti-communist Solidarity alliance emerged triumphant on June 4, 1989. The installation of a Solidarity officer, a Walesa ally, as Polish prime minister on August 19, signaled Poland's liberation from communist rule.

Poland was just the beginning. Hungary cast-off its Communist shackles on October 7, 1989. The vast exodus of East Germans from that nation via Poland led to the opening of East Germany's frontiers, prompting Berliners to level the infamous symbol of communist oppression, the Berlin Wall, a piece of which was donated to the Reagan Presidential Library. Rumania's communist ruler was captured and slain on Christmas Day 1989. This was followed, merely four days later, by the elevation to the Czechoslovakian presidency of Vaclav Havel, who, only a short time earlier, had been imprisoned by the communists. The formal reunification of East and West Germany into one nation became a reality on October 3, 1990. In April 1991, the Warsaw Pact formally ceased to exist.

Unsettled by their party's rapidly increasing loss of power, hard-line Soviet Communists in August 1991 seized both Gorbachev and the Parliament building on the grounds that they were sustaining communism and national unity. Mobilizing his countrymen, Russian Federation President Boris Yeltsin sent the army after the plotters, freed Gorbachev, and outlawed and ordered the termination of the Communist Party. The Soviet Union was no more.[2]

The theme of President Bush's State of the Union address the following year was unmistakable: "America won the Cold War." In the same address, Bush invoked a classic civil defense image of bygone times to tout the U.S. triumphant:

> Tomorrow our children will go to school and study history and how plants grow. And they won't have, as my children did, air raid drills in which they crawl under their desks and cover their heads in case of nuclear war. My grandchildren don't have to do that, and have the bad dreams that children once had in decades past. The threat is still there. But the long, drawn-out dread is over.

Under the terms of the START II accord, which Bush and Yeltsin signed in January 1993, the United States and Russia each were restricted to between 3,000 and 3,500 strategic warheads; the same accord also did away with all multiple-warhead intercontinental ballistic missiles.

During the Clinton presidency, the pace of arms control and disarmament greatly slowed, while federal backing and heed to guaranteeing the maintenance of government continued. Still, a pair of events — the collapse of Reagan's crisis relocation system and Bush's pronouncement that "duck and cover" was history — apparently indicated that civil defense as a means of protecting the public was history as well. The final confirmation of this was provided by President Clinton in 1999 when he signed legislation authorizing the building of the National Civil Defense/Emergency Management Monument at the old Federal Emergency Management Agency training area at Emmitsburg, Maryland. Built with private and some state contributions, the monument was dedicated three years later.[3]

Both the Cold War and Cold War–era civil defense were over in real life, but Cold War nuclear nostalgia continued to flourish on the movie screen.

Nuclear Nostalgia in the Clinton Years: Blast from the Past and Matinee

The Clinton years (1993–2001) witnessed the release of two films —*Matinee* (1993) and *Blast from the Past* (1999)— that were part of a wave of films released during the post–Cold War era, focusing on the Eisenhower-Kennedy years. These films, notes film historian Mick Broderick, differentiated from "the earlier 1980s nostalgia wave of period films (e.g., *Back to the Future* [1985], set principally in the 1950s) that promote the recent past as a golden age of prosperity and simplicity," far removed from the turmoil and alienation characterizing postmodern life. "Scrutiny of how nuclear issues are presented in recent cinema's recounting of the early 1960s provides an emblematic window on the often conscious narrative efforts to make problematic the era's retrospective construction as a stereotypically simple and unsophisticated sociopolitical environment."[4]

Blast from the Past opens in 1962 Los Angeles, where Calvin Webber (Christopher Walken), a teacher-turned-inventor, and his pregnant wife, Helen (Sissy Spacek), are hosting a cocktail party at their home when Kennedy's televised address on the Soviet missiles in Cuba airs. Cutting the party short, they enter their fallout shelter just as a malfunctioning jet fighter crashes into their house — creating the impression that a nuclear attack has begun. Shortly thereafter, Helen Webber gives birth to their son, whom they appropriately christen Adam.

The years pass. Completely unaware that no bomb has gone off, the Webbers carry on in their shelter, raising their son, watching reruns of Jackie Gleason's *Honeymooners* show, while the world above them passes from hippies to disco to grunge. During all this time, Adam (Brendan Fraser) has grown to adulthood without ever having seen the outside world. His mother, on the other hand, has begun to crack under the isolation of life underground after all this time.

Finally, the day comes when the shelter's sensory system detects that it is safe to go topside and automatically unlocks the entrance door. Clad in anti-radiation gear, Calvin Webber ascends to the surface, breaking through the floor of a restaurant-nightclub built on the site where his family's home used to stand. He then comes face to face with a pair of drugged-out derelicts, one of whom takes him to be a divine apparition. Venturing out further, Webber must contend with the Los Angeles of streetwalkers and adult book stores. The shock of what he finds proves too much for him. The fallout, he tells his wife, has "created a subspecies — mutants.... Some eat out of garbage cans. Others ... are multi-sexual. It seems they can be both masculine and feminine simultaneously." Traumatized, Calvin Webber has a heart attack.

To save his father, Adam volunteers to go topside for supplies. His mother offers simple words of advice: "Just act normal. If anyone asks, simply say, 'I'm from out of town. I'm here on business.'" When Adam asks her about meeting a girl — a subject he's been pondering "just these last 15 years or so" — his mother further counsels him to find one who isn't a mutant and who hopefully hails from Pasadena. Adam's father also tells him to stay out of the adult bookstore because that's where the poison gas is, and in the event that he finds "a healthy young woman," he should bring her down into the shelter.

Exiting up into the nightclub his father did, Adam encounters the same derelict, who now believes Adam is the "deity's" son. Stepping out into the daylight, Adam sees his first view of the sky: "I have never in my life seen anything like it before." For one who has, until now, lived his entire life underground, it's a wondrous moment, as is his first glimpse of (to use the idiom of an earlier time) "a Negro" — in this instance a black female letter carrier, who is clearly shocked at hearing herself described this way. Mick Broderick notes that Adam's "comic encounters with late-twentieth-century Los Angeles ... recall the common tropes of innocents abroad and fishes out of water. For Adam — a walking compendium of middle-American virtue and his parents' generational mores — the once virtual and phantomic world of texts, photos, and oral history is made flesh"; and he enjoys his real-life encounters with it. Broderick continues that a pair of themes constitutes much of the film's action: Adam's "idealized pursuit of knowledge and experience" and "the transformative power his near-messianic presence has on contemporary acquaintances." Regarding the latter theme, Broderick appropriates the title of a popular television series of the time to characterize Adam's impact on those he meets: "Adam leaves in his wake the previously cynical and disaffected Los Angelinos as if 'touched by an angel.'"[5]

Navigating his way around modern L. A., Adam makes his way to a baseball card shop, where he tries to sell his father's vintage Mickey Mantle cards. While there, he meets Eve (Alicia Silverstone), described by the DVD's package as "a modern L.A. woman, jaded about life and bummed by love," who is fired from her job at the store when she stops the store owner from buying Adam's cards at a price lower than their actual worth.

In exchange for one of his baseball cards, Eve agrees to drive Adam to a Holiday Inn. Along the way, they both discover a mutual interest: Perry Como. Adam grew up listening to Como's records in his family's shelter, while Eve gets "cranked" by them. Later, having a change of heart, Eve tries to give the baseball card she took as payment for driving Adam to the Holiday Inn back to him. Refusing to accept it, Adam instead convinces her to help him sell all his baseball cards to get enough money to buy supplies to restock his family's fallout shelter.

Adam then comes up with another request for Eve: That she help him find a non-mutant wife from Pasadena within two weeks — a request Eve says will take time to fulfill. For Eve, a contemporary woman with a cynical attitude toward marriage, Adam's request is a shock as are his courteousness and other perfect gentlemanly manners. Having been isolated from the real world, Adam epitomizes the total innocent in the world of the late 20th-century — one completely unfamiliar with the technological and social changes that have occurred since 1962, a "man child" in his parents' words.

The aforementioned "transformative power" Adam has over those he meets presently works its magic on Eve, who comes to realize that she's in love with him. When Adam tells her the truth about his family and his desire to take her back to their shelter, Eve, thinking Adam is mentally ill, calls the authorities to have him committed for treatment. Escaping them, Adam returns to his parents' shelter with the supplies while Eve searches for him. She eventually finds him at the adult bookstore above the shelter. Taking her into the sanctuary, Adam introduces Eve to his parents. Using the money from the stock certificates Adam brought with him, Adam and Eve build a new house for his parents, then bring them out of the shelter, reacquainting them with normal life in the new, post–Cold War world — a notion Adam's father finds hard to believe. In addition to validating traditional American values, the film's conclusion "suggests more than a hint of skepticism about the permanence of the fall of communism and the utopian promise of the post–Cold War Pax Americana"[6] — as illustrated by Calvin Webber's disbelief that the Soviet Union truly is no more. The film's affirmation of traditional values is evident even earlier by way of its illustration of the difference between the Los Angeles of 1962 and 1999 as symbolized by the adult bookstore standing where Adam's parents' home once stood. Eve's homosexual friend Troy (Dave Foley) explains that back then "cute little homes and ... fruit orchards" occupied the space the porn shop now occupies, to which Eve replies, "We've come a long way, haven't we?" Despite her surface veneer of cynicism, Eve, deep down, longs for the old-fashioned values upon which Adam was raised.

Like *Blast from the Past*, *Matinee*, released six years earlier, was set during the Cuban missile crisis and, in the words of its director Joe Dante, began "as a fantasy about Saturday matinees by Jerico Stone, and when we couldn't sell that, [screenwriter] Charlie Haas and I morphed it into the movie" it finally became. "The only thing in common between the two versions is" the film's "movie-within-a-movie" — *Mant!*[7]

Matinee opens with the impending arrival in Key West, Florida, of horror film producer Lawrence Woolsey (John Goodman), who has chosen Key West to debut his latest production, *Mant!* in which radiation exposure transforms a man into a mutant ant-like creature. In the midst of all this, the Cuban crisis erupts. Fifteen-year-old Gene Loomis (Simon Fenton), a 15-year-old fan of Woolsey's films, gets to meet his idol, who employs Gene to help him with the film. When Gene and his date attend the premiere, they get locked inside the theater's fallout shelter during a scare over a possible Russian attack touched off by Woolsey's special effects for his film. Scurrying out of the theater, expecting the worse, the theater audience discovers all's right with the world.[8]

Matinee fused the two related themes of nuclear war (personified by the missile crisis, school air raid drills, and fallout shelters) and Monster Culture (nuclear mutations, movie monster model kits, and magazines). For Woolsey, the timing of the film's release in Key West during the Cuban crisis is perfect: "This war stuff spooks them, and we come in. POW! The main event." He elaborates further:

> What a perfect time to open a new horror movie.... Millions of people looking over their shoulder, waiting for God's other shoe to drop. Never knowing if each kiss, each sunset, each malted milk ball might be their last.

Because of the era's war scares and international tensions, Woolsey's horror gimmicks are crucial to his film's success: "Takes a lot more to scare people these days," he says. "Too much competition.... Now they got bombs that'll kill half-a-million people. Nobody's had a good night's sleep in years. So you gotta have a gimmick ... something a little extra." Woolsey's observation that horror films are good for people during a time of crisis is noted in Kim Newman's judgment that *Matinee* strives "to provide a lighthearted assessment of the importance of mythical terrors to a terrified world."[9]

There was nothing lighthearted about the anxiousness the Cuban missile crisis generated — a point illustrated in *Matinee* by its depiction of the school "duck and cover" drill. One student, Sandra (Lisa Jakub), the daughter of liberal parents, incurs the wrath of school officials when she declines to take part in the drill. Her defiance was an exception. Looking back on the time, *Matinee's* director, Joe Dante, recalled that he and his fellow students thought these drills "every bit as futile as the girl in the movie does. But not many kids actually said anything. It was a very conformist era."[10] In contrasting *Matinee* with *Blast from the Past*, Mick Broderick has written that whereas the latter film focuses on the social and cultural dilemmas besetting modern urban America while only addressing the issues confronting Kennedy-era America in passing, "*Matinee* effortlessly touches on these ruptures in a way

Opposite and above: Cold War nostalgia in the post–Cold War era: Adam Webber (Brendan Fraser) emerged from his family's fallout shelter to face life in 1990s America in *Blast from the Past* (1999). *Matinee* (1993) recalled Cold War nuclear fears and popular culture against the backdrop of the Cuban missile crisis (New Line Features/Photofest; Universal Pictures/Photofest).

that deliberately makes problematic their historical recounting." After her defiance of the school's air-raid drill exercise earns her a trip to the principal's office, Sandra tells Gene, "all they teach you is lies. You bury your head while they build more bombs.' This rebel *with* a cause," Broderick continues, "explicitly challenges the convention of consensus, railing at institutionalized denial and the unquestioned social compliance of the inuring military-industrial complex. She also deflates Key West's own mythic status as a 'wonderful place to live.'" This is accentuated more vividly in a subsequent sequence showing Gene "gripped in a nuclear nightmare, one in which he imagines witnessing his neighborhood demolished in an atomic attack."[11]

The skepticism about official policy Sandra displays wasn't limited to the movie screen. In real life, educator Robert K. Munsil believed that the "duck and cover" drills played a significant part in incubating the student protests of the 1960s: "In many ways, the styles and explosions of the 1960s were born in those subterranean high school corridors, where we decided that our elders were indeed unreliable, perhaps even insane."[12] Confirmation of Munsil's thesis can be found in the aftermath of the Kent State shootings in 1970, when a sociology professor invited his students to explain why they were participating in the student strike following the tragedy on the Ohio campus; several of the students cited a shared experience from their childhood school days: Participating in weekly civil defense exercises. Such student reactions during the post–Kennedy-era protest movements, Henry Fairlie opined, stemmed in part from the tension levels of crisis the American people experienced during Kennedy's tenure — tensions, Fairlie argued, JFK fanned as a tool of his presidency to accustom Americans to accept confrontation: "When one has listened to the flower children and the hippies and the freaks, has one not also heard the barely suppressed echoes of a childhood in which they were told to think the unthinkable and, for a week in the fall of 1962, believed that the unthinkable was about to happen to them? On the one hand, the seeker after confrontation, on the other hand, the drop-out from confrontation. The country, and especially its youth, had been imaginatively prepared only for crisis, either to rush eagerly towards it, or to flee already weary from it."[13]

The old theme of the bomb shelter as a make-out place, witnessed in *Happy Days* and *Grease 2*, also appears in *Matinee,* when beatnik hoodlum Harvey Starkweather (James Villemaire) catches his former girlfriend Sherry (Kellie Martin) locking lips with Gene's friend Stan (Omri Katz). Chased by Starkweather, Stan finds a rifle in the theater fallout shelter, and uses the firearm to scare Starkweather off. Finding Stan in the shelter, Gene, Sandra, and Sherry explore the nuclear hideaway. When the shelter door begins closing, Stan and Sherry flee, leaving Gene and Sandra locked inside, leaving them to discuss their "Adam and Eve" responsibilities to the post-attack world.[14] Commenting on this theme, Joe Dante recalls "the discussions out on the gym field where boys would check out the girls from afar and claim this one or that one would 'do it' with them if they thought the bombs were falling." The fallout shelter, he continues, "was one of the only unpopulated make-out places in the house, especially for kids too young to get to the drive-in theater on their own."[15]

During the Cuban missile crisis, the number-one song on the American music charts was a hit about monsters: "The Monster Mash," by Bobby "Boris" Pickett and The Crypt Kickers. That same October of 1962, Aurora Plastics of Hampstead, Long Island, introduced youngsters to a new kind of plastic model kit: replicas of the Wolf Man, Frankenstein's Monster, and Dracula. Other monster kits featuring the Mummy, the Creature from the Black Lagoon, the Hunchback of Notre Dame, the Phantom of the Opera, King Kong, and Godzilla would follow. To the children who purchased these kits that anxious autumn, the monster figures held out the hope of survival in some form or another should the worst come to pass. Monsters, after all, can't die. This sense of immortality is conveyed in a scene from *Matinee* where Gene Loomis's younger brother sleeps with a Mummy figure next to his bed. Monsters are also a source of comfort to Gene, whose father is in the Navy. This, combines with the fact that his family is frequently forced to relocate, leaves Gene with few friends; hence, monster movies fill the void in his life. Gene also keeps up with the latest news from the world of horror through *Famous Monsters of Filmland* magazine — a real-life publication that initially appeared in 1958 and influenced not only Joe Dante, but Stephen King and Steven Spielberg as well. Recalling the impact of these manifestations of Cold War-era Monster Culture on his life, Dante explained that model building kept him off the streets. "But," he continues:

> I was less interested in the merchandise on the back pages of FM that I was in the contents, which opened up a whole world of old movies that I might otherwise never have discovered. At the time, once you saw a movie in theaters, you had to wait years for it to show up on TV, and if you missed it, well, it might be another year before it ran again. So monster magazines (and *TV Guide)* were an indispensable sources of info as to what was out there.[16]

Not only is *Matinee* a study of Kennedy-era nuclear fears, as illustrated by the Cuban missile crisis, school air raid drills, and fallout shelters; it also is an exercise in film history.[17] The latter is presented in the form of *Matinee's* movie-within-a-movie, *Mant!* This homage is a variation of such real-life Fifties atomic mutation films as *The Incredible Shrinking Man* and *The Amazing Colossal Man*— both of which depicted the harmful, albeit far-fetched, side-effects of radiation exposure. And, in the case of *Mant!*, the consequences of such exposure are truly implausible: The victim mutates into an ant-like creature as a result of being bitten by an ant while having his teeth X-rayed in his dentist's office! The opening *Mant!* trailer sequence in *Matinee* directly sets forth the pop-culture environment that nurtured science-fiction films of the time by joining two of the era's sci-fi classics — *Them!* (1954) And *The Fly* (1958) — to create *Mant!* and doing so "with great conviction, knowledge, and humor."[18] Adding to its credibility is the presence in the *Mant!* sequence of veteran Fifties sci-fi actors William Schallert (*Invasion U.S.A., The Incredible Shrinking Man*), Kevin McCarthy (*Invasion of the Body Snatchers*), and Robert Cornwaithe (*The Thing, The War of the Worlds*).

A final aspect of *Matinee's* Fifties sci-fi/horror origins can be found in the Lawrence Woolsey character. *Mant's* producer, Woolsey, is a master showman. His film is "Presented in Atomo Vision. With RUMBLE RAMA. The New Audience Participation Thrill That Actually Makes YOU Part of the Show!" Indeed, Woolsey's gimmicks prove life-saving at one point in *Matinee:* When the balcony of the theater presenting *Mant!* in Key West begins sagging, threatening to collapse, Woolsey speeds up the film to the scene featuring an atomic explosion; the audience, thinking a real explosion has occurred, exits the theater, clearing the sagging balcony — save for Gene Loomis's little brother, Dennis, whom Gene manages to save. Because of the mayhem, Woolsey's production is a success.

Woolsey's real-life counterpart was producer/director William Castle who promoted his films with such gimmicks as "Emergo," featuring a gleaming skeleton sailing out over the theatre audience, and "Percepto," in which theater seats were outfitted with electric vibrators to jolt those sitting in them. The effect of all this was to make the audience not merely spectators looking at a movie screen, but part of the film action itself. Castle's ultimate goal would have been for the audience to "taste the fog drifting through a cemetery. They'd smell the freshly dug grave. They'd feel the touch of ghastly fingers."[19] Joe Dante listed Castle as an inspiration for the character of Lawrence Woolsey in *Matinee*, but there were others: Roger Corman, Jack Arnold, Bert I. Gordon, and Ray Dennis Steckler. "Castle never actually made big bug movies," Dante notes, "and in any case that genre was played out before 1962. So we took a bit of license and it still seems true to the era." As for *Mant's* genesis: "*Mant!* owes a lot to *Them!* and *The Fly* for sure, but they were better movies than *Mant!*, which actually draws more on pictures like *Beginning of the End* and *The Giant Claw*, going so far as to incorporate large patches of verbatim dialog from each."[20]

Other films of the post–Cold War era repeatedly depicted the image of American cities being devastated by threats that, while non-nuclear in nature, nevertheless reflect what historian Joseph Masco sees as the lingering image of nuclear destruction Americans planned for by means of the nuclear tests of the Cold War era. In *Armageddon* and *Deep Impact*, both released in 1998, Earth is spared cosmic annihilation through the actions of Americans armed with nuclear weapons. Such films, Masco postulates, were part of "a moment of psychic release and cultural release from the Cold War arms race": Because the nuclear threat of that earlier time had greatly diminished, films could now present America's demise in other ways. Where the detonation of a nuclear blast during the Cold War was a serious event, one signifying the failure to avert nuclear conflict, the films of the post–Cold War era merely signify patriotism and pleasure — their goal is "to reinstall American identity through mass violence, suggesting that it is only threat and reactions to threat that can create national community."[21] Masco further notes:

> Regardless of its form (asteroids, or tsunamis, or alien invaders), these spectacles function as nuclear texts because they use mass destruction as a means of mobilizing the United States as a global superpower. As allegories of nuclear war, they both reproduce the emotional language of nuclear threat (mass death as a vehicle for establishing national community) and allow a productive misrecognition of its political content. This filmic genre also inevitably reinforces through aestheticized politics the ever-present need for war, and the ubiquity of external enemies with apocalyptic power. And in doing so, these texts relegitimize the need for nuclear weapons in the United States while offering an image of the United States as a reluctant superpower forced into global military action for the greater good.[22]

Modern thinking about civil defense-related matters such as air-raid drills and fallout shelters — considered quite serious in their day — judges such things as naïve and foolish. Thus, films like *Matinee* produce smiles and heads shaking when such images are presented to modern filmgoers. But an event occurring eight years after *Matinee*'s release — one Americans considered as equally unthinkable as a nuclear war — would resurrect the old civil defense images, making them seem relevant again.

September 11

In the aftermath of the September 11, 2001, terrorist attacks in New York and Washington, a Denver lay pastor at an inner city ministry generated, in *Time* magazine's words, a "huge — and frightened — response" to an Internet letter he sent advising people to study *Revelation* as a guide to what was happening: "People were asking themselves whether they were ready to die. Very sane, well-educated people have gone back to the storm cellar thing to make sure they have water and freeze dried stuff in their basements."

A Texas clergyman abdicated his pulpit to enlist himself full-time to enlist Christians in political activity. Vacating politics altogether, a Wyoming state senator was motivated to do so, in part, to help people get ready for the Second Coming.

"I would go for years without anyone asking about the End Times," observed the senior minister of the Fifth Avenue Presbyterian Church in midtown Manhattan. "But since September 11, hardcore, crusty cynical New York lawyers and stockbrokers who are not moved by anything are saying, 'Is the world going to end?,' 'Are all the events of the Bible coming true?' They want to get right with God. I've never seen anything like it in my 30 years in ministry."[23]

In addition to prodding some people to examine the state of their spiritual well-being, September 11 summoned forth comparisons with Cold War-era civil defense. Writing in the December 23, 2001, *New York Times*, Patricia Leigh Brown noted that where salesmen once went door-to-door, selling fallout shelters, their September 11 counterparts sold gas masks and Cipro — the latter an antidote to anthrax, a reminder of the anthrax scare that erupted immediately after the terrorist attacks. And where Cold War civil defense messages were beamed at specific groups (children and mothers), September 11 anxiety-prevention messages covered a wider range: The readers of one *Men's Health* issue were informed of the 25 best ways men could take to protect their families, including "leveling with them" and avoiding corpulence as "a fit man evacuates his family faster from a burning house." Post 9/11 reader surveys taken by *Ladies' Home Journal* indicated that sexual dreams had taken a back seat to revenge fantasies: 26 percent of poll respondents declared they had them at least once daily. The Office of Homeland Security intended to issue criteria to help ready Americans for possible domestic terrorist attacks. The State Department's online "Reward for Justice" program asserted that children of terrorists "often enroll in schools in the middle of the year and may leave prior to the end with little or no notice."

The similarities and differences between the two eras aside, Brown noted that they share one common element: Americans' habit of disregarding hysteria. Where most Americans didn't rush out to build fallout shelters, a sense of calm reasserted itself shortly after the terrorist attacks. "Sales of *nouveau* shelters are on the wane," Brown wrote, "and having now stashed away drinking water and duct tape, Americans appear to be overcoming their jitters and, lured by bargain fares, are beginning to fly again.... And no one has proposed the contemporary equivalent of 'Bert the Turtle' — yet."[24]

Several websites featured prefab or customized shelters for high-income earners and detailed directions for those less affluent to construct their own shelters. Author Cresson H. Kearney described one of these sites:

Having a permanent, ready-to-use, well-supplied fallout shelter would greatly improve millions of American families' chances of surviving a nuclear attack. Dual use family shelters — shelters that also are useful in peacetime — are the ones that Americans are most likely to build in normal peacetime and to maintain for years in good condition for use in a nuclear war.

The longer nuclear peace lasts, the more difficult it will be, even during a recognized crisis, to believe that the unthinkable war is about to strike us and that we should build expedient shelters and immediately take other protective actions. The lifesaving potential of permanent, ready-to-use family shelters will increase with the years.[25]

It would be necessary to continually upgrade the shelter's year-long storehouse of food to make certain such provisions remained garden-fresh. It would be wise to begin eating such rations in advance of doomsday:

> The emotional shock of suddenly being forced by war to occupy your shelter will be even worse if you have to adapt suddenly to an unaccustomed diet. It would be a good idea to occasionally practice eating only your survival rations for a day or two, and to store in your shelter a two-week supply of canned and dry foods similar to those your family normally eats. Then it will be easier if war forces you to make the changeover.[26]

At the time, numerous observers believed that more shelters should be immediately constructed in America. Deploring the fact that "fallout shelters fall short in the U.S.," a February 2002 article on the *NewsMax* website declared:

> In a 1999 survey by the Pew Research Center, 64 percent of those polled stated that they thought a major terrorist attack on the U.S. involving biological or chemical weapons would happen sometime over the next half century.... In the meantime, some Americans are voting with their pocketbooks and digging up their backyards just like the good old days of the Cold War. "They are treating me less like a crazy woman than they did before," Dr. Jane Orient of Tucson, Ariz., who promotes home shelters as head of Doctors for Disaster Preparedness, told *Newsmax.com*. If [Dr. Orient] had it her way, the U.S. would be more like the Russians, Chinese or Swiss. The Moscow subways double as shelters, equipped with blast doors. Much of the population of Beijing could be evacuated underground in about 10 minutes. And Switzerland has shelter for 110 percent of its population in private homes and public buildings.[27]

Equating the traumas of the September 11 era (the terrorist attacks, the anthrax scare, stories of missing and murdered children, war scares, and the Beltway Sniper's murderous rampage during the fall of 2002) with the terrors that had traumatized her generation ("duck and cover," polio epidemics, the Kennedy assassination), *Newsweek*'s Anna Quindlen wrote that, in her day, JFK's death was thought to be the greatest calamity her generation would ever know: "Our mothers wept, openly and unashamedly. The adults telegraphed the horrible importance of the occasion. Now," she continued, noting the impact of America's latest misfortunes on its children, the

> adults telegraph the horrible importance of one horribly important event after another. What kind of psychological price will these children pay for formative years in which a fireball of plane and passengers exploded within one of the nation's most triumphant landmarks, in which some of them missed soccer games or birthday trips to McDonald's because a man with a rifle was waiting to shoot passing strangers...? Most of us remember waking late on a crisp clear morning to blinding white beneath the window: no school because of snow! Now there are children who will remember school's being canceled because of a rain of bullets. The new normal: a sniper day.[28]

September 11 also spawned the federal government's latest civil defense agency: the Department of Homeland Security, which merged FEMA and 21 other federal agencies into a single organization employing 180,000 persons. Through four programs — border and transportation security; emergency preparedness and response; chemical, biological, radiological, and nuclear countermeasures; and information analysis and infrastructure protection — the department sought to discharge its mission of safeguarding the American people from disaster, whether man-made or natural in origin. Homeland Security director Tom Ridge's call to Americans during a "high" alert his department initiated in February 2003 (to purchase duct tape and plastic sheeting to secure their doors and windows against terrorist attack) evoked memories of past civil defense scares in that it prompted many Americans to hurry out to stores and buy up the available stocks of duct tape — undoubtedly pleasing merchants. But Ridge's duct tape pronouncement also engendered criticism of the Republican George W. Bush administration from Democrats, who accused it of providing spurious information and insufficient funding for domestic defense, and ridicule. Consequently, Homeland Security diminished the quantity of information the public knew about government intelligence regarding imminent terrorist activities — a move corresponding with prior civil defense history. Yet there was an important change regarding the critical evaluation of how civil defense operated: The government was accused of intentionally fabricating a "fear vote" for the purpose of sustaining Republicans in office, or creating a new big-money security market that filled the pockets of certain Bush champions in the business realm. Just the same, critics of September 11-era American civil defense, like civil defense critics of the past, apparently agreed on one point: Public civil defense is seriously deficient on all levels.

In one respect, Homeland Security marked a departure from earlier nuclear civil defense programs in that it conferred vast and unprecedented authority to intelligence and law-enforcement organizations. The provisions of the Patriot Act, approved by Congress with scant opposition just after 9/11, allowed the implementation of both searches and secret arrests to be made in the absence of warrants or judicial reviews, the holding of detainees without permitting them to talk to legal counsel, family, or friends for an indefinite period of time, and render sentences without permitting offenders access to their accusers. The law, furthermore, granted the FBI and other intelligence organizations new powers of surveillance and authority to spy on the actions and thoughts of both American citizens and immigrants.

In response, an enormous grassroots opposition materialized, initially taking the form of individual experts voicing their worries over the hazards parts of the law presented to the exercise of civil liberties and the right to lawfully dissent. Next, there came numerous significant legal motions on the part of large organizations determined to safeguard constitutional liberties. As had been the case with public opposition to Reagan's crisis relocation plans, opposition to the Patriot Act rapidly assumed a local character nationwide. "By May 2005, more than 382 cities and counties in 47 states, including Baltimore, Philadelphia, Denver, Detroit, Los Angeles, New York City, and Chicago, representing more than 61.5 million people, had approved formal local or state resolutions against portions of the Patriot Act, while hundreds of local and state protests" nationwide were gearing up for similar resistance. Seven states — Alaska, Colorado, Hawaii, Idaho, Maine, Montana, and Vermont — formally voted to resist parts of the act.[29]

Cold War nuclear imagery has also been involved in the "war on terror" as when President Bush declared to Americans in an address on Iraq in October 2002, "Facing clear evidence of peril, we cannot wait for the final proof, the smoking gun that could come in the form of a mushroom cloud."[30] Further evidence of such imagery can be seen in the color-coded system signifying the current likelihood of a terrorist attack — a system initially recommended by a 1952 civil defense study, *Project East River*, as a means of dealing with Soviet bombers. There was also the Homeland Security Administration's designation of shampoo bottles on planes as a potential terrorist weapons — which, Joseph Masco writes, are "official efforts to install and regulate fear in everyday life. In this regard, the 'war on terror' has been conducted largely as an emotional management campaign in the United States, using the tropes and logics developed during the early Cold War to enable a new kind of U.S. geopolitical project."[31]

A final link between the Cold War and the events of September 11 is the fact that, long before they were devastated in the terrorist attacks of 2001, both New York and Washington, D.C., had already been destroyed in the civil defense crusades of the Cold War era and Hollywood's summer blockbusters of the 1990s. Indeed, the images most often utilized to depict the magnitude of destruction arising from a nuclear blast during the Cold War were the Pentagon and the New York City skyline — as was the case when the AEC used these images to illustrate the enormity of the American H-bomb test of 1952. Thus, almost a half-century later, September 11 easily fit into talk of nuclear holocaust "precisely because our security council has imagined and rehearsed attacks on Washington and New York for generations, and because the specific symbols in the attacks (the Pentagon and the tallest building in the New York skyline) were also used by the nuclear state for three generations as part of its emotional management strategy. The Bush administration ... mobilized a well-established logic of nuclear attack to pursue its policy objectives, translating discrete, nonnuclear threats into the emotional equivalent of the Cold War nuclear crisis."[32]

Nuclear terrorism, international and domestic, had been recurring themes of popular culture in the pre–9/11 era. *The Sum of All Fears*, a 1991 Tom Clancy novel, found Iranian-backed Palestinians detonating a nuclear explosion at the Denver Skydome during the Super Bowl in the hope that America would accuse Russia of the foul deed and begin the Cold War anew. The 1994 feature film *True Lies* pitted Arnold Schwarzenegger against Islamic fundamentalists who threaten to nuke Florida. Three years later, George Clooney and Nicole Kidman confronted a Croatian Muslim terrorist who steals a nuclear missile from a Russian military train in *The Peacemaker*. A disgruntled ex–CIA operative seizes a U.S. Navy ship carrying nuclear missiles slated for decommissioning in *Under Siege* (1992), while another disgruntled American serviceman — an air force pilot — hijacks a pair of nuclear warheads, threatening to annihilate Denver with them, in *Broken Arrow* (1996). The latter two films proved especially timely as Americans confronted real life instances of domestic terrorism in the form of the Unabomber and the Oklahoma City bombing.[33]

But in the 9/11 era, as the Bush administration exhorted Americans to wage the "War on Terror" on the domestic and international fronts, escapism became the rule of the day in mass culture fare. The *Left Behind* novels, dramatizing the events surrounding the rapture of Christians as part of Jesus Christ's second coming, were bestsellers. Also popular were "reality television" shows. Among the most popular films of the immediate post–September 11 era were *Finding Nemo*, in which a cartoon clownfish seeks to return home; *Revenge of the Sith*, the final *Star* Wars film; the Harry Potter and Lord of the Rings series, and films about comic book superheroes (Spider-Man, Batman, The Incredibles, The Fantastic Four). In Steven Spielberg's 2005 remake of *War of the Worlds*, Tom Cruise must confront a Martian invasion with his own resources.[34]

Pop culture presentations of civil defense at the movies during the September 11 era were metaphorical. *Reign of Fire*, a 2002 release, couldn't have been timed any better for its debut. Its tale of an ancient menace (dragons) reawakened to jeopardize civilization in the early 21st century was a perfect metaphor for the contemporaneous real-life revival of another ancient threat (Islamic extremism). After a long slumber, the dragons awaken and, despite modern weaponry, leave the world a desolate ruin. A group of survivors, led by Quinn (Christian Bale) who, as a boy, witnessed the beginning of the dragons' reign of terror, has taken refuge in a castle in England. The menace is finally vanquished when Quinn, Benton Van Zan (Matthew McConaughey), a dragon slayer from America, and Alex (Izabella Scorupco), a member of Van Zan's team, journey to London and destroy the male dragon who fertilizes the female dragons' eggs — thereby guaranteeing that the dragon race will die out. During this final confrontation with the monster, Van Zan is killed, leaving Quinn and Alex to begin rebuilding a new world.

Reign of Fire might well be called "Civil Defense Meets Dragons." Shades of the Cold War are evident in the film. When the dragon threat initially appeared, there was a national civil defense alert for those who could hear it as well as the use of nuclear weapons against the monsters. The "duck and cover" era comes to mind when the children living in Quinn's castle sanctuary hide during a dragon's attack and, following the raid, recite a verse that could easily have been spoken by Bert the Turtle:

> What do we do when we wake?/Keep both eyes on the sky. What do we do when we sleep?/Keep one eye on the sky. What do we do when we see him?/Dig hard, dig deep, run for shelter, and never ever look back.[35]

Another 2002 release, Signs, directed by M. Night Shyamalan, places its civil defense imagery within the context of an alien invasion of Earth and its impact on a former clergyman and his family. Graham Hess (Mel Gibson), who left the clergy after the death of his wife in an automobile accident caused him to lose his faith, awakens one day to discover the presence of crop circles on his farm. The circles then begin appearing in other countries, followed by lights in the sky that are using the crop circles as a navigational aid. Hess and his family board up their home against the invasion, then take sanctuary in their basement. Graham's son Morgan (Rory Culkin) has an asthmatic condition that worsens, forcing them to leave their basement shelter to get medicine. The sequence of the Hess family emerging from their hideaway resembles one where a family emerges from hiding after a war. Once they're out of the basement, the Hesses discover an alien in their house — one who is threatening to kill Morgan with poison gas. While his brother does battle with the extraterrestrial, Graham Hess takes Morgan outside to give him his medicine — only to realize that his son's asthma wouldn't allow the alien's gas to enter his lungs. Morgan recovers, while his father regains his faith.[36]

Television turned retro in the immediate post–9/11 period, casting nostalgic eyes on the Cold War — an era when, in *Time* magazine's words, the
biggest concern for families was "the possibility that they might at any moment
be incinerated in a global nuclear war." The success of TV-series reunion spe-
cials in the months after 9/11 was one indication of this nostalgic trend. Shows
debuting during the fall 2002 season continued this vogue.[37] Set in Philadelphia in 1963, just before the Kennedy assassination, *American Dreams* focused
on the Pryors, a Catholic family, as they were buffeted by the turbulence of
the '60s — turmoil that engulfed the Pryors themselves. Wife Helen (Gail
O'Grady), feeling feminist urges, doesn't want to have another baby; son J.J.
(Will Estes) doesn't want to play football at Notre Dame; daughter Meg (Brit-
tany Snow) defies her father's orders by appearing on Dick Clark's *American
Bandstand*—all of which leaves the family patriarch Jack (Tom Verica) baffled
and resentful: "When did my dream become not enough?" he asks.

American Dreams's original purpose, explained the series' creator and
executive producer Jonathan Prince, "was to take the institutions of the late
Fifties and early Sixties — the Catholic Church, the football team, early television — and show the rebellion that happened in the Sixties." Shortly after
he submitted the series pilot to NBC, Prince received a call from a network
official who had assisted in the show's development, and was advised to turn
on the television. Prince then recounted what happened next:

> And I turned on the TV. It was September 11, and I'm watching buildings in
> flames. And he said, "I think your show just got a lot more relevant," because
> there's a generation of people ... who didn't know what it felt like to lose Presi-
> dent Kennedy.... We have a generation that lived pretty much without that. We
> saw Reagan got [*sic*] shot but he survived. The Pope. But this was epic — the
> tragedy of losing John F. Kennedy was epic.... There are those moments that
> unify us as a people, and often they're tragedy, sadly, and this is one of them.[38]

As the Pryors come to grips with the challenges the sixties are throwing
at the old ways, the old Cold War fears persist. At the dinner table one evening,
the Pryors' youngest son, Will, says he's heard the Russians have satellites
equipped with lasers aimed right at their house, an idea his mother later tells
him is nonsense: "They're not aiming lasers through your bedroom ... you
know the storm windows your father put in last month? They're super strong.
Laser beams would bounce right off 'em." At her Catholic high school, Meg
Pryor and her best friend, Roxanne Bojarski (Vanessa Lengies), are in the middle of an etiquette rehearsal when an air-raid siren sounds, signaling a drill.
Their instructor, Sister Claire, directs them to step outside single-file.

"I hate these drills ," says Meg, "especially in winter."

"If I were the Russians," opines Roxanne, "I'd bomb us on the first Thurs-
day of the month at exactly 10:00 A.M." She and Meg then avoid the chilly

temperatures outside by ducking behind the bleachers where Roxanne lights up a cigarette.

"What if Sister Claire finds us?" Meg asks.

"It's a drill," Roxanne reassures her. "We're practicing what we'd be doing if the Russians really did drop the bomb. I'm having my last cigarette."

Debuting the same season as *American Dreams, Oliver Beene* took a sardonic approach to Kennedy-era doomsday fears. The pilot episode featured the parents of the young protagonist waiting out the Cuban missile crisis in a basement bomb shelter, arguing over, of all things, whose responsibility it will be to remove any bodies they come upon outside the shelter ("It's always me!" the mother complains. "Doing the dishes, washing the windows, burying the dead!") Acknowledging his opinion that "any warm and fuzzy image of the past is wrong," *Beene*'s creator Howard Gewirtz continued, "I was around back then. There were dysfunctional families. If anything, the world situation was *more* threatening."

Picking up that thread, *Time*'s James Poniewozik observed: "And back then, we joked about it — if not on TV, then in movies like *Dr. Strangelove*," whereas television "worked more elliptically, through cold-war anxiety parables such as those" Rod Serling presented. Conceding that if a writer transformed *Oliver Beene*'s bomb-shelter sequence "into a bioterror scare in a sitcom set in the present," a top network would instantly veto it, Poniewozik wrote:

> Perhaps that's the hidden value of cultural nostalgia. It hints that the past was not better but worse than today, allowing us to exorcise forbidden thoughts about the present. Why do we believe the past was a happier, safer place than today? Maybe simply because we survived it. And because we didn't have love handles back then.

For his part, Jonathan Prince was annoyed with critics' objections to television's post–9/11 nostalgia wave. "In the shadow of 9/11, are people looking back for comfort? Well, yes. Shouldn't they be? That's what [TV] is supposed to do." Taking exception with this assessment and noting that "America's defiantly edgy, offensive, on-to-the-next-new thing pop culture is part of what defines us in the world (and, often, what enrages our enemies)," Poniewozik asked: "Is running into the warm skirts of the past what a vital, confident nation does?"[39]

Based on the crises of the past 40 years, the immediate answer is yes. The Kennedy assassination, Vietnam, Watergate, the cultural upheavals of the Sixties, and the energy crisis prompted nostalgic glances back toward the 1950s, making civil defense and its accompanying images — "duck and cover" drills and fallout shelters — seem quaint, amusing relics of the time. An explanation for this can be found in the skepticism and distrust of authority brought about by Vietnam and Watergate.

Civil defense was sold to the public to win their acceptance of nuclear deterrence as official policy: If the people believed they could survive a nuclear war should that become necessary, they would be more willing to accept such a possibility and take steps they were told would guarantee their survival. The reality was that very few people actually constructed fallout shelters. And when the post–Vietnam, post–Watergate era yielded revelations of government deception and violation of Constitutional laws and civil liberties and official abuses of power — actions justified as necessary to America's security during the Cold War — popular distrust replaced unquestioned acceptance of official pronouncements — including those regarding civil defense. Not only did Americans learn that their government had lied to them, they learned that American soldiers and civilians had been used as unwitting guinea pigs for nuclear tests and experiments with LSD. Bert the Turtle and 'duck and cover" became stock representations both of the duplicity and naïveté of an earlier time and the anti-nuclear movement. No better illustration of the latter can be found than *The Atomic Café*, the compilation film culled from Cold War–era newsreels and government propaganda films. Depicting nuclear tests (some of which involved soldiers), school civil defense drills, and fallout shelters, this 1982 film was released during the nuclear freeze movement of the early Reagan era, and meant to show just how ridiculous Cold War civil defense measures were. The shelters remaining from those years eventually were put to use for purposes other than they were originally intended — parties, wine cellars, or, usually, nothing at all.[40]

Pop culture's treatment of civil defense was equally as skeptical as the public's view of the subject. Even at the height of the Cold War, a Hollywood science-fiction film such as *The Deadly Mantis* presented a metaphorical, rather than a realistic, portrayal of civil defense operations, the theory being that audiences wouldn't pay to be entertained by the true horrors of nuclear war. Films like *The Deadly Mantis* and *Rocket Attack U.S.A.* subsequently became fodder for *Mystery Science Theater 3000*'s lampooning. By revealing the dehumanizing impact of just how far the Kennedy era's every-man-for-himself shelter mentality could turn neighbors against one another, *The Twilight Zone* played a major role in discrediting Kennedy's fallout shelter drive during the 1961 Berlin crisis. Similarly, *The Day After* may have persuaded President Reagan to alter his nuclear policy. Fifties nostalgia presented shelters as the perfect place for sexual hanky-panky. Whatever image pop culture put on civil defense (serious or humorous), what remained undeniable was the truth: Civil defense was intended to lessen the genuine horrors of nuclear war by making such a conflict seem less terrifying than it truly was and that it could be survived — if one took the necessary precautions beforehand and obeyed authority.[41]

Just how popular culture will address the present War on Terror is still unfolding, yet, as one film historian has written, cultural observers believe "the deeply inscribed Judeo-Christian narrative of apocalypse will no doubt be pressed into service to make sense of our (fictive or ideological) endings."[42]

Notes

Preface

1. Doris Kearns Goodwin, *Wait Till Next Year: A Memoir* (New York: Simon & Schuster, 1997), pp. 157–158.
2. *Ibid.*, pp. 159–160.
3. *Ibid.*, pp. 160–162.
4. Charles C. Alexander, *Holding the Line: The Eisenhower Era 1952–1961* (Bloomington: Indiana University Press, 1975), p. 101.
5. Richard M. Fried, *Nightmare in Red: The McCarthy Era in Perspective* (New York: Oxford University Press, 1990), pp. 4–5.
6. Alexander, *Holding the Line*, p. 101.
7. Spencer R. Weart, Chapter 2, "History of American Attitudes to Civil Defense," John Dowling and Evans M. Harrell, eds., *Civil Defense: A Choice of Disasters* (New York: American Institute of Physics, 1987), p. 11.
8. Dee Garrison, *Bracing for Armageddon: Why Civil Defense Never Worked* (New York: Oxford University Press, 2006), p. 32.
9. Neal Fitzsimons, "Brief History of American Civil Defense," Eugene P. Wigner, ed., *Who Speaks for Civil Defense?* (New York: Charles Scribner's Sons, 1968), pp. 30–31.
10. Garrison, *Bracing for Armageddon*, p. 32.
11. Cabell Phillips, *The 1940s: Decade of Triumph and Trouble* (New York: Macmillan, 1975), pp. 191–192.
12. Weart, Chapter 2, "History of American Attitudes to Civil Defense," Dowling and Harrell, eds., *Civil Defense: A Choice of Disasters*, p. 11.
13. Garrison, *Bracing for Armageddon*, p. 33.
14. Guy Oakes, *The Imaginary War: Civil Defense and American Cold War Culture* (New York: Oxford University Press, 1994), pp. 5–7.
15. Joseph Masco, "SURVIVAL IS YOUR BUSINESS: Engineering Ruins and Affect in Nuclear America," *Cultural Anthropology; Journal of the Society for Cultural Anthropology*," 23, Issue 2, May 2008, pp. 367–368.
16. *Ibid.*, p. 368.
17. *Ibid.*

Chapter 1

1. William M. Tuttle, Jr., "America's Children in an Era of War, Hot and Cold: The Holocaust, the Bomb, and Child Rearing in the 1940s," Peter J. Kuznick and James Gilbert,

eds. *Rethinking Cold War Culture* (Washington, D.C.: Smithsonian Institution Press, 2001), pp. 16–17.

2. *Ibid.*, p. 17.

3. *Ibid.*, pp. 18–20.

4. *Ibid.*, pp. 20–21.

5. *Ibid.*, pp. 21–22.

6. *Ibid.*, p. 27.

7. Laura McEnaney, *Civil Defense Begins at Home: Militarization Meets Everyday Life in the Fifties* (Princeton, NJ: Princeton University Press, 2000), pp. 12–15.

8. JoAnne Brown, "*A* Is for *Atom, B* Is for *Bomb*": Civil Defense in American Public Education, 1948–1963," *Journal of American History* 75, Number 1 (June 1988), pp. 69–70; Paul Boyer, *By the Bomb's Early Light: American Thought and Culture at the Dawn of the Atomic Age* (New York: Pantheon, 1985), p. 322.

9. Richard M. Fried, *The Russians Are Coming! The Russians Are Coming! Pageantry and Patriotism in Cold-War America* (New York: Oxford University Press, 1998), p. 46.

10. Garrison, *Bracing for Armageddon*, pp. 43–44; Michael J. Carey, "The Schools and Civil Defense: The Fifties Revisited," *Teachers College Record*, 84, Number 1, Fall 1982, p. 115.

11. Carey, "The Schools and Civil Defense," *Teachers College* Record, 84, Number 1, Fall 1982, p. 116.

12. *Ibid.*, pp. 116–117.

13. *Ibid.*, p. 117.

14. Garrison, *Bracing for Armageddon*, pp. 43–45.

15. http://conelrad.com/duckandcover/cover.php?turtle-01 (13 July 2009).

16. http://conelrad.com/duckandcover/cover.php?turtle+01a (13 July 2009).

17. *Ibid.*

18. *Ibid.*

19. http://conelrad.com/duckandcover/cover.php?turtle=01b (13 July 2009).

20. http://conelrad.com/atomicsecrets/secrets.php?secrets=04 (14 July 2009).

21. http://conelrad.com/duckandcover/cover.php?turtle=01b (13 July 2009).

22. *Ibid.*

23. Garrison, *Bracing for Armageddon*, p. 46. The Baby Boomers who grew up participating in the "duck and cover" and other civil defense drills in schools during the 1950s came to the realization that if they were to have a future at all, *they*—themselves—would have to assume the responsibility of changing the world in such a way as to guarantee a future would exist for them. An illustration of this attitude was presented, albeit metaphorically, in the 1958 science fiction film *The Blob*, in which a group of teenagers, unable to convince their parents and local authorities of the presence of a rapidly growing alien menace, are forced to take drastic measures of their own to force their elders to face the reality of the threat confronting their community. "All right," Steve, one of the adolescents, tells his peers, "we tried to do it the right way, now we're gonna wake this town up ourselves." In this manner, the teenage heroes of *The Blob*, in Robert A. Jacobs's view, presaged the counterculture and the New Left of the next decade, who, believing the older generation didn't understand the threat jeopardizing humanity's future, were compelled to sound the alarm themselves. In this way, Jacobs feels the message of "Duck and Cover" to its young viewers—that, in the absence of adults, they themselves would be responsible for their own survival in the event of an atomic attack—had come true. Robert A. Jacobs, *The Dragon's Tail: Americans Face the Atomic Age* (Amherst and Boston: University of Massachusetts Press, 2010), pp. 114–116.

24. Landon Y. Jones, *Great Expectations: America and the Baby Boom Generation* (New York: Ballantine, 1981), pp. 60–61. During the height of school civil defense programs, critics of the latter were a minority. Those who voiced objections presented their case normally within a physical, instead of a political, context. A. F. Corey, the executive secretary of the California Teachers' Association, opined: "Frightened children scanning the sky for Russian bombers is not a healthy aspect of national security." The same year Corey conveyed this sentiment, 1951, university professor Howard A. Lane observed: "The current press abounds

in pictures of teachers standing grimly erect over children prostrate in cover-drill." Lane was concerned that the combination of school lessons on the hazards of communism and careless talk about civil defense at home could needlessly alarm children. After being told in school that "communists are bad men that want to kill us," children might hear their parents say that "the neighbor who raises questions about the local civilian defense program is probably a communist!" The alternative to this, Lane proposed, was "hard, realistic study" of Russia, southeast Europe, and Asia. What children truly required protection from, in Lane's view, were "overwrought, anxious parents." Brown, *"A Is for Atom, B Is for Bomb," The Journal of American History,* June 1988, p. 75.

25. Garrison, *Bracing for Armageddon,* pp. 46–47.

26. Carey, "The Schools and Civil Defense," *Teachers College Record,* 84, Number 1, Fall 1982, pp. 123–124.

27. Boyer, *By the Bomb's Early Light,* pp. 323, 324–325.

28. http://conelrad.com/duckandcover/cover.php?turtle=01a (13 July 2009); http://conelrad.com/duckandcover/cover.php?turtle=01c (13 July 2009); http://conelrad.com/duckandcover/cover.php?turtle=09 (13 July 2009).

29. McEnaney, *Civil Defense Begins at Home,* pp. 36–37.

30. J. Fred MacDonald, *Television and the Red Menace: The Video Road to Vietnam* (New York: Praeger, 1985), p. 42.

31. Garrison, *Bracing for Armageddon,* p. 43.

32. Garrison, *Bracing for Armageddon,* pp. 48–51.

33. Oakes, *The Imaginary War,* p. 60.

34. Garrison, *Bracing for Armageddon,* p. 53.

35. Oakes, *The Imaginary War,* p. 60.

36. Garrison, *Bracing for Armageddon,* pp. 53–54.

37. Alice L. George, *Awaiting Armageddon: How Americans Faced the Cuban Missile Crisis* (Chapel Hill: University of North Carolina Press, 2003), p. 146.

Chapter 2

1. Douglas T. Miller and Marion Nowak, *The Fifties: The Way We Really Were* (Garden City, NY: Doubleday, 1975, 1977), pp. 334–335; Douglas Brode, *The Films of the Sixties* (Secaucus, NJ: Citadel Press, 1980), p. 45.

2. Melvin E. Matthews, Jr., *Hostile Aliens, Hollywood and Today's News: 1950s Science Fiction Films and 9/11* (New York: Algora, 2007), p. 71.

3. Douglas Brode, *Lost Films of the Fifties* (Secaucus, NJ: Citadel Press, 1988), p. 70.

4. Wheeler Winston Dixon, *Visions of the Apocalypse: Spectacles of Destruction in American Cinema* (London and NY: Wallflower Press, 2003), p. 66.

5. *Ibid.,* pp. 135–136.

6. *Ibid.,* p. 136.

7. Brode, *Lost Films of the Fifties,* pp. 70–71.

8. Dixon, *Visions of the Apocalypse,* pp. 136–137.

9. Bill Warren, *Keep Watching the Skies: American Science Fiction Movies of the Fifties. Volume I: 1950–1957* (Jefferson, NC: McFarland, 1982), pp. 78–79.

10. http://conelrad.com/pressbooks/callforaction.html; conelrad.com/pressbooks/civiliandefense.html; conelrad.com/pressbook/militarydefense.html.

11. Cyndy Hendershot, *Paranoia, the Bomb, and 1950s Science Fiction Films* (Bowling Green, OH: Bowling Green State University Popular Press, 1999), pp. 113–119.

12. Bill Warren, *Keep Watching the Skies! American Science Fiction Movies of the Fifties. Volume II: 1958–1962* (Jefferson, NC: McFarland, 1986), pp. 441, 764, 443.

13. Michael R. Beschloss, *Mayday: Eisenhower, Khrushchev and the U-2 Affair* (New York: Harper & Row, 1980), pp. 169–171.

14. Garrison, *Bracing for Armageddon,* pp. 85–86.

15. Alan M. Winkler, *Life Under a Cloud: American Anxiety about the Atom* (New York: Oxford University Press, 1993), p. 120.

16. Garrison, *Bracing for Armageddon*, pp. 86–87.

17. Michael Scheibach, ed., *"In Case Atom Bombs Fall": An Anthology of Government Explanations, Instructions and Warnings from the 1940s to the 1960s* (Jefferson, NC: McFarland, 2009), p. 96.

18. Margot A. Henriksen, *Dr. Strangelove's America: Society and Culture in the Atomic Age* (Berkeley and Los Angeles: University of California Press, 1997), pp. 103–104.

19. J. Ronald Oakley, *God's Country: America in the Fifties* (New York: Dembner Books, 1986), pp. 369–370).

20. Garrison, *Bracing for Armageddon*, pp. 68–71, 74.

21. *Ibid.*, pp. 73–78.

22. *Ibid.*, pp. 91–92, 94–96, 98–100.

23. Maurice Isserman, *If I Had a Hammer ... The Death of the Old Left and the Birth of the New Left* (New York: Basic Books, 1987), p. 145.

24. *Ibid.*

25. *Ibid.*, pp. 145–146.

26. *Ibid.*, p. 147.

27. *Ibid.*

28. Garrison, *Bracing for Armageddon*, p. 114.

29. Victoria O'Donnell, "Science Fiction Films and Cold War Anxiety," Peter Lev, Charles Harpole, gen. eds., *History of the American Cinema. Volume 7: Transforming the Screen 1950–1959* (New York: Charles Scribner's Son, 2003), pp. 169–170.

30. Matthews, *Hostile Aliens, Hollywood and Today's News*, p. 53.

31. O'Donnell in Lev and Harpole, eds., *History of American Cinema. Volume 7*, p. 170.

32. Joyce A. Evans, *Celluloid Mushroom Clouds: Hollywood and the Atomic Bomb* (Boulder, CO: Westview Press, 1998), pp. 136–137.

33. Kim Newman, *Apocalypse Movies: End of the World Cinema* (New York: St. Martin's Griffin, 2000), p. 104.

34. *Ibid.*, pp. 106–107.

35. *Ibid.*, p. 104.

36. Warren, *Keep Watching the Skies. Volume 1*, p. 255.

37. Mark A. Vieira, *Hollywood Horror: From Gothic to Cosmic* (New York: Harry N. Abrams, 2003), pp. 181–182; Evans, *Celluloid Mushroom Clouds*, p. 103.

38. Spencer R. Weart, *Nuclear Fear: A History of Images* (Cambridge, MA: Harvard University Press, 1988), p. 192.

39. Evans, *Celluloid Mushroom Clouds*, p. 100.

40. Weart, *Nuclear Fear*, p. 192.

41. Scheibach, *"In Case Atom Bombs Fall,"* p. 88.

42. *Ibid.*, pp. 92–93.

43. *Ibid.*, pp. 88–91.

44. Christopher John Bright, "'Out in the Open': Popular Representations of Some American Nuclear Weapons in the Early Cold War," Rosemary B. Mariner and G. Kurt Piehler, eds., *The Atomic Bomb and American Society: New Perspectives* (Knoxville: University of Tennessee Press, 2009), pp. 329–330.

45. *Ibid.*, p. 330.

46. *Ibid.*, pp. 332–333.

47. *Ibid.*, p. 333.

48. *Ibid.*, p. 334.

49. *Ibid.*

50. *Ibid.*, pp. 334, 335.

51. *Ibid.*, pp. 336–337.

52. Dana M. Reems, *Directed by Jack Arnold* (Jefferson, NC: McFarland, 1988), p. 122.

53. Warren, *Keep Watching the Skies. Volume II*, p. 324.

54. Tony Shaw, *Hollywood's Cold War* (Amherst: University of Massachusetts Press, 2007), p. 139.

55. *Ibid.*

56. Reems, *Directed by Jack Arnold*, p. 122.

57. William Manchester, *The Glory and the Dream: A Narrative History of America 1932–1972* (New York: Bantam Books, 1975), p. 677.

58. Reems, *Directed by Jack Arnold*, pp. 134–135.

59. Warren, *Keep Watching the Skies. Volume II,* pp. 324, 325.

60. Reems, *Directed by Jack Arnold*, p. 126.

61. *Ibid.,* p. 127.

62. *Ibid.,* p. 130.

63. Shaw, *Hollywood's Cold War*, pp. 152–153.

64. G. Tom Poe, "Historical Spectatorship Around and About Stanley Kramer's *On the Beach*," Melvyn Stokes and Richard Maltby, eds., *Hollywood Spectatorship: Changing Perceptions of Cinema Audiences* (London: BFI, 2001), p. 91.

65. *Ibid.*

66. Shaw, *Hollywood's Cold War*, pp. 153–155.

67. Poe, "Historical Spectatorship Around and About Stanley Kramer's On the Beach," Stokes and Maltby, eds., *Hollywood Spectatorship*, pp. 93–94.

68. *Ibid.,* p. 94.

69. *Ibid.,* pp. 94–95.

70. *Ibid.,* p. 95.

71. *Ibid.*

72. *Ibid.,* pp. 95–96.

73. *Ibid.,* p. 96.

74. *Ibid.*

75. *Ibid.,* pp. 96–97.

76. *Ibid.,* pp. 97–98.

77. *Ibid.,* p. 98.

78. *Ibid.*

79. *Ibid.*

80. *Ibid.*

81. *Ibid.,* pp. 98–99.

82. *Ibid.,* p. 99.

83. *Ibid.,* p. 100.

84. Shaw, *Hollywood's Cold War,* p. 158.

Chapter 3

1. George, *Awaiting Armageddon*, p. 39. The opening of one television series struck the network airing it as too evocative of a real-life nuclear war alert. Debuting on ABC in the fall of 1963, *The Outer Limits* was a science-fiction anthology series similar to Rod Serling's *The Twilight Zone*. Each installment began with a disquieting whining sound heard over the image of an oscillating sine wave and simulated video interference, followed by a somewhat menacing "Control Voice":

There is nothing wrong with your television set. Do not attempt to adjust the picture. We are controlling transmission. If we wish to make it louder, we will bring up the volume. If we wish to make it softer, we will tune it to a whisper. We will control the horizontal. We will control the vertical. We can roll the image; make it flutter. We can change the focus to a soft blur, or sharpen it to crystal clarity. For the next hour, sit quietly and we will control all that you see and hear. We repeat: There is nothing wrong with your television set. You are about to experience the awe and mystery that reaches from the inner mind to *The Outer Limits*.

The series' initial title, "Please Stand By," is a phrase heard as part of a statement from a radio or television that the latter is "experiencing technical difficulties," or that a significant official announcement is impending. In the case of *The Outer Limits*'s Control Voice, the latter, in the opinion of historian Rick Worland, resembled the intermittent television and radio tests of "The Emergency Broadcast System" (EBS). While the this has been used to warn people of natural disasters, during the Cold War its purpose was to disseminate official information during a "national emergency," i.e., a nuclear attack. The fact that production on *The Outer Limits* began in the immediate post–Cuban missile crisis era, Worland writes, it "gave its apocalyptic tales a more than hypothetical edge," something that didn't escape the network's attention:

> [ABC] … objected to *Please Stand By* as a title. It was still less than a year after the Cuban Missile Crisis, and they did not want the program's opening to be misconstrued as a bonafide emergency alert. [*Outer Limits*'s creator Leslie] Stevens took a cue from his Control Voice speech, briefly renaming his new show *Beyond Control.*

The change in the series' title in no way changed either its opening sequence or the latter's resemblance to the EBS tests and announcements. Established by President Truman at the behest of the Defense Department at a time when it was feared that the Korean War might become a major American/Soviet conflict, the EBS was, in Worland's words "wholly a product of the Cold War." In addressing national defense, the Federal Communications Commission's 1952 Annual Report candidly declared: "An efficient communications system is invaluable in time of peace but is vital in time of cold war." Indicative of the extent of both American nuclear unease and the cognizance of the EBS during the pre–Cuban missile crisis period were a series of 30-minute nationwide tests, which were required of all broadcasting stations, conducted yearly from 1959 to 1961. Appearing on air during the 1961 test, President Kennedy characterized the EBS as "vital for our national defense," and the collaboration of private broadcasters "essential to the survival of this Nation." "In this context," Worland concludes, "*The Outer Limits*'s distinctive opening sequence shrewdly invoked a reality both quotidian and alarming." Rick Worland, "Sign-Posts Up Ahead: *The Twilight Zone, The Outer Limits,* and TV Political Fantasy 1959–1965," *Science Fiction Studies* 68, Volume 23, Part 1, March 1996, pp. 110–112.

2. McEnaney, *Civil Defense Begins at Home*, p. 112.

3. *Ibid.*, pp. 35–36.

4. Oakes, *The Imaginary War*, pp. 105–106.

5. *Ibid.*, pp. 106–108.

6. *Ibid.*, pp. 120–123.

7. *Ibid.*, pp. 123–129.

8. MacDonald, *Television and the Red Menace*, pp. 40–42.

9. *Ibid.*, pp. 43–44.

10. *Ibid.*, pp. 44, 45.

11. Oakes, *The Imaginary War*, pp. 101–104.

12. MacDonald, *Television and the Red Menace*, p. 45.

13. Thomas Doherty, *Cold War, Cool Medium: Television, McCarthyism, and American Culture* (New York: Columbia University Press, 2003), pp. 8–9.

14. *Ibid.*, pp. 9–10.

15. *Ibid.*, p. 10.

16. MacDonald, *Television and the Red Menace*, p. 46.

17. Doherty, *Cold War, Cool Medium*, pp. 10, 11.

18. *Ibid.*, p. 12.

19. MacDonald, *Television and the Red Menace*, pp. 46–47.

20. Michael Uhl and Tod Ensign, *GI Guinea Pigs: How the Pentagon Exposed Our Troops to Dangers More Deadly Than War: Agent Orange and Atomic Radiation* (New York: Playboy Press, 1980), pp. 74–75.

21. Masco, "SURVIVAL IS YOUR BUSINESS," *Cultural Anthropology* 23, Issue 2, May 2008, p. 373.

22. Uhl and Ensign, *GI Guinea Pigs*, pp. 76–77.

23. *Ibid.*, pp. 77–78.

24. *Ibid.*, pp. 79, 82, 83; MacDonald, *Television and the Red Menace*, p. 47.
25. *Ibid.*, p. 83.
26. *Ibid.*, p. 85.
27. *Ibid.*
28. *Ibid.*
29. MacDonald, *Television and the Red Menace*, p. 47.
30. James T. Patterson, *Grand Expectations: The United States, 1945–1974* (New York: Oxford University Press, 1996), pp. 348–349; The Editors of Time-Life Books, *This Fabulous Century. Volume VI: 1950–1960* (New York: Time, 1970), p. 274.
31. Andrew J. Falk, *Upstaging the Cold War: American Dissent and Cultural Diplomacy, 1940–1960* (Amherst and Boston: University of Massachusetts Press, 2010), pp. 121–123, 124.
32. *Ibid.*, p. 125.
33. *Ibid.*, pp. 125, 127.
34. *Ibid.*, p. 127.
35. *Ibid.*
36. *Ibid.*, pp. 128–129.
37. *Ibid.*, pp. 131–134.
38. *Ibid.*, pp. 134–135.
39. *Ibid.*, p. 142.
40. *Ibid.*, pp. 142–144.
41. *Ibid.*, p. 153.
42. Quoted in *Ibid.*, p. 155.
43. *Ibid.*, p. 158.
44. *Ibid.*, pp. 160–161.
45. *Ibid.*, pp. 161–162.
46. *Ibid.*, p. 162.
47. *Ibid.*, p. 163.
48. Michael Scheibach, *Atomic Narratives and American Youth: Coming of Age with the Atom, 1945–1955* (Jefferson, NC: McFarland, 2003), p. 169.
49. Quoted in MacDonald, *Television and the Red Menace*, p. 45.
50. Andrew D. Grossman, *Neither Dead nor Red: Civilian Defense and American Political Development During the Early Cold War* (New York: Routledge, 2001), p. 85.
51. *Ibid.*, p. 87.
52. *Ibid.*, pp. 87–88.
53. Oakes, *The Imaginary War*, pp. 3–5.
54. Quoted in Cyndy Hendershot, *Anti-Communism and Popular Culture in Mid-Century America* (Jefferson, NC: McFarland, 2003), p. 98.
55. Quoted in *Ibid.*, pp. 98–99.
56. *Ibid.*
57. Quoted in *Ibid.*, pp. 99–100.
58. *Ibid.*
59. *Ibid.*, pp. 100–101.
60. Arthur Shulman and Roger Youman, *How Sweet It Was. Television: A Pictorial Commentary* (New York: Bonanza, 1966), p. 249.
61. Jacobs, *The Dragon's Tail*, pp. 136*n*, 70–71.
62. *Ibid.*, p. 71.
63. Patterson, *Grand Expectations*, p. 349.
64. Mary Ann Watson, *The Expanding Vista: American Television in the Kennedy Years* (New York: Oxford University Press, 1990), pp. 36–37.
65. Harry Castleman and Walter J. Podrazik, *Watching TV: Four Decades of American Television* (New York: McGraw-Hill, 1982), p. 144.
66. "Rough Road," *Newsweek*, January 2, 1961, p. 60.
67. Miller and Nowak, *The Fifties: The Way We Really Were*, p. 60.
68. Garrison, *Bracing for Armageddon*, p. 61.

69. Miller and Nowak, *The Fifties*, pp. 61–62.
70. Garrison, *Bracing for Armageddon*, p. 88.
71. Oakley, *God's Country*, p. 370.
72. Isserman, *If I Had a Hammer...*, p. 149.
73. Oakley, *God's Country*, p. 370.
74. Isserman, *If I Had a Hammer...*, pp. 149–150.
75. *Ibid.*, p. 150.
76. *Ibid.*, pp. 151–155.
77. Oakley, *God's Country*, pp. 370–371.

Chapter 4

1. Quoted in Herbert S. Parmet, *JFK: The Presidency of John F. Kennedy* (New York: Dial Press, 1983), p. 197.

2. Norman Gelb, *The Berlin Wall: Kennedy, Khrushchev, and a Showdown in the Heart of Europe* (New York: Times Books, 1986), pp. 113–114.

3. John F. Kennedy: "Radio and Television Report to the American People on the Berlin Crisis, July 25, 1961," John F. Kennedy Presidential Library & Museum, Boston, Massachusetts. www.jfklibrary.org/Historical+Resources/Archives/Reference+Desk/Speeches/JFK/003 POO3BerlinCrisis07251961.htm.

4. Michael R. Beschloss, *The Crisis Years: Kennedy and Khrushchev 1960–1963* (New York: HarperCollins, 1991), p. 260.

5. Gelb, *The Berlin Wall*, pp. 116–117.

6. Fred Kaplan, *The Wizards of Armageddon* (New York: Simon & Schuster, 1983), p. 307.

7. Garrison, *Bracing for Armageddon*, pp. 110–111.

8. Jeremy Isaacs and Taylor Downing, *Cold War: An Illustrated History, 1945–1991* (Boston: Little, Brown, 1998), p. 172.

9. Winkler, *Life Under a Cloud*, p. 126.

10. Manchester, *The Glory and the Dream*, p. 909.

11. Bernard A. Weisberger, *Cold War, Cold Peace: The United States and Russia Since 1945* (New York: American Heritage, 1984), pp. 210–211.

12. Isaacs and Downing, *Cold War*, pp. 172–174.

13. Walter Karp, "When Bunkers Last in the Backyard Bloom'd," *American Heritage*, 31, Number 2, February/March 1980, pp. 85–86.

14. Beschloss, *The Crisis Years*, p. 278.

15. Karp, *American Heritage*, February/March 1980, p. 86.

16. The Soviet resumption of testing helped Khrushchev in several ways. Unable to frighten the West into recognizing East German sovereignty and letting Berlin come under Soviet control by brandishing his nuclear sword, Khrushchev had at least terminated the exodus into West Berlin with his wall and achieved a minor propaganda triumph by demonstrating that the Soviet Union could violate its postwar accords without incurring significant wrath on the West's part. Be resuming nuclear testing, Khrushchev could improve his standing with his generals, who wondered why he hadn't countered Kennedy's defense buildup with one of his own and pushed matters to the brink, and with leaders of disregard Third World and other countries who might view his willingness to enter negotiations as an implicit acknowledgment that, despite his assertions to the contrary, America's nuclear might vastly exceeded Soviet power in this area. In the event of negotiations on the Berlin matter, Khrushchev desired to be in a strong position. Beschloss, *The Crisis Years*, pp. 294–295.

17. Manchester, *The Glory and the Dream*, p. 912.

18. Aleksandr Fursenko and Timothy Naftali, *Khrushchev's Cold War: The Inside Story of an American Adversary* (New York: W. W. Norton, 2006), p. 410.

19. Karp, *American Heritage*, February/March 1980, pp. 86–87.

20. Kenneth D. Rose, *One Nation Underground: The Fallout Shelter in American Culture* (New York: New York University Press, 2001), p. 93.

21. "Gun Thy Neighbor?" *Time*, August 18, 1961, p. 58.

22. Henriksen, *Dr. Strangelove's America*, p. 205.

23. Karp, *American Heritage*, February/March 1980, p. 92; L. C. McHugh, S. J., "Ethics at the Shelter Doorway," *America*, September 30, 1961, pp. 824–826.

24. Jacobs, *The Dragon's Tail*, p. 76.

25. Joel Engel, *Rod Serling: The Dreams and Nightmares of Life in* The Twilight Zone (Chicago: Contemporary Books, 1989), p. 185.

26. Don Presnell and Marty McGee, *A Critical History of Television's* The Twilight Zone, *1959–1964* (Jefferson, NC: McFarland, 1998), pp. 11–12.

27. Engel, *Rod Serling*, pp. 187–188, 189.

28. Gordon F. Sander, *Serling: The Rise and Twilight of Television's* Last Angry Man (New York: Dutton, 1992), p. 172.

29. *Ibid.*, p. 155.

30. *Ibid.*, p. 181.

31. Martin Grams, Jr., The Twilight Zone: *Unlocking the Door to a Television Classic* (Churchville, MD: OTR Publishing, LLC, 2008), pp. 422–423.

32. *Ibid.*, p. 420.

33. *Ibid.*, pp. 423, 420.

34. Jacobs, *The Dragon's Tail*, p. 77.

35. The class prejudice evinced here paralleled the reaction among Kennedy's White House staff to the class bias in the draft of a fallout–shelter booklet intended for distribution to the American people. One section of the brochure declared: "The anticipation of a new market for home shelters is helpful and in keeping with the free enterprise way of meeting changing conditions in our lives." The brochure featured illustrations of office buildings and suburban dwellings with huge basements and gardens — yet ignored urban tenements and apartment buildings, and factory laborers. Another drawing depicted a family fleeing the nuclear holocaust in a cabin cruiser. An outraged John Kenneth Galbraith, the Harvard economist and JFK's ambassador to India, informed the president: "The present pamphlet is a design for saving Republicans and sacrificing Democrats.... I am not at all attracted by a pamphlet which seeks to save the better elements of the population, but in the main writes off those who voted for you." The pamphlet was ultimately revised, with 25 million copies distributed to 790 civil defense offices and 30,954 post offices across the nation. Kaplan, *The Wizards of Armageddon*, pp. 311, 313.

36. Bob Crane interview with Rod Serling about *The Twilight Zone* episode "The Shelter," KNX Los Angeles, October 1961. CONELRAD.com and Youtube.com. During the same broadcast, Crane, referring to a panel discussion on shelters he had recently viewed, noted one man's position that "until the government starts building them themselves, public shelters, I can't see where there's this immediacy.... Why should I go out and spend two or three thousand dollars to build one if the government isn't bothering?" Such skepticism extended to such key officials of the Kennedy administration as the members of National Security Council, Vice President Lyndon Johnson, Attorney General Robert Kennedy, and Assistant Secretary of Defense Steuart Pittman — none of whom went to the effort of constructing a shelter for the safety of their families. And, in Pittman's case, the refusal to do so was ironic as the responsibility for civil defense became *his* once it was transferred to the Defense Department. Gerald H. Clarfield and William M. Wiecek, *Nuclear America: Military and Civilian Nuclear Power in the United States 1940–1980* (New York: Harper & Row, 1984), p. 250.

37. Grams, *The Twilight Zone*, pp. 423–424.

38. Karp, *American Heritage*, February/March 1980, p. 92.

39. *Ibid.*, p. 93.

40. *Ibid.*, p. 92.

41. Winkler, *Life Under a Cloud*, p. 131.

42. Karp, *American Heritage*, February/March 1980, pp. 92–93.

43. Quoted in Henriksen, *Dr. Strangelove's America*, pp. 214, 216–217.

44. Karp, *American Heritage*, February/March 1980, p. 93.

45. Garrison, *Bracing for Armageddon*, pp. 120–122.

46. *Ibid.*, pp. 122–123, 125–126.

47. Thomas C. Reeves, *A Question of Character: A Life of John F. Kennedy* (New York: The Free Press, 1991), p. 308.

48. Rose, *One Nation Underground*, p. 112. Placing *Twilight Zone's* "Shelter" episode within the context of the criticism of bomb shelters and thermonuclear war in American culture during and after the Berlin crisis, Margot A. Henriksen feels that the victory scored by those opposing the shelter mania and the government's civil defense program not only signaled "the first unambiguous Atomic Age victory for the forces of dissent in America" but that the spirit of such dissent entered American television as well, calling further attention to the lessons Americans had learned: that preparing for a thermonuclear conflict was transforming Americans into "monsters" and that no amount of shelter could shield American families from the hazards of the Atomic Age. Henriksen continues that in the wake of *The Twilight Zone*, numerous "bizarre" television sitcoms became popular: *Mister Ed* (1961–1965), *The Beverly Hillbillies* (1962–1971), *My Favorite Martian* (1963–1966), *Bewitched* (1964–1973), *The Munsters* (1964–1966), *The Addams Family* (1964–1966), and *I Dream of Jeannie* (1965–1970). The success of these programs, which featured such offbeat "mutants" as a talking horse, a genie, a witch, and monstrous-looking families may have been due to the fact that physical change due to radiation had entered the American consciousness as a result of the real-life changes experienced by the victims of the atomic bombs dropped on Japan during World War II and the mutation themes of 1950s science fiction films and novels, thus conditioning Americans to such grotesqueries. Bizarre television shows also reflected the dehumanization and debasement of the caliber of life that had become an issue during the "shelter morality" debate arising from the Berlin crisis as well as the shattering of the celebration of the traditional nuclear family as the bastion of security against the hazards of the Cold War — a model personified by the family sitcoms of the 1950s. "The family had been seen as the one institution crucial to protect in nuclear war, as indicated by the focus on family fallout shelters, and the mutant families in bizarre television sundered the idea that it was possible to protect the family from the 'nightmare civilization' being constructed during the Berlin crisis and the entirety of the Atomic Age in America. With the atomic bomb America had created families of Frankensteins — as one could characterize the bevy of bizarre beings in 60s television shows — and they attacked the system which had created them." Henderson continues, "By challenging the traditional character of American families, and by breaking out of the confining conformity of the 1950s, bizarre television families undercut the cold war and Atomic Age system that so depended on the family to contain and blunt subversive and dissenting sentiments in America." Margot A. Henriksen, "The Berlin Crisis, the Bomb Shelter Craze and Bizarre Television: Expressions of an Atomic Age Counterculture"; Alison M. Scott and Christopher D. Geist, eds., *The Writing on the Cloud: American Culture Confronts the Atomic Bomb* (Lanham, MD: University Press of America, 1997), pp. 162–165, 167, 169.

49. George, *Awaiting Armageddon*, pp. 167–168.

50. *Ibid.*, p. 169.

51. Garrison, *Bracing for Armageddon*, pp. 128–131.

52. Jacobs, *The Dragon's Tail*, pp. 61–62.

53. *Ibid.*, pp. 72–73.

54. Warren, *Keep Watching the Skies. Volume II*, p. 761.

55. Newman, *Apocalypse Movies*, p. 151.

56. *Ibid.*

57. Jack G. Shaheen, ed., *Nuclear War Films* (Carbondale and Edwardsville: Southern Illinois University Press, 1978), p. 46.

58. Commenting on the transformation of Milland's character in the film into a merciless survivalist, Milland's co-star Mary Mitchel felt, "And probably everybody would get that way [after an atomic attack]. Because you obviously have to look after yourself. There are a lot of people who, when the ship is sinking, would become [ruthless]. It probably would be

scary." Tom Weaver, *Earth vs. the Sci-Fi Filmmakers: 20 Interviews* (Jefferson, N: McFarland, 2005), p. 296.
59. Rose, *One Nation Underground*, pp. 98–100.
60. Shaheen, ed., *Nuclear War Films*, p. 48.
61. Toni A. Perrine, *Film and the Nuclear Age: Representing Cultural Anxiety* (New York: Garland, 1998), p. 172.
62. Shaheen, ed., *Nuclear War Films*, p. 49.
63. Warren, *Keep Watching the Skies. Volume II*, p. 684.
64. Perrine, *Film and the Nuclear Age*, p. 173.
65. Shaheen, edit., *Nuclear War Films*, p. 46.
66. *Ibid.*, p. 48.
67. Warren, *Keep Watching the Skies. Volume II*, pp. 681–682.

Chapter 5

1. Perrine, *Film and the Nuclear Age*, pp. 11–12.
2. Clarfield and Wiecek, *Nuclear America*, p. 258.
3. Winkler, *Life Under a Cloud*, pp. 132–133.
4. Kendall R. Phillips, *Projected Fears: Horror Films and American Culture* (Westport, CT: Praeger, 2005), pp. 129–130.
5. Miller and Nowak, *The Fifties: The Way We Really Were*, pp. 4–5.
6. Oakley, *God's Country*, p. 429.
7. "Back to the '50s," *Newsweek*, October 16, 1972, p. 78.
8. Castleman and Podrazik, *Watching TV*, pp. 250–251.
9. John Gregory Stocke, "'Suicide on the Installment Plan': Cold-War-Era Civil Defense and Consumerism in the United States," Scott and Geist, eds., *The Writing on the Cloud*, p. 46.
10. *Ibid.*, p. 47.
11. *Ibid.*, p. 48.
12. *Ibid.*, pp. 48–49.
13. *Ibid.*, pp. 49–50.
14. *Ibid.*, p. 53.
15. *Ibib.*
16. *Ibid.*, pp. 54–56.
17. Henriksen, *Dr. Strangelove's America*, p. 415n; Newman, *Apocalypse Movies*, p. 65.
18. George, *Awaiting Armageddon*, p. 153.
19. David Obst, *Too Good to Be Forgotten: Changing America in the '60s and '70s* (New York: John Wiley & Sons, Inc., 1998), pp. 32–40.
20. George, *Awaiting Armageddon*, p. 153.

Chapter 6

1. Phillips, *Projected Fears*, p. 132.
2. Richard Gid Powers, *Not Without Honor: The History of American Anticommunism* (New York: The Free Press, 1995), pp. 345–346, 386–387, 389.
3. Garrison, *Bracing for Armageddon*, pp. 133–134.
4. Boyer, *By the Bomb's Early Light*, p. 356.
5. Steven F. Hayward, *The Age of Reagan: The Conservative Counterrevolution 1980–1989* (New York: Crown Forum, 2009), pp. 334–335.
6. Phillips, *Projected Fears*, p. 142.
7. Isaacs and Downing, *Cold War: An Illustrated History*, pp. 333–334.
8. Powers, *Not Without Honor*, p. 400.

9. Richard J. Barnet, *The Rockets' Red Glare: When America Goes to War. The Presidents and the People* (New York: Simon & Schuster, 1990), p. 387.

10. Powers, *Not Without Honor*, pp. 396–397.

11. Garrison, *Bracing for Armageddon*, pp. 148–149.

12. Barnet, *The Rockets' Red Glare*, p. 392.

13. Winkler, *Life Under a Cloud*, p. 133.

14. *Ibid.*, pp. 133–134.

15. *Ibid.*, p. 134.

16. *Ibib.*; email from the Reverend Fred Small to Melvin E. Matthews, Jr., December 22, 2010. The lyrics were written by Small and copyrighted 1983 Pine Barrens Music (BMI).

17. Winkler, *Life Under a Cloud*, pp. 134–135.

18. Barnet, *The Rockets' Red Glare*, pp. 393–394.

19. *Ibid.*, p. 395.

20. *Ibid.*

21. Tony Shaw and Denise J. Youngblood, *Cinematic Cold War: The American and Soviet Struggle for Hearts and Minds* (Lawrence: University Press of Kansas, 2010), p. 33.

22. Paul S. Boyer, "Nuclear Themes in American Culture, 1945 to the Present," Mariner and Piehler, eds., *The Atomic Bomb and American Society*, p. 10.

23. Title drawn from *Newsweek*, November 21, 1983, p. 66.

24. "Fallout Over *The Day After*," *Newsweek*, October 24, 1983, p. 126.

25. Newman, *Apocalypse Movies*, pp. 230–232.

26. "Fallout Over *The Day After*," *Newsweek*, October 24, 1983, p. 126.

27. "TV's Nuclear Nightmare," *Newsweek*, November 21, 1983, p. 70.

28. Nicholas Meyer, *The View from the Bridge: Memories of Star Trek and a Life in Hollywood* (New York: Viking Penguin, 2009), pp. 139, 140.

29. *Ibid.*, pp. 140–141.

30. *Ibid.*, pp. 141–142.

31. *Ibid.*, pp. 142–143.

32. *Ibid.*, pp. 144–147.

33. *Ibid.*, pp. 147–148.

34. *Ibid.*, pp. 148–149, 150.

35. *Ibid.*, pp. 150–151.

36. *Ibid.*, p. 151.

37. *Ibid.*, pp. 151–152.

38. *60 Minutes*, "The Week Before *The Day After*," November 13, 1983 (New York: Columbia Broadcasting System, Inc., 1983), pp. 7–8, 9.

39. Hayward, *The Age of Reagan*, p. 335; Ronald Reagan, *The Reagan Diaries*, Douglas Brinkley, ed. (New York: HarperCollins, 2007), pp. 185–186.

40. Hayward, *The Age of Reagan*, p. 335.

41. "TV's Nuclear Nightmare," *Newsweek*, November 21, 1983, p. 66.

42. Newman, *Apocalypse Movies*, p. 234.

43. Hayward, *The Age of Reagan*, p. 335.

44. Powers, *Not Without Honor*, p. 399.

45. Hayward, *The Age of Reagan*, p. 335.

46. Powers, *Not Without Honor*, p. 399.

47. Barnet, *The Rockets' Red Glare*, p. 395.

48. Garrison, *Bracing for Armageddon*, pp. 174–176.

49. Meyer, *The View from the Bridge*, pp. 153–154.

Chapter 7

1. Garrison, *Bracing for Armageddon*, pp. 183–184.

2. Powers, *Not Without Honor*, pp. 421–422.

3. Garrison, *Bracing for Armageddon*, pp. 184, 230*n*.

4. Mick Broderick in Scott C. Zeman and Michael A. Amundson, eds., *Atomic Culture: How We Learned to Stop Worrying and Love the Bomb* (Boulder, CO: University Press of Colorado, 2004), p. 136.

5. *Ibid.*, p. 138.

6. *Ibid.*, p. 139.

7. Email from Joe Dante to Melvin E. Matthews, Jr., February 28, 2010.

8. Matthews, *Hostile Aliens, Hollywood and Today's News*, pp. 135–134.

9. Newman, *Apocalypse Movies*, p. 69.

10. Email from Joe Dante to Melvin E. Matthews, Jr., February 27, 2010.

11. Zelman and Amundson, eds., *Atomic Culture*, p. 141.

12. Matthews, *Hostile Aliens, Hollywood and Today's News*, p. 134.

13. Henry Fairlie, *The Kennedy Promise: The Politics of Expectation* (New York: Dell, 1974), pp. 232–233, 254–255.

14. Matthews, *Hostile Aliens, Hollywood and Today's News*, p. 134.

15. Email from Joe Dante to Melvin E. Matthews, Jr., February 27, 2010.

16. Matthews, *Hostile Aliens, Hollywood and Today's News*, pp. 135, 136; email from Joe Dante to Melvin E. Matthews, Jr., February 27, 2010.

17. Zelman and Amundsen, eds., *Atomic Culture*, p. 139.

18. *Ibid.*, p. 140.

19. Matthews, *Hostile Aliens, Hollywood and Today's News*, pp. 134, 135–136.

20. Email from Joe Dante to Melvin E. Matthews, Jr., February 27, 2010.

21. Masco, "Survival Is Your Business," *Cultural Anthropology* 23 Issue 2, May 2008, pp. 384–385.

22. *Ibid.*, pp. 385–386.

23. Matthews, *Hostile Aliens, Hollywood and Today's News*, p. 69.

24. *Ibid.*, pp. 6–8.

25. Dixon, *Visions of the Apocalypse*, p. 81.

26. *Ibid.*, pp. 81–82.

27. *Ibid.*, p. 82.

28. Anna Quindlen, "Young in a Year of Fear," *Newsweek*, November 4, 2002, p. 68.

29. Garrison, *Bracing for Armageddon*, pp. 194–196.

30. Masco, "Survival Is Your Business," *Cultural Anthropology* 23 Issue 2, May 2008, p. 387.

31. *Ibid.*, pp. 387–388.

32. *Ibid.*, p. 388.

33. Boyer, "Nuclear Themes in American Culture, 1945 to the Present," Mariner and Piehler, eds., *The Atomic Bomb and American Society*, p. 10.

34. *Ibid.*, p. 14.

35. Matthews, *Hostile Aliens, Hollywood and Today's News*, pp. 142–143.

36. *Ibid.*, pp. 146, 147–148.

37. James Poniewozik, "Look Back in Angst," *Time*, September 23, 2002, p. 73.

38. "Pilot" Commentary with Executive Producer Dick Clark and Creator and Executive Producer Jonathan Prince, *American Dreams*.

39. Poniewozik, *Time*, September 23, 2002, p. 74.

40. Miller and Nowak, *The Fifties: The Way We Really Were*, p. 78*n*.

41. *Ibid.*, p. 56.

42. Zelman and Amundson, eds., *Atomic Culture*, p. 142.

Bibliography

Books

Alexander, Charles C. *Holding the Line: The Eisenhower Era 1952–1961.* Bloomington: Indiana University Press, 1975.

Barnet, Richard J. *The Rockets' Red Glare: When America Goes to War. The Presidents and the People.* New York: Simon & Schuster, 1990.

Beschloss, Michael. *The Crisis Years: Kennedy and Khrushchev 1960–1963.* New York: HarperCollins, 1991.

_____. *Mayday: Eisenhower, Khrushchev and the U-2 Affair.* New York: Harper & Row, 1986.

Boyer, Paul. *By the Bomb's Early Light: American Thought and Culture at the Dawn of the Atomic Age.* New York: Pantheon Books, 1985.

Brode, Douglas. *The Films of the Sixties.* Secaucus, NJ: Citadel Press, 1980.

_____. *Lost Films of the Fifties.* Secaucus, NJ: Citadel Press, 1988.

Castleman, Harry, and Walter J. Podrazik. *Watching TV: Four Decades of American Television.* New York: McGraw-Hill, 1982.

Clarfield, Gerard H., and William M. Wiecek. *Nuclear America: Military and Civilian Nuclear Power in the United States.* New York: Harper & Row, 1984.

Dixon, Wheeler Winston. *Visions of the Apocalypse: Spectacles of Destruction in American Cinema.* London and New York: Wallflower Press, 2003.

Doherty, Thomas. *Cold War, Cool Medium: Television, McCarthyism, and American Culture.* New York: Columbia University Press, 2003.

Dowling, John, and Evans M. Harrell, eds., *Civil Defense: A Choice of Disasters.* New York: American Institute of Physics, 1987.

The Editors of Time-Life Books. *This Fabulous Century. Volume VI: 1950–1960.* New York: Time, 1970.

Engel, Joel. *Rod Serling: The Dreams and Nightmares of Life in* The Twilight Zone. Chicago: Contemporary Books, 1989.

Evans, Joyce A. *Celluloid Mushroom Clouds: Hollywood and the Atomic Bomb.* Boulder: Westview Press.

Fairlie, Henry. *The Kennedy Promise: The Politics of Expectation.* New York: Dell, 1974.

Falk, Andrew J. *Upstaging the Cold War: American Dissent and Cultural Diplomacy, 1940–1960.* Amherst and Boston: University of Massachusetts Press, 2010.

Fried, Richard M. *Nightmare in Red: The McCarthy Era in Perspective.* New York: Oxford University Press, 1990.

_____. *The Russians Are Coming! The Russians Are Coming! Pageantry and Patriotism in Cold-War America.* New York Oxford University Press, 1998.

Fursenko, Aleksandr, and Timothy Naftali. *Khrushchev's Cold War: The Inside Story of an American Adversary.* W. W. Norton, 2006.

Garrison, Dee. *Bracing for Armageddon: Why Civil Defense Never Worked.* New York: Oxford University Press, 2006.

Gelb, Norman. *The Berlin Wall: Kennedy, Khrushchev, and a Showdown in the Heart of Europe.* New York: Times Books, 1986.

George, Alice L. *Awaiting Armageddon: How Americans Faced the Cuban Missile Crisis.* Chapel Hill, NC: University of North Carolina Press, 2003.

Goodwin, Doris Kearns. *Wait Till Next Year: A Memoir.* New York: Simon & Schuster, 1997.

Grams, Martin, Jr. *The Twilight Zone: Unlocking the Door to a Television Classic.* Churchville, MD: OTR, 2008.

Grossman, Andrew D. *Neither Dead nor Red: Civilian Defense and American Political Development During the Early Cold War.* New York: Routledge, 2001.

Hayward, Steven F. *The Age of Reagan: The Conservative Counterrevolution 1980–1889* New York: Crown Forum, 2009.

Hendershot, Cyndy. *Anti-Communism and Popular Culture in Mid-Century America.* Jefferson, NC: McFarland, 2003.

_____. *Paranoia, the Bomb, and 1950s Science Fiction Films.* Bowling Green, OH: Bowling Green State University Popular Press, 1999.

Henriksen, Margot A. *Dr. Strangelove's America: Society and Culture in the Atomic Age.* Berkeley and Los Angeles: University of California Press, 1997.

Isaacs, Jeremy, and Taylor Downing. *Cold War: An Illustrated History, 1945–1991.* Boston: Little, Brown, 1998.

Isserman, Maurice. *If I Had a Hammer ... The Death of the Old Left and the Birth of the New Left.* New York: Basic Books, 1987.

Jacobs, Robert A. *The Dragon's Tail: Americans Face the Atomic Age.* Amherst and Boston: University of Massachusetts Press, 2010.

Jones, Landon Y. *Great Expectations: America and the Baby Boom Generation.* New York: Ballantine, 1981.

Kaplan, Fred. *The Wizards of Armageddon.* New York: Simon & Schuster, 1983.

Kuznick, Peter J., and James Gilbert, eds., *Rethinking Cold War Culture.* Washington, D.C.: Smithsonian Institution Press, 2001.

Lev, Peter, and Charles Harpole, eds. *History of the American Cinema. Volume 7: Transforming the Screen 1950–1959.* New York: Charles Scribner's Sons, 2003.

MacDonald, J. Fred. *Television and the Red Menace: The Video Road to Vietnam.* New York: Praeger, 1985.

Manchester, William. *The Glory and the Dream: A Narrative History of America 1932–1972.* New York: Bantam Books, 1975.

Mariner, Rosemary B., and G. Kurt Piehler, eds., *The Atomic Bomb and American Society: New Perspectives.* Knoxville: University of Tennessee Press, 2009.

Matthews, Melvin E. Jr. *Hostile Aliens, Hollywood and Today's News: 1950s Science Fiction Films and 9/11.* New York: Algora, 2007.

McEnaney, Laura. *Civil Defense Begins at Home: Militarization Meets Everyday Life in the Fifties.* Princeton, NJ: Princeton University Press, 2000.

Meyer, Nicholas. *The View from the Bridge: Memories of Star Trek and a Life in Hollywood.* New York: Viking Penguin, 2009.

Miller, Douglas T., and Marion Nowak. *The Fifties: The Way We Really Were.* Garden City, NY: Doubleday, 1975, 1977.

Newman, Kim. *Apocalypse Movies: End of the World Cinema.* New York: St. Martin's Griffin, 2000.

Oakes, Guy. *The Imaginary War: Civil Defense and American Cold War Culture.* New York: Oxford University Press, 1994.

Oakley, J. Ronald. *God's Country: America in the Fifties.* New York: Dembner Books, 1986.

Obst, David. *Too Good to Be Forgotten: Changing America in the '60s and '70s.* New York: Wiley & Sons, 1998.

Parmet, Herbert S. *JFK: The Presidency of John F. Kennedy.* New York: The Dial Press, 1983.

Patterson, James T. *Grand Expectations: The United States, 1945–1974.* New York: Oxford University Press, 1996.

Perrine, Toni A. *Film and the Nuclear Age: Representing Cultural Anxiety.* New York: Garland, 1998.

Phillips, Cabell. *The 1940s: Decade of Triumph and Trouble.* New York: Macmillan, 1975.

Phillips, Kendall R. *Projected Fears: Horror Films and American Culture.* Westport, CT: Praeger, 2005.

Powers, Richard Gid. *Not Without Honor: The History of American Anticommunism.* New York: The Free Press, 1995.

Presnell, Don, and Marty McGee. *A Critical History of Television's The Twilight Zone, 1959–1964.* Jefferson, NC: McFarland, 1998.

Reagan, Ronald. *The Reagan Diaries.* Ed. Douglas Brinkley. New York: HarperCollins, 2007.

Reems, Dana A. *Directed by Jack Arnold.* Jefferson, NC: McFarland, 1988.

Reeves, Thomas C. *A Question of Character: A Life of John F. Kennedy.* New York: The Free Press, 1991.

Rose, Kenneth D. *One Nation Underground: The Fallout Shelter in American Culture.* New York: New York University Press, 2001.

Sander, Gordon F. *Serling: The Rise and Twilight of Television's Last Angry Man.* New York: Dutton, 1992.

Scheibach, Michael. *Atomic Narratives and American Youth: Coming of Age with the Atom, 1945–1955.* Jefferson, NC: McFarland, 2003.

_____, ed. *"In Case Atom Bombs Fall": An Anthology of Government Explanations, Instructions and Warnings from the 1940s to the 1960s.* Jefferson, NC: McFarland, 2009.

Scott, Alison M., and Christopher D. Geist, eds., *The Writing on the Cloud: American Culture Confronts the Atomic Bomb.* Lanham: University Press of America, 1997.

Shaheen, Jack G., ed. *Nuclear War Films.* Carbondale and Edwardsville: Southern Illinois University Press, 1978.

Shaw, Tony. *Hollywood's Cold War.* Amherst: University of Massachusetts Press, 2007.

_____, and Denise J. Youngblood. *Cinematic Cold War: The American and Soviet Struggle for Hearts and Minds.* Lawrence: University Press of Kansas, 2010.

Shulman, Arthur, and Roger Youman. *How Sweet It Was. Television: A Pictorial Commentary.* New York: Bonanza Books, 1966.

Stokes, Melvyn, and Richard Maltby. *Hollywood Spectatorship: Changing Perceptions of Cinema Audiences.* London: BFI, 2001.

Uhl, Michael, and Tod Ensign. *G.I. Guinea Pigs. How the Pentagon Exposed Our Troops to Dangers More Deadly Than War: Agent Orange and Atomic Radiation.* New York: Playboy Press, 1980.

Vieira, Mark A. *Hollywood Horror: From Gothic to Cosmic.* New York: Harry N. Abrams, 2003.

Warren, Bill. *Keep Watching the Skies: American Science Fiction Movies of the Fifties. Volume I: 1950–1957.* Jefferson, NC: McFarland, 1982.

_____. *Keep Watching the Skies! American Science Fiction Films of the Fifties. Volume II: 1958–1962.* Jefferson, NC: McFarland, 1986.

Watson, Mary Ann. *The Expanding Vista: American Television in the Kennedy Years.* New York: Oxford University Press, 1990.

Weart, Spencer R. *Nuclear Fear: A History of Images.* Cambridge, MA: Harvard University Press, 1988.

Weaver, Tom. *Earth vs. the Sci-Fi Filmmakers: 20 Interviews.* Jefferson, NC: McFarland, 2005.

Weisberger, Bernard A. *Cold War, Cold Peace: The United States and Russia Since 1945.* New York: American Heritage, 1984.

Wigner, Eugene P., ed. *Who Speaks for Civil Defense?* New York: Charles Scribner's Sons, 1968.

Winkler, Alan M. *Life Under a Cloud: American Anxiety About the Atom.* New York: Oxford University Press, 1993.

Zeman, Scott C., and Michael A. Amundson. *Atomic Culture: How We Learned to Stop Worrying and Love the Bomb.* Boulder: University Press of Colorado, 2004.

Articles

"Back to the '50s," *Newsweek,* October 16, 1972, 78.

Brown, JoAnne. "*A* Is for *Atom, B* Is for *Bomb*": Civil Defense in American Public Education, 1948–1963." *Journal of American History 72,* no. 1 (June 1988): 69–70, 75.

Carey, Michael J. "The Schools and Civil Defense: The Fifties Revisited." *Teachers College Record.* Volume 84, Number 1, Fall 1982. 115–117, 123–124.

Crane, Bob Interview with Rod Serling about *The Twilight Zone* episode "The Shelter." KNX Los Angeles, October 1961. CONELRAD.com and Youtube.com.

Dante, Joe. Email to Melvin E. Matthews, Jr., February 28, 2010.

"Fallout Over *The Day After,*" *Newsweek,* October 24, 1983, 126.

"Gun Thy Neighbor?" *Time,* August 18, 1961, 58.

http://conelrad.com/duckandcover/cover.php?turtle=01 (13 July 2009).

http://conelrad.com/duckandcover/cover.php?turtle+01a (13 July 2009).

http://conelrad.com/duckandcover/cover.php?turtle=01b (13 July 2009).

http://conelrad.com/duckandcover/atomicsecrets/secrets.php?secrets=04 (14 July 2009).

http://conelrad.com/duckandcover/cover.php?turtle=01c (13 July 2009).

http://concelrad.com/duckandcover/cover.php?turtle+09 (13 July 2009).

http://conelrad.com/pressbook/callforaction.html;conelrad.com/pressbooks/civilian defense.html;conelrad.com/pressbook/militarydefense.html.

Karp, Walter. "When Bunkers Last in the Backyard Bloom'd." *American Heritage* 31, Number 2 (February/March 1980): 85–87, 92–93.

Kennedy, John F. "Radio and Television Report to the American People on the Berlin Crisis, July 25, 1961." John F. Kennedy Presidential Library & Museum, Boston, Massachusetts. www.jfklibrary.org/Historical+Resources/Archives/Reference+Desk/Speeches/JFK/003P003BerlinCrisis07251961.htm.

Masco, Joseph. "'SURVIVAL IS YOUR BUSINESS': Engineering Ruins and Affect in Nuclear America." *Cultural Anthropology; Journal of the Society for Cultural Anthropology* 23, Issue 2 (May 2008): 367–368.

McHugh, L. C. S. J. "Ethics at the Shelter Doorway." *America,* September 30, 1961, 824–826.

"Pilot" Commentary with Executive Producer Dick Clark and Creator and Executive Producer Jonathan Prince. *American Dreams.*

Poniewozik, James. "Look Back in Angst." *Time,* September 23, 2002, 73–74.

Quindlen, Anna. "Young in a Year of Fear." *Newsweek,* November 4, 2002, 68.

"Rough Road." *Newsweek,* January 2, 1961, 60.

60 Minutes. "The Week Before *The Day After,*" November 13, 1983. New York: Columbia Broadcasting System, 1983, 7–9.

"TV's Nuclear Nightmare." *Newsweek,* November 21, 1983, 66, 70.

Worland, Rick. "Sign-Posts Up Ahead: *The Twilight Zone, The Outer Limits* and TV Political Fantasy 1959–1965." *Science-Fiction Studies,* Volume 23, Part 1, March 1996.

Index